THE RESURRECTION
Narrative and Belief

Also published by SPCK:

Jesus and the Ethics of the Kingdom
J. I. H. McDonald and Bruce Chilton
(*Biblical Foundations in Theology series*)

The Resurrection

NARRATIVE AND BELIEF

J I H McDonald

First published in Great Britain 1989
SPCK
Holy Trinity Church
Marylebone Road
London NW1 4DU

British Library Cataloguing in Publication Data

McDonald, James I. H. (James Ian Hamilton), 1933–
The Resurrection: narrative and belief.
1. Bible. N.T. Special subjects: Jesus
Christ. Resurrection
I. Title   II. Series
232.9′7

ISBN 0-281-04400-7

Printed in Great Britain at
the University Press, Cambridge

Contents

Foreword

by James P Mackey

Death makes religious believers of us – death, which we never think about, or try not to think about, or pretend we don't think about … and which we certainly do not wish to talk about very often. So we don't wish to talk about religious faith very often either, except to keep it at a distance … like death.

Professional believers have always been the worst enemies of religious faith, and they still are so to this day. One wonders why. Perhaps because they too are commonly engaged in the common cultural denial of death: it is only a transition, after all, to a far better place than we have ever known. And what of its daily harbingers, the personal loneliness, the political betrayals, the stale taste of success, the onset of gout? These do pose some practical problems – no doubt they do – but no more serious, surely, than death … and it can't be all that serious, considering what's beyond.

There is an odd collusion between modern atheistic humanists and professional Christians. The humanists, with great and sustained superficiality, hide the existential question which death poses under the morally neutral cloak of the image of extinction, a kindly promise of total ontological amnesia. Then, with the same sustained superficiality, they act as if the problem of evil were a problem for Christians. But Christians, too, bury the problem, together with its deep, dark prospects, under a written promise of better things beyond.

When death is denied, in any way whatever, the one thing that gives depth to human life is missing, the thing that can give to every instant of survival the *frisson* of the miraculous, and to every small gesture, to every ordinary achievement, a surprising significance. Then we are left without real death and without real life, and the substitute is a mere puzzling existence grinding onwards towards a pale *post mortem* future, each one of us clutching a barely decipherable old promissory note of uncertain authorship.

The modern humanist, with some ostentation, bravely throws the note away; the gesture is slightly reminiscent of the self-satisfaction with which he commits the problem of evil to the Christian, and equally irresponsible. But his gesture does raise the question, for those who had not seen it already lying round their feet: What earthly reason is there to believe that another life could be better than this one? And if God, or we, really could make life better, why did God, and we, fail to do so the first time round? Is this God's practice match, and ours?

The escapist mentality, to which so very much of Christian rhetoric contributes, must do a very great deal to explain why most of the people are indifferent to religion most of the time, and why, in the modern world, increasing numbers are indifferent to religion all of the time. And those of us who do not wish to be indifferent can still quite fail to see how the stature of sons of God can be achieved on the factory floor, or the stirrings of eternal life could be sensed in every winter's breaking up by spring.

Christianity being the kind of religion it is, a religion to which the plain person of the founder is so utterly central, our failure can never be reversed until we are led to *see* the stature of divine sonship and the source of eternal life in the man like us who walked the dust paths of Galilee. And we cannot be satisfied if they are only visible to us after his death: for then the story of his life is reduced to a supply of miracles to assure us that he was something we could not see; or, alternatively, it is reduced to a supply of cosy, vague pieces of moralizing about love, to keep us going until we could see that stature and that source of eternal life in his, and our, hereafter. As I walk with the shadow of death ever shortening before me I want to know his risen life now, and know that he knew it before his death and in his death, and then I will live and die in the inestimable happiness of hope.

I have myself raised the problem of life before and in death in a systematic way, and, in *Modern Theology* (Oxford, Oxford University Press, 1987), I took a typical systematician's short cut to a possible Christian solution, based as it must be upon the life, death and destiny of Jesus. Eucharist, I said to myself, is surely where the real presence of Jesus as Lord is known, where his Spirit makes us part of his body, where he 'appears' in life-giving power … and Eucharist is part of Jesus' ministry and prominent at his death, just as much as it is prominent in his risen appearances. Then (typical once more of the systematician who first makes up his mind and then goes looking for the proof-texts!) I asked the Scripture scholar if he could show how 'risen' life could be attributed to Jesus before his death and consequently felt by us before ours. I have read each chapter of the resulting book in draft. I soon had the narrowness of the eucharistic base for my theory exposed. I still pressed my question with undiminished determination, but instead of seeing it criticize the material that came my way, I found it ever more fully and richly answered with each chapter written, each New Testament author analysed. So it remains for me only to recommend Ian McDonald's book to other readers with gratitude and enthusiasm, and to give the following brief foretaste of its argument.

From the opening chapter, in which the emergence of Christian resurrection imagery from Jewish apocalyptic thought is described, the unique character of Christian faith becomes obvious: instead of idealized figures symbolizing a glorious future, having often escaped death, we have a future already effective for us in a man who is victorious precisely by living and dying like all of us.

This one Paul encountered, much in the way any of us can encounter him, by granting entry (under sudden and unexpected pressure, in his case), to the life, the spirit, that made Jesus what he was and is, 'God with us', and so becoming one body with him so that the same life could flow to others and into all the world.

This one Mark depicts in metaphorical story. Metaphor is a surprising and mind-opening union of things otherwise held apart, if not in opposition. Mark's metaphorical narrative detects divine power in the story of a man – a story, moreover, of a man vulnerable as seed scattered on hard and hostile ground. And if only by refusing to add any final and unambiguous encounter with a risen and victorious Lord, Mark lets us know that we can encounter this one still in the obstacles and failures of life.

With Matthew and Luke, as they are treated in this book, scenes from the ends of the Gospels are shown to contain the key to the whole structure of the Gospels, and to be therefore as much beginnings as ends: Matthew's sense of the power and presence of Jesus from his great closing scene on the mountain top; Luke's equally powerful sense of the glory of the Lord caught by human eyes in human lives in the structure of a journey, the interpretation of Scripture, the fellowship of a meal – all in the Emmaus story at the end – and then (as in Matthew's case also) proving to be the visible formula which holds together the whole Gospel.

This kind of exegesis carries our conviction by its own intrinsic virtuosity – but it is also a parable of the main point of the book: that resurrections are ends, in the true sense of emergences of what was there all along; and so they are also beginnings of what is always there for us all.

And finally there is John's massive and intricate deployment of symbolism in order to reveal what Jesus reveals: eternal life, like eternal beauty, wandering on her way underneath the fragility of all finite existence.

In the old days we had doctrines of Christ which proved his divinity from the miracles he performed in life and which crowned the proof with the greatest miracle of all, his self-raising from the dead. Thus was Christ proved to have been the same divine being both before and after death. But this was all in aid of proving further that he had paid the price for our forgiveness. The moral teaching of Scripture then defined the sins from which by a heavenly transaction we were to be forgiven, and the virtues by which, once forgiven, we really ought to live. Power and presence were dealt with by means of lesser doctrines of 'created' grace; and written morality was all we could have because Jesus' divinity quite eclipsed his humanity.

More recently in theology we had a return to Jesus' full and true humanity. Now we had inspiration for our lives from a man like us in all things, sin alone excepted. At the same time in theology we saw the dawning realization that resurrection had much more to do with the divinity of Jesus than the mere provision of extraneous proof material to those who doubted it. But since resurrection was still commonly imagined to have taken place *only after* death, it was never quite clear if this inspiration for our lives from Jesus' life was merely humanitarian example after all; and, correspondingly, it was not clear whether he became divine after his death or was then for the first time shown to be, or to have been, divine. The divine, the 'exalted', the 'raised', was still, one suspected, as in the previous scheme, a matter of someone's existence, or someone's status, which might ultimately affect us; but it was still not seen to be a matter of powerful presence in every particle of our world which was living in and through us, or else killing us, in every instant.

This book moves us to the point we must reach, where the question of God is for Jesus, and for the members of his body in the world, a question of how to live and how to die from day to day.

James P Mackey

Acknowledgements

It is a pleasant duty to acknowledge the encouragement and stimulation I have received from many people in writing this book. The suggestion that I should embark on this study came, as he explains in the Foreword, from Professor James Mackey. As far as I can recall, his interest was initially aroused by a paper I presented to a group of colleagues on the structure of Mark's Gospel, towards the end of which I raised the question of Mark's understanding of the resurrection. With a theologian's eye for issues of fundamental concern, Professor Mackey led me to concentrate on the interpretation of the resurrection in the New Testament: a subject on which he himself had reflected in several of his writings. At first we thought that the theme of the book might be 'Eucharist and Resurrection'; but soon it became apparent that exegetical explorations were indicating a wider canvas. Professor Mackey describes our collaboration with characteristic generosity, but I must emphasize my great indebtedness to him for his invaluable comments on the early drafts, for his acute and helpful criticism as the book developed, and for the patience and constant good humour with which he responded to the demands I made on him.

My grateful thanks are also due to Professor James Dunn, who read the completed draft of this book and commented helpfully on it. I should add that I myself must accept responsibility for the style of exegesis. It is an attempt to move towards a more consciously holistic understanding of the text, but in a non-doctrinaire manner and without ignoring the positive results of the more traditional diachronic approaches. Here I should acknowledge the stimulation received from membership of the Society for New Testament Studies seminar on the role of the reader in the interpretation of the New Testament. My understanding of the theory is undoubtedly incomplete. Readers must judge whether the imperfections are equally evident in practice in this book.

Many of my friends and colleagues have taken a kindly interest in this project. Professor John O'Neill in particular has afforded me every encouragement. He gave generously of his time to discuss in depth some historical aspects of the subject which in the end did not figure largely in the published work. My debt to him is therefore much greater than appears. Professor Duncan Forrester has taken an active interest in the book, even though the final version is less directly related to eucharistic studies than was the original intention. Many colleagues – in New Testament studies, Christian ethics and across the Divinity disciplines – have enriched my understanding and made Edinburgh such a rewarding place in which to study and teach.

In addition, one could not hope to have a more helpful and co-operative publishing editor than Philip Law. To him and his colleagues at SPCK I am truly indebted.

Last, but by no means least, the person who has invested more time and energy in this book than any other apart from myself is my wife Jenny. Not only has she cheerfully endured my preoccupation with it, but she has typed several drafts, helped with the bibliography and proof-reading, and properly castigated occasional infelicities of style or vocabulary. Her patience and understanding, support and encouragement have provided the context in which I could attempt the work. To her I owe the greatest debt of all.

J I H McDonald
Edinburgh, January 1989

Introduction

To study the theology of the resurrection in the New Testament is to engage with living reality.

To some, such a statement may sound like a rash foray beyond the safe limits of historical criticism. Surely it would be more defensible to describe the resurrection faith as a living reality for the New Testament writers and the communities they addressed or represented! Their faith and thought are the proper object of study and provide the data for investigation. Only in this way can we ensure that New Testament study is properly scientific!

There is, however, a growing recognition today that the rigid subject–object division which such a viewpoint presupposes is a misconception.[1] It assumes that we who read and study the New Testament are somehow 'above' the material it contains, as its judges or critics. We develop expertise in determining its text, elucidating its historical milieu, identifying its sources and examining its authorship. As critics, we remain detached, aloof and invulnerable. Yet, while such approaches reveal much about the New Testament (a fact which is not disputed here), they may well ignore or distort its true nature. For the New Testament *addresses* and *involves* the reader, whoever the reader may be. It proclaims a message, the 'good news' of salvation for all humankind: the critic is not exempted! It tells a story which intersects our own story and demands response. It has a strong educational and pastoral concern.[2]

The treatment which is most likely to penetrate to the heart of the New Testament is that which enables the reader – as critic, historian, sociologist, liturgist or inquirer – to *hear* its message. This is to be inducted, as participant, into a living realm of discourse: that is, one which is concerned with the issues of life and death and which challenges one's most basic assumptions about faith, identity, values and destiny. The theme of resurrection is a particularly good example.

Compared to the old subject–object relation, this holistic understanding of New Testament studies unites ancient writers and readers with their modern counterparts in a common exploration of truth and life. It must be emphasized, however, that it does *not* represent a return to a pre-critical approach, nor does it bypass critical studies. The term 'post-critical' is also eschewed, if only to avoid the suggestion of presumption. The insistence is rather that critical studies are means to an end, not the end itself. That the creative use of critical studies is inherent in all intelligent interpretation emerges clearly from a brief consideration of the basic process.

To interpret the New Testament involves the recognition that each writer – be he evangelist, letter-writer or seer – projects a world within

1

which certain actions take place. This is the world of the text, in which the reader is invited to participate.[3] Readers become engrossed in the action, the interplay of characters or the plot, or the unfolding of a given issue. It is within such interaction that they encounter, for example, the language and concept of resurrection: perhaps in a narrative or story of an event in Jesus' ministry; or in a story about Jesus after his crucifixion; perhaps as part of a debate in the early Church about what it means to believe in the resurrection; or as an essential component of an apocalyptic vision.[4]

The language and concept of resurrection, however, also reflect a wider cultural context. Hence, in order to appreciate their connotation, if not their full import, it is necessary to make a foray into the extra-textual world which they presuppose. To understand 'resurrection' in the New Testament, it is essential to consider what its cultural antecedents have been, and how the New Testament writers relate to this heritage. In other words, the term 'resurrection' has a realm of meaning which can be explored only through critical historical study. This task is essayed in Chapter 1.

No less important, however, is the way in which the author uses the term in the text. It is at this point that readers are drawn into the discourse between the author and the readers he is addressing in the text. The world of the text reveals something of the author, for he participates in the action within the text in so far as he communicates through it with his readers. Hence we can speak of the author-in-the-text, as well as the readers-in-the-text, for the interaction of ancient author and ancient receptors is evident throughout.

Paul provides an obvious example. One cannot read 1 Corinthians 15 – a prime resurrection text – without realizing that this is a highly personal dialogue between Paul and at least a section of the Christian community at Corinth (see Chapter 2, pp. 37–40). The text shows us something of the apostle as he communicates a basic understanding of what faith in the resurrection means; and it shows us something also of a community or a group which is operating within a cultural framework which differs in certain important respects from that of Paul and which prompts a different – and, so far as the apostle understands it, a seriously defective – view of resurrection. Yet the whole exchange is more than a friendly debate about an interesting subject. Paul's presentation encompasses the apostles' proclamation (*kerygma*) of basic Christian belief ('what he handed on to them as of first importance', 1 Cor. 15.1–3; my paraphrase) and the united apostolic teaching (*didache*) on the subject. The element of authority relates to the witness (*martyria*) to the truth as it has been disclosed to the apostles. In the course of a rather long argument, Paul confronts his readers with the truth claim and demands their commitment to it.

The evangelists – named in the later gospel superscriptions as Matthew, Mark, Luke and John, though their identity is not known to us with certainty – follow a similar procedure, even though it is less evident at first glance. They personally do not intrude into the text in the way that Paul does – with complete propriety – in his letters, yet each leaves his mark, unmistakably, on the text of his Gospel: and he does so in spite of the fact that he is transmitting traditional material in a much tighter framework than Paul. Each Gospel is the evangelist's statement of the 'good news' (Mark 1.1) of Jesus Christ, the word (*logos*) become flesh (John 1.14). Each Gospel presents, as its plot, the story of Jesus in which God's concern for the salvation of humankind is conveyed. Each Gospel is an invitation to the reader not only to get to know the story of Jesus but also to find in it grounds for believing in the God who speaks in Christ: 'that believing you may have life in his name' (John 20.31b). In the first instance, of course, the ancient reader – the 'reader in the text' – is addressed. In Luke's Gospel, he is identified as Theophilus (1.3). But these Gospels are also read today, whether in a liturgical context or in private study; and the modern reader is addressed no less directly than the reader in the text.

To interpret the New Testament is therefore to be drawn into its world and to find meaning there. It is to take seriously its witness to 'the deep things of God' (1 Cor. 2.10) and to be challenged by it. Critical scholarship is essential to this end, for the witness is encapsulated in an ancient context. The complete model of interpretation, however, transcends that of subject–object. The New Testament is not simply a set of verbal propositions to be analysed grammatically or formally as one might dissect a specimen under the microscope. The reader is part of the larger whole with which the New Testament deals. To study the New Testament is to 'hear' its message. It is to be addressed by its 'word'. It is not only to judge its text critically, it is to be judged critically by the text.[5]

To interpret the resurrection is therefore a complex process. It involves the critical study of the source documents as well as an elucidation of the cultural context in which word and concept are used. It involves a study of the way in which New Testament writers use the term: whether in relation to the resurrection of Jesus or the resurrection of the faithful. It may involve a historical study of the grounds on which resurrection claims are based, as well as theological reflection on the meaning of resurrection. But the process moves readers, inexorably, to consider their own finitude and to view the new perspectives which resurrection opens up as live options for themselves. They are thus confronted with a new understanding of life and death, hope and despair, goal and purposelessness, the scope of 'bodily' existence and mortality. The perspective of resurrection, therefore, impinges on worldly or everyday existence, as it does in the story of Jesus 'in the flesh'. It evokes a power or dynamic which enables one to transcend the apparent hopelessness of a given human situation and to lay hold of the new creative possibilities of faith and hope.

This book is an attempt to capture something of these perspectives in a study of the theology of the resurrection in the New Testament. It carries no presumptuous claim to the effect that the holistic approach provides all the answers where others have failed! In fact, much previous work is assumed rather than recapitulated here,[6] and the limitations of the study which follows are felt most keenly by the author himself. If it succeeds in raising for the reader the wider implications of the fact that the resurrection, so far from being an appendix to the story of Jesus, is implicit in the entire message of the New Testament, it will bear its own witness to the truth which liberates and renews.

1 cf. J. O. Martin (1987). The following passage is particularly pertinent:

> Classical historical-criticism was objectivist, pursuing mechanical analysis and working with Cartesian split consciousness. It was strongly archaeological in direction, oriented to the past-historical, operating on assumptions of single efficient causality. Within an emerging holistic paradigm, historical-critical analysis now functions within the historical-political task of interpretation. It functions not only to discern the dynamics of the social-political world of the text in its past context, but also to discern the same dynamics in the contemporary context of the interpreter (p. 381).

cf. also Torrance (1976), *passim*.
2 Paul's paraenesis in 1 Corinthians is an example of educational concern. For a concise survey of the New Testament and pastoral care, see my article in Campbell (1987), pp. 172–4.
3 cf. Fowler (1983).
4 The Septuagint had already translated Hebraic language into Greek verbs: *chaya* was translated as *zen*, 'to live'; *hequis* as *anastenai*, 'to rise'; and *qum* as *egerthenai*, 'to be raised up'. The basic vocabulary was thus inherited from the Hebrew Scriptures: cf. 2 Kings 4.31; 13.20–1; Isa. 26.14, 19; Jer. 51.39, 57; Hos. 6.2. Cf. Rigaux (1973), pp. 8–9.
5 cf. Dunn and Mackey (1987), chapter 1.
6 In particular, one would mention Grass (1962), Schenke (1968), von Campenhausen (1968), Marxsen (1970), Rigaux (1973), Wilckens (1977), Perkins (1984). On the theology of the resurrection, the classic is still Künneth (1965). On the resurrection narratives in particular, there are works by Fuller (1972), Alsup (1975), Perrin (1977).

1

The Resurrection in Context

*When they heard of the resurrection of the dead, some mocked; but others said,
'We will hear you again about this'.*

ACTS 17.32

A classic culture barrier emerged when Paul was preaching at Athens (Acts 17.22–31). It was not that Paul was unable to relate to the Hellenistic ethos: the recorded summary suggests that he did so rather well (cf. 17.24–29). His mastery of the diatribal style and his familiarity with Jewish approaches to the Gentile world enabled him to hold his audience.[1] But the punchline was specifically Christian: the resurrection of the one appointed by God to judge the world (17.31). It was at this point that the hearers distanced themselves from the apostle. There was nothing in their cultural experience to enable them to come to terms with such a claim. They were worlds apart.

Modern readers may share something of the Athenians' dilemma, although many centuries of Christian tradition may have helped a little. The modern world-view, however, is very different from that of Jewish apocalyptic, which Paul's statement presupposed. Some mapwork of the latter must therefore be supplied.

1 THE EMERGENCE OF
THE RESURRECTION HOPE IN ISRAEL

Only in its later phases does the Old Testament evince any interest in life beyond the grave. Characteristically, Israel's religious interest focused on the span of life from birth to death. The reward of piety was a long life 'in the land which the Lord your God gives you' (Exod. 20.12). It was good to die, like Abraham, 'an old man and full of years' and be gathered to one's people (Gen. 25.8). Premature death was to be lamented.[2] It is the lot of humankind to return to the dust (Ps. 90.3). Amid the uncertainties of life, it is well to apply oneself to divine wisdom (Ps. 90.12). Personal experience of divine deliverance centres on recovery from life-threatening trouble (Ps. 116.3–4, 8–9). The perfect pattern, which belongs to 'the latter days' (Mic. 4.1), portrays the blessings of obedience in this-worldly, even homely, images. Swords are made into ploughshares, spears into pruning-hooks; war and the arts of war are neither practised nor studied, 'but they shall sit every man under his vine and under his fig tree, and none shall make them afraid' (Mic. 4.4).

Yahweh, King and Creator, has graciously chosen Israel to be his special people. Such a status involves responsibility, especially moral responsibility. According to the Deuteronomist, his choice of them was an act of love (Deut. 7.8), engendering in them the response of love and obedience (7.9). Covenant-love (or mercy), faithfulness, steadfastness and obedience are the watchwords of Israel's faith. Blessings attend the obedient – this-worldly blessings at that (cf. 28.1–14). 'You shall tend upward only, and not downward' (28.13). The lot of the disobedient is singularly unattractive. For them there is a veritable regression to the condition of Israel in Egypt before the great deliverance – and they may bring down the whole nation with them (cf. Deut. 28.15–68, esp. 60, 68).

The difficulty with this kind of picture is that it is idealized and therefore vulnerable to empirical reality. The prosperity of the wicked contradicted this cosy moral dualism. The adversity of the faithful caused even greater difficulty, as is evident in the Psalms and in the deep anger of Job (cf. Pss. 31.1 ; 44.9, 23 ; Job *passim*). The problem is not, as is sometimes suggested, that 'history contradicts both the doctrine of God's benevolence to the individual and the doctrine of the election and special position in God's esteem of the people of Israel'.[3] It is that such doctrines, *if combined with a simplistic reward-and-punishment theory*, are contradicted by human experience. The narrow frame of reference excludes much of human pain and suffering, as well as human failure and adversity, from positive assessment.

The necessary widening and deepening of human perception involved different dimensions of faith. One was the reassessment of suffering and adversity, even death. MacNeile Dixon, in his Gifford Lectures, after reviewing attempts from Descartes onwards to posit an undeniable proposition ('I think, therefore I am') as an epistemological foundation, offered the following suggestion:

> No philosophers, or men of science, have so far had the hardihood, as far as I know, to deny us our pains. They relieve us of all else. They have taken from us our personality, our freedom, our souls, our very selves. They have, however, left us our sorrows. Let us take, then, as our foundation the proposition 'I suffer, therefore I am'. And let us add to it the converse and equally true statement, 'I am, therefore I suffer'. The privilege, if it be a privilege, of existence is ours, and we have paid the price required. We have discharged our debts. We have not had something for nothing. We have free minds, and can look round us with a smile. Nothing can any longer intimidate us.[4]

Israel, too, was searching for fundamental understanding, though not in terms of philosophy. There emerged the recognition not only that the life of the present generation is bound up with its forefathers but that it is also heir to the consequences of the sins of the forefathers. 'The fathers have eaten sour grapes, and the children's teeth are set on edge' (Ezek. 18.2). In this situation, one can only have recourse to the compassion of Yahweh (Ps. 79.8). There also emerged the acknowledgement that loyal service can be costly and incur undeserved reverses:

> All this has come upon us,
>   though we have not forgotten thee,
>   or been false to thy covenant   (Ps. 44.17).

The most impressive development is the picture of the servant of Yahweh as taking upon himself the full weight of human sorrow and suffering, and yet affirming a positive purpose in it all (Isa. 53). Suffering and death can have a vicarious element: they can be undertaken for others' benefit (53.4–5, 10–12). The canvas is therefore stretched in order to affirm the good outcome (53.10–11) and to give assurance of divine vindication (53.12). A somewhat thinner version of this scenario interprets suffering as discipline and testing, but the righteous thus afflicted have a hope that is 'full of immortality' (Wisd. 3.4–6).

Thus we arrive at the point at which we may observe, with Wilckens, that 'the question of *resurrection* in Jewish thinking stands in the *context* of the *theodicy* question':[5] theodicy being the attempt to affirm the goodness and omnipotence of God in face of the operation of evil in the world. It is important, however, not to over-intellectualize the problem. To do so frequently ends in serious reductionism.[6] The way forward is to follow the inner logic of Israel's thinking as it wrestles with such problems. Its procedure is probably best described by a term such as 'apperception': the perceiving of the pattern of interaction between the great symbols of Israel's faith (kingdom, covenant, creation, salvation) and the problematic human scene, in the perspective both of history and of eternity.[7]

In the Old Testament, Yahweh is Creator, King of the universe, victorious over the chaos monster, and providential sustainer of the earth (cf. Ps. 96.10). Indeed, this creation motif, standing as it does in tension with the more limited covenantal theology, conserves the idea of divine sovereignty over the entire cosmos. It is for this reason that it is reasserted in apocalypticism, which effectively transfers the old chaos/creation conflict into the future. Hence, when the chaos of destruction and death overtakes Israel at the hands of Babylon, it is not surprising to find a prophetic vision, like that of Ezekiel's valley of dry bones (Ezek. 37.1–14), in which Yahweh alone has the power to re-create the life of the nation: '"Son of man, can these bones live?" And I answered, "O Lord God, thou knowest"' (37.3). Then comes the resurrection image: 'Behold, I will open your graves, and raise you from your graves, O my people; and I will bring you home into the land of Israel' (37.12). The language of resurrection is metaphorical: it constitutes an iconic symbol.[8] A historical reality is indicated: the restoration of Israel to her own land and the renewal of the nation. This historical reality is to be effected by the power of the sovereign God, with whom are the issues of life and renewal.

A difficult passage in Isaiah seems to make a similar point, also by the use of resurrection imagery:

> Thy dead shall live, their bodies shall rise.
>   O dwellers in the dust, awake and sing for joy!
> For thy dew is a dew of light,
>   and on the land of the shades thou wilt let it fall
>
> (Isa. 26.19).

7

Difficulties attach to text, translation and date; but it is clear enough that the image of bodily resurrection is used to demonstrate that the power of Yahweh will secure the increase of the nation (cf. Isa. 26.15).[9]

If Yahweh has the power of creation and re-creation, he also exercises the royal prerogative of judgement within history. The judgement against Babylon is a judgement against evil, arrogance, ruthlessness and oppression (Isa. 13.11; 14.4), and is effected within history by the Medes. The oppressor is cut down to size, so that the shades of former earthly potentates in Sheol bestir themselves sufficiently to welcome the new arrival with the words: 'You too have become as weak as we! You have become like us!' (Isa. 14.10). A cause and effect sequence operates in history, whereby the wicked eventually bring judgement upon themselves and the righteous eventually receive blessing. But the process is no longer regarded as simple. It is as complex as history itself, and can leave the individual with a feeling of helplessness or emptiness (cf. Eccles. 1.2).

Thus the simple morality of the Deuteronomic model – the 'two way' theology[10] that has its roots in covenantal thinking and relates right and wrong behaviour to reward and punishment – is eventually reworked at a much more sophisticated level of understanding. The process involves the use of metaphor and imagery – for example, the language of resurrection and the Sheol scene – to suggest perspectives unavailable at the level of literal description. In other words, the immanent forces in history are projected, for clarification, on to a metaphorical screen which allows a deeper appreciation of their meaning. Yet this screen, while imaginative, is not mere make-believe. It is a parable[11] of history and experience, interpreted in the context of the eternal purpose of God.

The later parts of the Old Testament overlap with the so-called intertestamental literature. Here, four leading theological characteristics are readily identifiable. These are, as J. H. Charlesworth has put it, 'the problems of sin and theodicy, emphasis upon God's transcendence, speculations about the Messiah, and the ideas concerning the afterlife'.[12] To be sure, these are in keeping with the expanding scenario of Israel's religious awareness which we have noted above in embryo, although the widening of vision is undoubtedly assisted by 'the influence of an exotic and Gentile climate of thought, namely Iranian Zoroastrianism'[13] mediated to Judaism through the Persian Empire. While the Sadducees resisted such innovations, this kind of 'transcendentalism' was firmly embraced by deeply pious and committed movements in Judaism: in particular, by the Hasidim (or 'Pious Ones') from whom both Pharisees and Essenes derived. It was their judgement, therefore, that such a development was far from being alien to Israel's religious tradition but rather provided the wider scope essential for the expression of the essence of their faith in the traumatic times of the Maccabees and their successors.

Several aspects of this transcendental world-view are particularly relevant to our concerns:

(a) Cosmic conflict and the court of heaven

Historical Israel continued to be at the mercy of mighty powers which had crushed her in the past and, in Maccabean times, threatened her very being. They are the predatory beasts of Daniel 7, the birds of prey in 1 Enoch. Yet Israel was God's flock, God's people. Hence, the conflict was of cosmic dimensions: between the power of God and the powers of evil. The writer to the Ephesians reflects this world-view when he states: 'We are not contending against flesh and blood, but against the principalities, against the powers, against the world rulers of this present darkness, against the spiritual hosts of wickedness in the heavenly places' (Eph. 6.12).

The historical powers have therefore a transcendental counterpart: 'the prince of the kingdom of Persia' (Dan. 10.13, 20) is opposed by Michael, Israel's prince and guardian angel (Dan. 10.21; 12.1). The Gentile nations have each their guardian angel: the seventy shepherds of 1 Enoch. At the head of the powers stands Satan, the great adversary of God. Hence, the scene is set for the ultimate conflict between God and Satan, the war of the sons of light and the sons of darkness, Armageddon. In this transcendental view of cosmic conflict, the outcome is beyond doubt. The great powers, symbolized in Daniel 2.31–5 as a mighty statue with feet partly of clay, are shattered by a 'stone cut out by no human hand' and destroyed without trace, while the stone is seen to be the mountain of the Lord that fills the earth.

The transcendental scenario is perhaps best illustrated by the court of heaven (cf. Dan. 7.9–10). The 'Ancient of Days' presides enthroned over the heavenly hosts. 'The court sat in judgment, and the books were opened' (7.10c). The court is, of course, directly concerned with human history, dominated as it has been by the bestial powers. The last and worst beast – no prizes are given for recognizing the kingdom of Antiochus IV Epiphanes – is instantly executed (7.11), the others stripped of their power (7.12):

> and behold, with the clouds of heaven
> there came one like a son of man,
> and he came to the Ancient of Days
> and was presented before him.
> And to him was given dominion... (7.13–14a).

Here is the creation of the eternal, humane and universal Kingdom which, under God, fulfils the longings of the faithful. The lesson is spelt out: 'the saints of the Most High shall receive the kingdom, and possess the kingdom for ever...' (7.18). Thus the demands of theodicy and justice, as well as the vindication of covenantal loyalty, are fully met.

(b) Vindication and judgement

The presupposition of this picture of the court of heaven is the resurrection, at least of the faithful. The beasts are not hauled before the divine court when judgement is given against them. The heavenly decree is executed on earth, while the saints of the Most High inherit the eternal Kingdom. The saints may be supposed to have performed signal service on earth, especially in opposing the bestial powers. There is thus a close interrelation between the court of heaven and historical events. Judgement in heaven represents the final definitive verdict on earthly action and looks to the completion of God's purpose for his cosmos.

The interaction of heaven and earth is well illustrated by memorable chapters in the Wisdom of Solomon. As the wisdom tradition emphasized, it is important for humankind to follow the precepts of Wisdom on earth. The ungodly court death (Wisd. 1.12–16). They recognize their own finitude and mortality, sketched most beautifully in Wisdom 2.1–5. But the practical conclusion they draw is not only to live by the pleasure principle (2.6–9) but to oppress and exploit (2.10). 'Might is right': the lame duck has no utilitarian value (2.11). To them, the person of principle and faith is an inconvenience and a burden (2.12–16) to be harassed and taunted (2.17, 19). The underlying charge is that the faith of the righteous is not borne out by the evidence of human experience (2.18, 2,0). The problem of theodicy is used as a pretext by sinners, who take no account of the mystery of God's purposes:

> Thus they reasoned, but they were
>   led astray,
> for their wickedness blinded them,
> and they did not know the secret
>   purposes of God,
> nor hope for the wages of holiness,
> nor discern the prize for blameless
>   souls;
> for God created man for
>   incorruption,
> and made him in the image of his
>   own eternity,
> but through the devil's envy death
>   entered the world,
> and those who belong to his party
>   experience it   (2.21–4).

The perspective of eternal life is then explored. Too late, the wicked see the folly of their ways: 'it was we who strayed from the way of truth' (5.6a); 'so we also, as soon as we were born, ceased to be...' (5.13). In the court of heaven the righteous are vindicated:

> the righteous live for ever,
> and their reward is with the Lord;
> the Most High takes care of them.
> Therefore they will receive a glorious crown,
> and a beautiful diadem from the hand of the Lord...
>   (5.15–16).

One theological strand, which came into prominence about the second century BC, had a background of persecution and 'posited post-mortem judgment as a means to adjudicate this injustice'.[14] Daniel 12 belongs to this category. When Michael intervenes to save the elect, there is an awakening of 'many of those who sleep in the dust of the earth': some to everlasting life, some to 'shame and everlasting contempt' (12.2). Here one may discern both bodily resurrection and the two-way motif of reward and punishment hereafter. A similar model is found in the Assumption of Moses 10 and in Jubilees 23.27–31.[15] There are also impressive similarities in the Testament of Judah 25, although in this passage there is a much more general concern with the restoration of Israel. The twelve tribal chiefs will be resurrected, along with the founding fathers (Abraham, Isaac and Jacob) and the faithful in Israel. A judgement scene of the conventional type is presupposed.[16] This exaltation tradition stands in continuity with Isaiah 13, 14 and 52—53.2, where the fate of Israel's enemies is sealed and the grievously oppressed servant community exalted and vindicated.

Similar motifs are indicated in the impressive seventh chapter of 2 Maccabees. Pledged to die rather than transgress the laws of their fathers, the brothers and their mother invoke God's compassionate care in the face of horrific torture (7.6). As the second brother is about to die, he addresses the king thus: 'You accursed wretch, you dismiss us from this present life, but the King of the universe will raise us up to an everlasting renewal of life, because we have died for his laws' (7.9). Thus, loyalty to the heavenly King and covenant is linked indissolubly with vindication and eternal life. The fourth brother, cherishing the hope of resurrection, tells his persecutor: 'for you there will be no resurrection to life!' (7.14).[17] The mother invokes the notion of God the Creator:

> I do not know how you came into being in my womb. It was not I who gave you life and breath, nor I who set in order the elements within each of you. Therefore the Creator of the world, who shaped the beginning of man and devised the origin of all things, will in his mercy give life and breath back to you again, since you now forget yourselves for the sake of his laws (7.22–3).

The punishment of Antiochus is emphasized throughout (cf. 7.31, 34–6). The brothers accept suffering because of their own sins, as rebuke and discipline at the hands of the living God, but reconciliation will follow (7.33). For all such martyrs who 'have drunk of everflowing life under God's covenant', vindication is complete hereafter.

There is another strand of theology, represented in both early and late sources, which does not arise in the context of persecution and simply takes eternal life and death as the reward and punishment for one's actions on earth. The Psalms of Solomon provide many examples. As the result of God's judgement, the righteous will rise to eternal life while 'the destruction of the sinner is forever' (3.11). The sinners' inheritance is Sheol (Hades), darkness and destruction (14.9). Their memory will no longer be found (13.11). Later books such as 4 Ezra and the Sibylline Oracles imply a general resurrection and judgement. The wicked are punished in Gehenna; the righteous dwell in light. In the Testament of Benjamin, 'all will rise, some to glory and some to dishonour'. Thus it is clear that there are different ways of relating the resurrection to the parties concerned – especially to the unrighteous.

11

Some light is thrown on this matter by the remarkable twenty-second chapter of 1 Enoch. In the course of his cosmic travels, Enoch arrives at a great mountain in the west containing four hollow places, deep and wide and smooth. Here, it is explained, the spirits of the souls of the dead await the day of judgement. Although there are problems of interpretation, it would appear that there are four groups. There are the righteous, who dwell by the water-spring and live in the light (22.9b). There are the wicked who have not been punished during their earthly life: here they are separated 'for this great torment' until judgement day, when it seems they will be constrained for ever in Gehenna (22.10–11). There are those who have suffered death at the hands of sinners (22.12) – like Abel, murdered by his brother Cain and still crying out for retribution (22.5–7). Finally, there are the wicked who have already paid for their misdeeds, whose place is with the wrongdoers for ever: for them there is neither final punishment nor resurrection to life.

In spite of its difficulties, a consistent logic may be discerned in the passage, if perhaps at the risk of over-simplification. The first and the last groups – the righteous and the reprobate – are similar in that they already enjoy their eternal reward: the righteous life, the reprobate extinction. Neither the wholly righteous nor the wholly reprobate require to be raised to final judgement, for the balance of reward and punishment has already been effected in their cases. The problem rests with the two intermediate categories where 'fullness' – or, in modern terms, fulfilment – has not been reached. The victims of murder have been cut off prematurely in their earthly existence and their demand for retribution has yet to be met. The wicked who have not incurred the penalty of their sin before their death have begun to pay their dues through torment before being assigned to their final dire destination. The logic, therefore, affirms and underscores 'the old view of the correspondence between what one does and what one has to endure, between one's actions and one's conditions'.[18] The point of the whole passage is that God effects the salvation of his covenanted people, while the unfaithful are delivered to death; and that the inequalities evident in history are finally sorted out by the divine Judge.

The danger of this kind of solution is that it is simply too neat and therefore may represent a rationalization of the evidence. It is only fair to say that it is not completely clear that those who have suffered violent death are righteous martyrs or themselves implicated in sin: there is a suggestion, in a text that is probably secondary, that three chambers are dark and only one bright. And although no resurrection is assigned to the righteous, their location suggests a 'rest in peace' scenario prior to everlasting life, rather than beatification itself. As Nickelsburg observes, 'it would be a unique passage if it envisioned only a resurrection of the sinners'.[19] General solutions must be treated with suspicion. Complete consistency can hardly be expected in this kind of literature, just as complete consistency is not to be found in relation to judgement and life after death. But it is fair to say that the general principle of judgement and vindication holds firm. In this way, a final solution is sought to the problem of theodicy and a sketch offered of the outworking of the sovereign purpose of the Creator, bound in covenant to his people and faithful to the end.

(c) The mode of resurrection

'Some one will ask, "How are the dead raised? With what kind of body do they come?"' (1 Cor. 15.35). It is little wonder that the Corinthian Christians put this question to Paul. Greek cultural presuppositions about life after death differed markedly from at least some views held in the Jewish world, but the latter was by no means uniform in its understanding or in the imagery it used, and a simple contrast between Greek and Jewish models (or Greek and Christian models) cannot be drawn.

To be sure, if one goes back five centuries or so before Christ, resurrection language related, as we have seen, to the restoration of Israel from its grave in exile to the expected new life of the nation in its own land. The metaphor of resurrection could hardly have had a more this-worldly application. The new Israel, while spiritually renewed, was flesh and blood. The basic concept is of Yahweh's eternal covenant with Israel. From that, Israel derived its hope of eternity; and the fulfilment of these hopes was essentially located in this world. Israel lives on and looks for the fulfilment of its destiny. The dead, as individuals, know only the shadowy reality of Sheol; and this is in no sense life. Certainly, if one were to contrast this view with, say, Socrates' belief in the immortality of the soul, once released from the constraints of the body, one might conclude that the Greeks believed in the after-life and the Hebrews, by and large, did not.

As part of the complex development of belief in ancient Judaism, involving not only the question of theodicy but also the apperception of the operation of the God of the covenant, Creator and King over history and Judge of the cosmos, a new emphasis was placed on the final scenario of judgement. The dead are still thought of as sleeping in the dust of the earth (Dan. 12.2). The image of awakening is thus as appropriate as that of resurrection. As we have seen, some presuppose the appearance of the righteous and the wicked before the throne of judgement; others that the wicked are already condemned to death. Later expressions of the Pharisaic tradition in particular, with their scriptural appeal to 'law and prophets', reinforced the 'solid' concept of the resurrection body. Indeed, the fourth Sibylline oracle holds that, prior to the final judgement, God will remake mortals from dust and bones into their former form. This stereotype is sometimes assumed to represent the Jewish view as a whole and to have passed *simpliciter* into the Christian tradition. O. Cullmann in particular, in an influential essay, drew a sharp distinction between this view and the Greek belief in the immortality of the soul.[20]

Yet the Jewish tradition of the intertestamental period is in fact much more complex. The Wisdom of Solomon presupposes the immortality of the soul or the spirit; it has no place for the resurrection of the body.

Human beings were created for immortality but lost it through 'the devil's envy' (Wisd. 2.23–4). Nevertheless, 'the souls of the righteous are in the hand of God', safe from all torment (3.1); 'their hope is full of immortality' (3.4); 'they are at peace' (3.6). To be sure, the writer does not hesitate to combine this notion of immortality with the more traditional idea of the Kingdom (3.7–8): both being comprehended by the notion that the faithful abide in God's love (3.9). Grace and mercy are upon the elect, but the ungodly are punished (3.9–10).

This Hellenistic-type model of immortality is well attested in earlier Hasidic and apocalyptic writings, and tended to dominate in Essene circles. Thus, Jubilees states: 'their bones shall rest in the earth, and their spirits shall have much joy' (23.32). 1 Enoch 103 ascribes goodness, joy and honour to 'the souls [*psychais*] of the pious dead: their spirits [*pneumata*] will rejoice and not perish'. The Qumran writings have a preference for speaking of 'eternal life' (or 'joy' or 'salvation'), though they provide a few examples of resurrection language which, however, need not imply resurrection of the flesh. Such language can be used of the soul, which can in turn be endowed with bodily attributes.

There may be a tendency on the part of some modern interpreters to exaggerate the antithesis between body and soul or spirit, especially in Hellenistic Judaism. In so far as the language of immortality presupposed Hellenistic concepts, it might well be – as in Stoicism – that the difference between them was one of degree only: the soul was conceived as an ethereal bodily substance, such as fire.[21] As Paul explains to the Corinthians, each type of being has its own body: 'If there is a physical body, there is also a spiritual body' (1 Cor. 15.44). What is certainly true is that in the Jewish tradition one did not think in terms of the liberation of the soul from the prison of the body. Bodily existence, however, need not be physical or 'in the flesh'.

There is thus considerable variety and fluidity in relation to the mode of resurrection in ancient Jewish writings. As Hengel puts it, 'spiritualized and realistic conceptions stand side by side with relatively little connection'.[22] Nickelsburg writes in the same vein: 'The evidence indicates that in the intertestamental period there was no single Jewish orthodoxy on the time, mode, and place of resurrection, immortality, and eternal life'.[23] It would be wrong to assume that the flux arises simply because of the importation of alien ideas, to which some groups were more open than others; and that we are justified in going back to the original 'pure' corporeal notion of resurrection. As we have seen, the latter belongs to a different context and is transposed into the celestial judgement scenario. There is evidence that the Hebrew tradition was itself on the move, irrespective of outside influences. Consider Psalm 73:

> Thou dost guide me with thy counsel,
>   and afterward thou wilt receive me to glory...
> My flesh and heart may fail,
>   but God is the strength of my
>   heart and my portion for ever   (Ps. 73.24, 26).

It is possible that, with his deep spirituality, the psalmist is already groping for the essential notion of eternal life as the fulfilment of his relationship with God on earth. Whatever doubts remain about the precise meaning of being received 'afterward' into glory or honour, it clearly refers to the fulfilment of a life of faith and obedience on earth. It does not in any sense denigrate life in the flesh. That is the scene of our service, the first realization and expression of our dependence on God. Its completion lies 'afterward' in the future.

(d) Divine intervention

It would be wrong to interpret the concern for the vindication of the righteous and the judgement of the wicked as evidence of a headlong flight into pure individualism in post-exilic Judaism. The emphasis on the nation is as strong as ever. The emphasis on divine vindication was at its strongest in time of national threat: Maccabean times present the prime example, when Judaism struggled for its life against Antiochus IV Epiphanes. In such contexts, divine vindication was bound up with divine intervention in history. In Daniel, the expectation of imminent divine deliverance is strong (cf. 9.23–7): an expectation strengthened by the witness of the Scriptures and the visions or dreams of the prophet. In the Enoch circle, there is a similar expectation, related to the same threat (1 Enoch 83—90, 91–3). Even after the fall of Jerusalem, 4 Ezra and 2 Baruch place weight on divine deliverance, their aim being 'to vindicate the existence of the orthodox in Israel in the present, and to vindicate their view of orthodoxy as the true mode of Jewish identity'.[24]

A particular feature of this scenario is the emergence of certain figures, including messianic figures, who play a significant role in the divine deliverance which Israel was awaiting. Frequently, these figures are attached to particular groups: for example, Melchizedek was linked with Qumran. The Enoch group is of considerable interest. The mysterious account in Genesis 5.24 – Enoch 'spent his life in fellowship with God, and then he disappeared, for God took him away' (GNB) – was filled out by later tradition (cf. Heb. 11.5).

In the orthodox tradition represented by Jubilees, he is a heavenly scribe who annotates the judgement of the world and the priest who burns the incense in the Lord's sanctuary (Jub. 4.16–25). In 2 Enoch, he emerges not only as heavenly scribe but as redeemer (2 Enoch 64.5). But it is in the Similitudes of Enoch (1 Enoch 37.71) that the fullest picture emerges. Lifted on the chariots of the Spirit (71.2), he was shown all the secrets of the universe in 'the heaven of heavens' (71). In the second parable (45—57), he sits as the Elect One on the seat of glory in a transformed heaven and at the centre of the life of the righteous (45.3–6). In a strong evocation of Daniel 7,[25] he is designated 'that son of man' by whose power the might of arrogant and oppressive kings is overthrown (46). He is a pre-existent heavenly being, the antecedent of time (48), full of divine wisdom and power (49), righteous in judgement and destroyer of the unrepentant (50):

In those days, Sheol will return all the deposits which she has received and hell will give back all that it owes. And he shall choose the righteous and the holy ones from among [the risen dead], for the day when they shall be selected and saved has arrived (51.1–2).[26]

In the climax of the book (70—1), Enoch is addressed as the 'Son of Man', on whom rests 'the righteousness of the Antecedent of Time':

Everyone…shall [follow] your path, since righteousness never forsakes you. Together with you shall be their dwelling places; and together with you shall be their portion. They shall not be separated from you forever and ever and ever. So there shall be length of days with that Son of Man, and peace to the righteous ones…(71.16–17).

Such a passage seems to presuppose an 'eschatological community': a sub-group within Judaism, as M. Casey describes it, who treasure the secret knowledge of salvation invested in the name of Enoch.

The description of the translation of Enoch owes something to the biblical account of the translation of Elijah (2 Kings 2.11). The return of Elijah as the harbinger of the Day of the Lord was expected in the later prophets (cf. Mal. 3.1; 4.4–6). The return of Enoch was based on 1 Enoch 90.31. In the Apocalypse of Elijah, the two figures come down to fight Antichrist for seven days; they will be killed and lie dead for three and a half days, but on the fourth day they will arise and denounce him. 'Do you not know that we live in the Lord?' (cf. 4.7, 13–15).[27] But there are a number of other prominent messianic or intermediary figures in Israel's hope of salvation. The return of Moses was deduced from Deuteronomy 18.15: 'The Lord your God will raise up for you a prophet like me from among you, from your brethren – him you shall heed…' He was the greatest of all prophets, 'whom the Lord knew face to face' (Deut. 34.10). References to his divine elevation are found in a number of Jewish sources, including Josephus (who implies his translation rather than his death),[28] Philo and the rabbinic tradition. The expectation of the Davidic king-messiah is another example, but there is in fact no lack of candidates.[29]

A review of material such as that discussed above underlines the fact that resurrection language is essentially eschatological and relates particularly to the apocalyptic world-view which gave expression to the hopes and expectations of ancient Judaism. To the modern reader, it is a strange, almost closed world; yet when the followers of Jesus – or Jesus himself – used resurrection language, it was this realm of discourse which provided the frame of reference. At the same time, symbols of prime importance were implicit in it: God as King and Judge, who exercises his sovereign will over a wayward cosmos; the God of the covenant, bound to his people in covenant-love, and the God who delivers his people by his divinely commissioned servant. In the interaction of these faith symbols is to be found Israel's answer to the problem of theodicy.

How far did the Christians presuppose this symbolic system, and how far did they modify it in the light of new experiences which gave rise to new symbols? That question will be reviewed in the next section and will be part of the agenda for the rest of the book.

2 THE RESURRECTION OF JESUS AND THE APOCALYPTIC WORLD-VIEW

Strictly, the resurrection of Jesus in the New Testament belongs to the eschatological rather than the apocalyptic realm of discourse.[30] It is part of the final action of God for the liberation and salvation of his people. Nevertheless, the apocalyptic world of ancient Judaism provides a broad frame of reference for affirming that the Jesus who lived and died is part of the transcendent world and participates centrally in the destiny of the cosmos.

In Revelation, the court of heaven is portrayed with all the furniture of Jewish apocalyptic (cf. Rev. 4—5). The mission of Jesus can be read into the essentially apocalyptic scene: 'the Lion of the tribe of Judah, the Root of David, has conquered' (5.5). The Lamb stands in the place of honour (5.6): the Lamb who was slain (5.12). The sacrificed/glorified Christ is installed at the centre of heavenly worship and power (5.12–14). He it is who unseals the last great cosmic events (Rev. 6—8). He it is who reigns for a thousand years with the resurrected saints (20.4). The Lamb is wedded to the city of God (21.9); with God himself, the Lamb is the city's temple (21.22), and its lamp (21.23–4); from the throne of God and of the Lamb, the river of the water of life flows (22.1). Meanwhile, the faithful on earth, beset with trouble, pray for the fulfilment of the envisioned end: 'Come, Lord Jesus!' (22.20).

If the mission of Jesus is to be seen as the focal cosmic event, his followers eagerly await the consummation of his work. The death of the faithful, as at Thessalonica (1 Thess. 4.13), causes concern. Will they participate in the final glory? In answer, Paul relates the centre of the Christian kerygma – the death and resurrection of the Messiah (cf. 1 Cor. 15.3–5) – to messianic functions within the Jewish apocalyptic framework, and emerges with the assurance that 'God will bring with him those who have fallen asleep' (1 Thess. 4.14). The Jewish apocalypse known as 2 Baruch describes the consequence of the appearance of the Messiah in this way:

> And it will happen at that time that those treasuries will be opened in which the number of the souls of the righteous were kept, and they will go out and the multitudes of the souls will appear together, in one assemblage, of one mind. And the first ones will enjoy themselves and the last ones will not be sad (30.2).

In 1 Thessalonians, the risen Lord descends from heaven with divine command, archangelic summons, and trumpet blast; the Christian dead arise from their graves, the living are 'caught up together with them in the clouds to meet the Lord in the air; and so we shall always be with the Lord' (4.17). Much of the imagery is related to Jewish apocalyptic:

the archangel, the trumpet and the clouds; even the notion of the return of the divine figure. The meeting 'in the air' may be understood simply as the language of transcendence. The total statement brings comfort to believers (4.18).

It needs no great effort to demonstrate that 1 Corinthians 15 also draws heavily on Jewish apocalyptic. Given the distinctively Christian proclamation of the death and resurrection of Jesus, the Messiah (15.3–5, 12), the notion of the eternal messianic community underpins the argument against those who deny the resurrection of the dead (15.12). The idea of victorious messianic rule (cf. 15.24–8) is found in several Jewish apocalypses, as is the transformation of the righteous (15.51). Nor can one fail to recognize the dependence of the little apocalypses in the New Testament (such as Mark 13) on conventional Jewish imagery.

What are we to make of all this? Are we left with no more than a revamped apocalyptic world-view? Have the historical elements in the story of Jesus simply been submerged in a tidal wave of cosmic speculation? And does the use of resurrection language mark the point at which the flood gates were opened?[31] If so, is there any way in which we can 'comfort one another' with such words? These are substantial questions, relating to the heart of the enterprises we term New Testament theology and hermeneutics. At this stage, discussion of them can be no more than preliminary, for answers should emerge in the course of the subsequent chapters of this book. However, it may be helpful to comment in a preliminary way on some aspects of the problem which underlie our later discussion.

(a) The appearances of the risen Jesus

Attempts have been made to show that apocalypticism provides the essential context for the understanding of the appearances of the risen Jesus. J. M. Robinson finds in Revelation 1.13–16 'the only resurrection appearance in the New Testament that is described in any detail'.[32] The passage is as follows (my translation):

> When I turned round I saw seven golden lampstands, and in the midst of the lampstands one like a son of man, clad in a long robe and with a golden girdle around his breast. His head and his hair were white as white wool – like snow; and his eyes like flaming fire. His feet resembled burnished bronze, refined as in a furnace; and his voice was like the sound of many waters. He held in his right hand seven stars, from his mouth proceeded a sharp two-edged sword, and his face was like the sun shining in full strength.

Here indeed is rich, imaginative apocalyptic imagery, but the passage itself is astonishingly composite: 'made up of elements found in various representations of God, of angels, of the Messiah and perhaps of a pagan deity as well'.[33] The Christology of Revelation presupposes both the resurrection – 'first-born of the dead' (1.5) – and the atoning death of Christ, 'who loves us and has freed us from our sins by his blood' (1.5). He is the Coming One (1.7), sending prophetic messages by his inspired prophet to the seven churches (1.10–11). While the image of 'one like a son of man' is derived from Daniel 7.13, the messianic overtones – as in 1 Enoch – are unmistakable (cf. 1 Enoch 46.1–8). The details of the description portray Christ in the aspect of divinity. It is the Ancient of Days who has hair 'like pure wool' in Daniel 7.9; 'white like wool' in 1 Enoch 46.1; 'like snow' in the Apocalypse of Abraham 11. The picture is of the cosmic Christ, whose power eclipses all astral powers (cf. Col. 1.16) and whose coming will effect dread vengeance on his enemies (cf. Isa. 11.4; 1 Enoch 62.6; 2 Esdras 13.9–13; 2 Thess. 2.8). One is bound to ask whether there is anything in common between this composite apocalyptic extravaganza and the appearances of the risen Jesus in the Gospels.

Robinson's argument is that they have in common the quality of 'luminosity'. John of Patmos saw the Christ in glory; Stephen 'gazed into heaven and saw the glory of God, and Jesus standing at the right hand of God' (Acts 7.55). A 'light from heaven' flashed about Saul on the Damascus road (Acts 9.3); Jesus was so transfigured on the mountain that 'his garments became glistening, intensely white, as no fuller on earth could bleach them' (Mark 9.3). This luminosity, Robinson further argues, is evidence not only that the appearance stories are rooted in apocalypticism but that they enshrine an important Gnostic element, expressed above all in the language of light and focusing upon a radiant, disembodied Christ. The suggestion is that this early 'gnosticizing trajectory' was offset by the evangelists, who deliberately emphasized the 'bodiliness' of Jesus and played down the 'luminous appearances'.

Robinson's hypothesis has been challenged on a number of scores. Evidence of Gnosticism is hard to find in the first century, though one is forced to recognize its precursor – 'a kind of *gnosis*', as R. McL. Wilson has put it.[34] Robinson seems to have overstretched his case and indulged, at least to a degree, in what G. O'Collins has termed 'scholarly retrojection'.[35] That issue apart, the luminosity to which Robinson appeals may be no more than a shared convention in the narratives, the primary aim of which is to testify that in the risen Jesus one encounters the transcendent – or the divine. In contrast, the vision in Revelation 1.13–16 is concerned with the divine source of prophetic inspiration for the messages to the seven churches. It is not in itself the revelation or realization that he who was dead yet lives, nor is it directed to the commissioning of the apostles or the formation of the apostolic community. It is connected instead with the prophetic edification of the community.

In any case, while apocalyptic and apologetic elements are undoubtedly present in the narratives,[36] the focus is on the reality and particularity of Jesus, whom the disciples knew intimately in the days of his ministry and whose death had been all too real to them. In other words, the focus is on personal identity rather than luminosity. To be sure, the visionary elements have their own function, and the perception involved is more than ordinary 'seeing'. Such perception, however, presupposes a spiritual sensitivity developed in fellowship with Jesus. The resurrection faith has therefore some kind of correlative within the community of disciples prior to Jesus' death. The resurrection appearances cannot be understood as isolated phenomena, but only as integral parts of the story of Jesus.

(b) The ministry of Jesus

The story of Jesus' ministry and death is also set in the context of the Jewish or Hellenistic Jewish apocalyptic world-view. There are 'little apocalypses' such as Mark 13, with their focus on the coming of the Son of Man 'in clouds with great power and glory'. Elements of apocalyptic imagery are found in the narratives of Jesus' baptism, ministry and transfiguration. The transfiguration, indeed, locates Jesus on the mountain with two translated figures, Moses and Elijah (cf. the discussion above, pp. 15–16); but its immediate context is the prospect of the death of Jesus. Commanded to 'listen to him' (Mark 9.7 par.), the disciples learn that 'the son of man must suffer ... and be rejected ... and be killed, and after three days rise again' (8.31 par.). Although in communion with Moses and Elijah, Jesus is not translated but raised up from death.

'Son of Man' is one of the most distinctive terms applied to Jesus. As a symbol, it seems to face at least two ways. On the one hand, it suggests that the evangelists, their sources and presumably the communities they represented, understood Jesus' mission as fulfilling apocalyptic expectation. His ministry had its climax with the saints in the court of heaven: the whole vision reflecting Daniel 7 and its derivatives. On the other hand, the Son of Man symbol encapsulates the fundamental characteristics of Jesus' ministry: forgiveness, poverty, the reclamation of the lost, humble service, and complete self-giving. Between these two positions, the Son of Man 'passion' sayings recognize the 'necessity' for Jesus' ministry to involve conflict, rejection, suffering and death – and so fulfil the Scriptures.[37] Vindication would come, not by a last-minute deliverance from death as in an Enoch-type translation (was this in Jesus' mind at Gethsemane?) but by undergoing the death of his historical being and entering by resurrection into eternal glory.

However, it is not only in the Son of Man sayings that one encounters the dialectic between historical ministry and the transcendent realm. It is central to Jesus' presentation of the Kingdom of God. In Jesus' ministry, the reign of God has begun to be actualized. The initiative comes from God; the invitation is to humankind. Jesus enacts in his ministry both the divine approach and the human response. The parables articulate and dramatize aspects of common life-experience in such a way that the activity of God in the world is portrayed; and they thereby stimulate the hearers to respond in moral action consistent with God's reign.[38] Thus in Jesus and his ministry the transcendent intercepts the historical and the historical responds to and reflects the transcendent purpose. Even the cross is parabolic. Confronted with it, one is challenged to see not the death of a law-breaker, nor merely a tragic end to a noble life, but the expression of a transcendent hope which human sin cannot destroy. Jesus' ministry and death – indeed, his whole story – are properly characterized as eschatological. His ministry and teaching

20

constantly signal the transcendent in the midst of history. Apocalyptic elements simply underline this point.

The presence of the eschatological in the midst of history necessitates the use of images of new life, renewal and resurrection. One must become like a child; one must be reborn; the Kingdom is like seed growing in the ground towards harvest; human conditions are transformed; the dead are raised! The motif of resurrection is thus encapsulated in Jesus' ministry: not simply as an anticipation of Jesus' own resurrection but as an expression of the power of God at work in the world to transform and renew it. Here is no facile adaptation of apocalyptic elements. Rather, the language of resurrection is employed to interpret the eschatological significance of Jesus' life and death as the end of the 'old' aeon and the opening up of the 'new'.

(c) Resurrection as a transformation of the apocalyptic world-view

Our preliminary investigation suggests that Jesus and his story were by no means submerged in an apocalyptic tidal wave. Rather, eschatological perspectives were expressed and transformed by Jesus in his enactment of the Kingdom in word and deed. 'Resurrection' is a powerful statement of this transformation. It has become the pivot of a new interpretation of the cosmos, in which the figure of Christ – crucified and risen – is definitive. In Christian apocalypses, such as the book of Revelation, the focus is on the glorified and exalted Christ.

1 Peter is a good example of a new understanding – beginning as it does with a joyful recognition of the world-shattering and life-transforming significance of the resurrection of Jesus Christ from the dead (1 Pet. 1.3–9). The Christian or messianic community develops its solidarity with him in its sufferings (1.6–7) as well as in its 'subsequent glory' (1.11). Hence, the baseline for exploring the meaning of Christ's resurrection is now the people of God itself (1.14–21; 2.4–10) and the perspectives of faith, hope, love and obedience which it enshrines. Baptism, the rite of initiation into the community, is also an identification with the Christ who brought life out of death; for as he was 'put to death in the flesh but made alive in the spirit' (3.18), so the believer is called upon to transcend the passions of the flesh and 'live the life of God in the spirit' (4.6; my translation). The concept of resurrection therefore embraces the work of Christ in salvation, the experience of the believer and the believing community in solidarity with Christ, and the cosmic implications of Christ's glorification. It is in the last-mentioned sphere that the imagery of apocalyptic continues to be of service, whether denoting Christ's sovereignty (cf. 3.22) or suggesting the scope of his salvation in terms of his preaching to the imprisoned spirits (3.19; cf. 4.6).[39]

To study the ways in which the theme of resurrection is developed in the New Testament, we must turn to the New Testament writers themselves. They alone can reveal the possibilities of the concept of resurrection in Christian perspective. Their realm of discourse is not limited to apocalyptic but develops revealing perspectives within the communities of faith: in the common life of the people of God, in table fellowship and sacrament, in the perspective of growth and becoming, in universal mission... In such contexts the Christian understanding of resurrection is fully articulated. The focus is, of course, the death and resurrection of Jesus himself. Yet to treat the resurrection of Jesus as some kind of appendix to his life is to caricature and misrepresent the quality of the New Testament understanding of it. The resurrection represents a transforming and dynamic power which transcends the old apocalyptic world-view and energizes the people of God as it energized Jesus' own ministry.

Locked into their own culture, the Athenians found Paul's talk of resurrection incomprehensible and, in some cases, unworthy of serious consideration. It would be foolish to presuppose that modern readers are not similarly disadvantaged by cultural presuppositions.[40] For this reason, a fresh exploration of the concept of the resurrection in terms of narrative and belief may help to open up new possibilities of understanding. In subsequent chapters, therefore, New Testament perspectives on the resurrection invite consideration as valid interpretations of the human condition.

1 cf. McDonald (1980), pp. 53–4; Gärtner (1955), pp. 70–1. Gärtner describes Paul's approach as 'a typical exemplar of the first Christian sermons to the Gentiles'.
2 cf. David's lament for Saul and Jonathan, 2 Sam. 1.17–27; and for Abner, 2 Sam. 3.33–4.
3 Hayman (1975–6), p. 28.
4 Dixon (1937), p. 90.
5 Wilckens (1977), p. 86: italics as in text. With the approach developed here, cf. Rigaux (1973), pp. 3–15.
6 cf. Hayman (1976), pp. 461–2.
7 'Apperception' was used by Leibnitz to denote a higher degree of perception or reflective knowledge; and by Herbart to denote the appropriation or absorption of an idea by a more complex idea or system already present in the mind. Macmurray (1961), pp. 110–11, uses the term to denote the process by which we select from what is presented to us at any moment and organize it in our consciousness in terms relevant to our interests.
8 cf. Nida (1960), p. 66. 'Iconic', as distinct from 'pure', symbols 'partake of some of the properties of their referents'; they *portray* something of the reality they symbolize – as in the picture of the dead being raised from their graves. The painter Stanley Spencer made much of this image.
9 cf. Kaiser (1974), pp. 215–20.
10 cf. Nickelsburg (1972), p. 173–4.
11 cf. 'the parable of Enoch', 1 Enoch 1.3; cf. Charlesworth (1983) in loc.; Knibb (1978), p. 58. The notion of 'similitude' incorporates analogy and metaphor.
12 Charlesworth (1983), p. xxxiii.
13 Förster (1964), p. 44.
14 Nickelsburg (1972), p. 173; cf. p. 27.
15 ibid., pp. 28–33.
16 ibid., pp. 34–7.
17 Notice that this is a different concept of the fate of the wicked from that recorded, for example, in Dan. 12.2.

18 Wilckens (1977), p. 90.
19 Nickelsburg (1972), p. 136.
20 Cullmann (1958).
21 cf. Hengel (1974), I, pp. 199–200.
22 ibid., p. 198.
23 Nickelsburg (1972), p. 180.
24 Casey (1987), p. 16. A copy of this unpublished essay was kindly made available by Dr Casey to the present writer, who acknowledges his debt to it, especially in this section.
25 cf. 4 Ezra 13. In 1 Enoch, the influence of Ezek. 1 is also apparent. The derivative nature of the references to 'that Son of man' in 1 Enoch suggests that the vision of the heavenly court in Dan. 7 is a recurring and creative element in apocalyptic and messianic discourse. Cf. Perrin (1967), pp. 167–70; Allison (1985), pp. 129, 132.
26 In the Dream Visions (83—90), the righteous who are resurrected and meet the Messiah include converts from the nations.
27 Elijah and Enoch were expected in a number of Christian texts: cf. Bousset (1896), pp. 203–8. The passage cited, however, bears a close relation to Rev. 11.7–11, where the two figures in the text are usually taken to be Elijah and Moses. It is highly likely that a Jewish source has been used: cf. Wilckens (1977), p. 106. In that case, we find the resurrection of individual figures playing a key role in the eschatological drama.
28 *Antiquitates* IV, 326. Josephus also reports the veneration of the Essenes for Moses: *De bello Judaico* II.145.
29 Casey (1987), p. 17, lists the following figures: 'a future Davidic king, an eschatological high priest, Abel, Abraham, Asenath, Elijah, Enoch, Isaac, Jacob, Joseph, Melchizedek, Michael, Moses, Wisdom and Word'.
30 cf. Rowland (1982), pp. 23–48.
31 In this kind of discussion, one must beware of committing what sociologists and others call 'the genetic fallacy': that is, the belief that to explain the source of origin is sufficient to dispose of the question of validity.
32 J. M. Robinson (1982), p. 10.
33 Rist (1957), p. 377.
34 R. McL. Wilson (1982), p. 111–12.
35 O'Collins (1987), p. 211. The reader's attention is drawn to his discussion of Robinson's position in an Appendix, pp. 210–16.
36 Apocalyptic elements include angels, being 'taken up to heaven' and other visionary features; apologetic elements relate to the solidity or 'bodiliness' of the figure of Jesus and physical characteristics such as eating.
37 There has, of course, been a long-standing debate among New Testament scholars about the precise nature of 'Son of Man' references in the Gospels. Most notably, G. Vermes has argued that Jesus' use of the term was as an Aramaic periphrasis (*bar nasha*) for the first person singular; but debate still continues about the linguistic accuracy of this case: cf. Vermes (1973), pp. 160–91; Vermes (1978), pp. 123–34; Casey (1979), pp. 224–27. M. Casey has argued that the phrase always has a more general reference: 'a man...', and that reflections of Dan. 7 represent later church interpretation. However, the criterion of differentiation is a blunt instrument and its application in distinguishing the historical Jesus from the Church's view of Jesus may well cause distortion: cf. Casey (1979), pp. 224–40. This is particularly so when the linguistic problem underlying 'Son of Man' usage is as intractable as both the debate and the evidence suggest it is.
38 cf. Chilton and McDonald (1987), pp. 79–109.

39 Though inevitably dated, the discussion of the subject in Selwyn (1964), pp. 314–62, is a standard work of reference.
40 The subject is discussed exhaustively, and somewhat negatively, in Nineham (1976).

2

Discerning the Body
The Resurrection in Pauline Theology

...[not] discerning the body.

1 COR. 11.29

You are the body of Christ...

1 COR. 12.27

To pursue the theme of resurrection in Paul's theology is to be drawn into the living heart of his apostleship and his life in the people of God. Implicit in all his writings, the resurrection receives explicit expression in a number of passages, most of which are discussed below. Our purpose, however, is not so much to present an in-depth study of a few passages in isolation, but to relate Paul's statements of resurrection faith to the totality of his theological understanding and his self-understanding as these emerge in the reading of his letters.

1 APOSTLE AND WITNESS

'Am I not free? Am I not an apostle? Have I not seen Jesus our Lord?' (1 Cor. 9.1). For Paul, commissioning as an apostle and Christian freedom have their immediate source in his encounter with Jesus, the risen Lord. Paul claims *to have seen* Jesus: the nuance of the perfect tense suggesting that this was not simply a passing event nor even a recurring event in his experience but, in modern language, an existential or life-transforming event issuing in a new freedom and in apostolic service.

Such an encounter cannot be equated with catching sight of Jesus in Jerusalem prior to his death (cf. 2 Cor. 5.16), as if Paul were simply countering the suggestion that, unlike the twelve, he had never seen Jesus in his life (cf. Acts 1.21–6). Nor can it be equated *simpliciter* with 'visions and revelations of the Lord' (2 Cor. 12.1), ecstatic experiences which apparently befell Paul from time to time and which could have significance for him (cf. 2 Cor. 12.2–10). This does not, of course, rule out the possibility that his first experience was of a visionary nature: nor does it prevent Paul from citing any of his experiences, early or late, for apologetic purposes. Paul, however, singles out his first 'seeing' of Jesus as an event which was unrepeatable by its very nature. It was the encounter which released him from bondage into a new freedom and which made him an apostle of Jesus Christ.

So far, so good! But there is more to it than that. If we went no further, we should leave Paul exposed to the charge that his experience might have been of the 'subjective vision' variety: which, if not devastating to his case, would rob it of much of the significance it might otherwise have for others. Less kind critics are found who describe him as a hallucination-prone fanatic. A range of questions is thus raised, not only about the objective element, if any, in the experience by which he set such great store, but also about its validation. If we are concerned to investigate the substance of his transforming experience – viz. 'the Lord', 'the risen Christ' – such questions might even be called pressing. But do we have sufficient access to the data to make a judgement?

Fortunately for us, the fact that Paul was called upon to defend the validity of his apostleship opens up the issue, even for the modern reader. The case he presents is, of course, the case for the defence; but the prosecution charges are not hard to find. In 1 Corinthians 15.5–9, for example, Paul has to find an answer to several basic objections. His encounter with the risen Christ was 'last of all' – later than that of the other apostles and well outside the pale of 'forty days' postulated by Luke–Acts as the span of special appearances to the apostolic group (cf. Acts 1.3). And he had been a persecutor of the Church and therefore, in his own words, unfit to be called as an apostle. Paul is, on his own admission, both last and least: in human terms, he suffered ostensibly from a double disqualification which he turns to theological advantage.

His apostleship – both the fact of it and its productivity – he ascribed only to the grace of God and not to any merit on his own part (1 Cor. 15.10). All the earlier indications were against such an eventuality; only the transforming action of God in Christ could have made it a reality. That action was for Paul, the receptor, a violent experience: like being 'untimely ripped' (*ektroma*, 1 Cor. 15.8) from the womb of Pharisaic Judaism into apostolic ministry. Though the phrase 'last of all' implies that Paul was a late entrant to that exclusive group who had 'seen the Lord', what Paul emphasizes is that he came *prematurely* to this new world: *ektroma* implies premature birth, not late birth.[1] The other apostles, with whom there is an implied contrast, had been prepared for their encounter with the risen Christ through their previous association with Jesus. Paul, later in time, had been unceremoniously thrust into witness to the resurrection and into apostolic ministry without any positive preparation. His record was a disqualification, rather than the reverse. It was God's action alone that could have made him an apostle and witness to the risen Christ. His opponents have to reckon with the remarkable nature of his calling and with its evident results.

An earlier clash with critics is found in Galatians. Here, the case against Paul appears to be fairly specific. In the interests of winning popular favour (1.10), he has departed from the rigour of God's requirements in the Law. His position, it is alleged, is one of accommodation to human weakness and is therefore a dilution of divine requirements. In this important respect, it has been disowned by the leading apostles (cf.

2.1–2, 11–14). The case is part of a wider crisis affecting Paul's ministry and the Gentile mission as a whole.

The defence statement opens with an *exordium* that presents Paul's basic position.[2] The gospel he preached is not a merely human message; it does not have a human source, nor is it based on human teaching (1.11–12). It comes through an objectively given 'revelation of Jesus Christ' (1.12). To locate the *source* of Paul's message, one must look beyond him to Christ. Paul does not proceed to relate the tradition about Christ – which would have been one way to substantiate his position. Rather, in his *narratio* of story, he recounts his former life in Judaism, his zeal for the Jewish faith, and his persecution of 'the church of God'. The dramatic change, the sense of a destiny marked out for him before he was born (cf. Isa. 49.1; Jer. 1.4–5), was brought about by God's action. Conversion and calling are telescoped.

The divine–human encounter has as its issue Paul's apostleship to the Gentiles, for 'it pleased [God] to reveal his Son [in] me' (*en emoi*, 1.16). To translate 'to me' is too weak and possibly misleading. The revelation took him over. It became incarnate *in him* (cf. 2.20; 4.6): a concept that would be familiar to those who made much of their experience of the Spirit of Christ (cf. 3.2–5). The purpose, however, was not simply to secure Paul's own salvation, still less to afford him spiritual satisfaction (cf. 1 Cor. 14.1–5, 18–19): it was specifically 'in order that I might preach him among the Gentiles' (1.16). There is a unity, in Paul, of message and messenger, of gospel and apostle. Hence Paul is an apostle – however late in time his calling may be and however premature it might be in terms of his preparedness – because he is part of God's salvation for his creation. Other apostles – James, Peter, John (2.9) – were sent to the Jews; Paul had been made 'an apostle to the Gentiles' (2.8).[3] The revolution had thus been created not by the human action or aspirations of Paul but by the act of 'God the Father, who raised [Christ] from the dead' (1.1).

The risen Christ, from whom Paul claimed to derive his commission, signalled a new age in the dealings of God with humankind. There could be no reversion to the old ways of the Law, no building up again of what had been torn down (2.18). It was not that Paul, now a servant in the Church he once tried to destroy, had become anti-Jewish! But he could not 'nullify the grace of God' (cf. 2.21) by insisting that salvation was by 'works of the Law'. Christ has lived, died and is Lord: that makes a tremendous difference! 'If justification were through the law, then Christ died to no purpose' (2.21). But since Christ, the Messiah, has come, then faith in Christ is the fulfilment of Judaism, 'the end of the law' as well as the ground of salvation for all. God's action in Christ thus issues in mission, and in this mission Paul is called to a key role. The apostles, indeed, give him 'the right hand of fellowship' (2.9) in token of their fundamental accord. Contention arose only when apostolic practice was, for whatever reason, at variance with the gospel of Christ (2.14).

The case for the defence, as set out by Paul, is convincing. It rests on the objectivity of the 'Christ event', the act of God's grace, the substance of the gospel. This is the Archimedean point that has levered the world of Jewish religion into a new orbit: or, in theological terms, the eschatological world-picture has been decisively remade by the 'Christ event'. Into this event Paul himself has been drawn; by it he has been transformed. In him Christ lives; through him, Christ is writing a new page of latter-day history. This depth of conviction and clarity of insight presumably explains why Paul is not unduly exercised by the thought that the apostles were commissioned at an earlier point than he himself was, or that his own experience was therefore of a secondary or derivative order. The explicit case is that Paul had 'seen Jesus our Lord' and had received his commission from him precisely when the mission to the Gentiles was ripe for launching. If further accreditation is required, it is supplied by his churches – the 'seal' of his apostleship. The hidden agenda, implicit in the redrawn eschatology, is that the mission to the Gentiles is itself an essential part of the 'event of Christ'.

If witness to the risen Christ and commissioning as an apostle are inseparable in Paul, can this logic be applied retrospectively to the others cited in 1 Corinthians 15.5–8? The passage itself is complex and condensed. It is primarily concerned with the fundamental message which Paul shared with the others cited as witnesses (15.1–2, 11). The witness of Cephas (Peter) is accorded priority, along with that of the twelve (15.5). Thus Paul aligned himself with the original cadre. The addition of James to the list is probably an astute move by Paul. Doubtless, James' witness to the risen Lord was frequently cited as that of 'the most significant of the early recruits to the young church',[4] but it also gave Paul the opportunity to make the point that appearances of the risen Lord were not confined to a small original group: hence his wide indeterminate reference to 'all the apostles'. Even more boldly, he cites 'more than five hundred brethren' (15.6). A specific connection with mission cannot be maintained here, nor is a simple identification of this event with Pentecost possible. Paul clearly recognized a substantial group of people, including 'all the apostles', as witnesses to the risen Lord. There is no way of telling whether he thought this list exhaustive. He seems to contemplate an early messianic community, built on the witness of its leading members to the exalted Christ. Not all these witnesses were apostles; nor did the appearances of the risen Christ provide the sole matrix of the commissioning of those who were. Again, in the messianic community, there was a diversity of gifts and ministries, as in Paul's own churches: James is associated more with presidency of the church in Jerusalem, rather than with mission as such. Paul's position is distinctive. For the traditional content of the *kerygma* Paul was dependent on church sources (15.3) and never attempted to conceal the fact (cf. Gal. 1.18). While the witness of Peter and the twelve referred to a wide experience of Jesus' ministry, death and resurrection, Paul's apostleship and witness to the risen Christ derived directly from one intense encounter. But the well-being of his mission and the demands of truth itself required that he unashamedly list himself with the original witnesses and thus claim for the Gentile churches an immediate source in the messianic event that brought in the new era.

How is the modern reader to approach the question of the validity of the apostolic witness? In his famous essay 'The New Testament and Mythology', Rudolf Bultmann refused to accept 1 Corinthians 15.3–8 as part of the *kerygma*, and claimed that Paul was following the 'fatal' procedure of trying to 'prove' the miracle of the resurrection by adducing a list of eyewitnesses.[5] The resurrection being an article of faith which by its very nature is not open to proof, all that can be demonstrated as historical is the faith of the disciples. Julius Schniewind pointed out, not unreasonably, that the preaching of the Church 'gives us not the Easter faith but the Easter *testimony* of the original disciples'. 'To accept the word of the apostles and to believe in the risen Lord are one and the same thing.'[6] No sooner had Bultmann apparently accepted the force of this contention than he repeated his objection to Paul's attempt 'to adduce a proof for the *kerygma*'.[7]

Bultmann's exegesis is uncharacteristically unsound at this point, and fails to take seriously the nature of witness. The exegete has no option but to accept the witness to the risen Christ as a given part of the *kerygma* – at least, the Pauline *kerygma*. *Kerygma*, after all, is not a timeless concept: it is what somebody actually proclaims, and 1 Corinthians 15.3–8 indicates what Paul and the other apostles proclaim (15.11). And witness is not about adducing proof: it is concerned with 'a living relationship with reality as it presents itself to the human subject'.[8] Paul, like his fellow witnesses, identifies that reality as 'Jesus our Lord'. Such witness may be no more than a glimpse of an inexhaustible reality, but it suggests also being in living touch with that reality, even (in Paul's case) being transformed by it. Indeed, to read Paul's letters today is to accept the possibility of encountering that same reality – and being transformed by it.

2 WITNESS TO CHRIST

For Paul, 'seeing Jesus' was *at one and the same time* life-transforming encounter, apostolic commission (1 Cor. 9.1) and divine revelation (Gal. 1.12). It was at once existential and cognitive; it involved commitment and vocation; and it simultaneously de-centred and re-centred his life and world-view. Taken by themselves, experiences of 'seeing the risen Christ' would probably represent psychic phenomena of significance to the experiencing subject but otherwise of direct moment only to the psychical researcher. Like *glossolalia* ('speaking in tongues'), they would stand for 'mysteries in the Spirit' that edify oneself rather than the Church at large (cf. 1 Cor. 14.1–5). Paul, however, never treats them in isolation, but always in the context of the foundational event which the *kerygma* proclaims (cf. 1 Cor. 15.1–8). In this context, they represent much more than visionary awareness of Jesus beyond the grave. Whatever their visual or visionary content, they disclose the totality of the ministry of Jesus, the Messiah: that is, a ministry of vicarious suffering and death in fulfilment of Scripture (1 Cor. 15.3) and, in spite of the burial with its sense of human finality, a ministry vindicated by

God, who raised him 'on the third day in accordance with the scriptures' (1 Cor. 15.4). To 'see' Christ is in some sense to see and identify with the whole 'Christ event'. Paul's witness is to an event which transcended his previous perceptions of reality and confronted him with the Lord, victorious over suffering and death, and now demanding his commitment and service. To recognize the trans-formation – the transfiguration – of Christ is to surrender oneself to his transforming or transfiguring power.

The hymn Paul cites in Philippians 2.5–11 depicts the 'Christ event' (cf. 2.5) in a great poetic sweep which leads from God in heaven through a servant ministry to exaltation and cosmic glory:

> He shared in God's mode of being,
> But never did he contemplate the equality he enjoyed
>   as an act of lese-majesty against God.[9]
> Rather, he gave of himself utterly,
>   taking upon himself the servant's mode[10]
> And sharing the lot of mankind.
>   It is within such constraint that we find him – a man indeed:[11]
>   A man who humbled himself,
> Becoming obedient to the point of death,
>   even death on a cross.
> For that reason, God himself has exalted him
> and given him the name
>   above all names,
> that at the name of Jesus
> every knee should bow
>   in heaven above and upon the earth and in the regions below,
>   and every tongue confess that
> Jesus Christ is Lord –
>   to the glory of God the Father.[12]   (my translation)

The picturesque form of the poem is derived from apocalyptic messianism. Its first movement is from God to mankind. It is not an imperialist or self-seeking movement, like that of Adam in the Garden or the rebellious angels who would be as God. Here, as in the Logos concept (cf. John 1.1), the divine agent is not an inferior minion in the court of heaven, but stands in the closest relationship to God. The Christ-mind in heaven could not contemplate turning equality with God, which was already his, into an act of rapaciousness against God.

It is only fair to indicate that this interpretation is at variance with other views commonly advanced. Recently, the tendency has been for commentators to opt for an 'anthropological' interpretation of the passage which focuses on the contrast between Adam and Christ:[13] unlike Adam, Christ did not 'grasp at' equality with God. Apart from the fact that this approach involves a doubtful rendering of the Greek word *harpagmos*,[14] it falls short of providing a wholly adequate account of the first section of the poem. The more traditional view, on the other hand, has been excessively coloured by later theological notions of pre-existence.[15] What is of note, however, is the variety and elaboration of the role of intermediary figures in intertestamental Judaism. 'The

30

Davidic king, an eschatological High Priest, an eschatological prophet, Abel, Elijah, Enoch, Melchizidek, Michael, Moses, Wisdom, all these were held by some Jews in this period to be of unusually elevated status and to have performed or to be about to perform some function of evident significance.'[16] Even rabbinic Judaism had to come to terms with the notion of two powers in heaven.[17] As Casey has argued, it is not that Paul and others simply borrowed static concepts from Judaism; they also harnessed the dynamic or creative possibilities of the material. With the figure of Jesus the Messiah at the centre of interpretative concern, rapid christological development was possible, not least in the setting of Hellenistic Christianity. Hence, in the Philippian hymn, the Christ figure spurns all imperialistic designs and effects a self-emptying: not so much a laying aside of divine attributes (as the traditional forms of kenotic Christology required) as a total self-giving, characterizing not only the move from heaven to earth but also the form of existence lived out on earth.[18]

The focus of the poem, the point at which mere mortals can find him, is thus the ministry on earth. It comprises a life whose whole substance is poured out in the service of others: an expression of authentic humanity, with its own particular dynamic of service which takes it by an inescapable logic to 'death on a cross'. Here is the bottom line of the gospel message. Whatever doubts the quest of the historical Jesus may have raised about the biographical features of Jesus' life, its overall pattern or *Gestalt* is unimpaired: a servant ministry, a crucified Messiah. Viewed in worldly terms – that is, in terms of the logic and values of worldly power or religious triumphalism – such a proposition presents a stumbling-block to Jews and is mere folly to Gentiles (1 Cor. 1.23). Yet with whom do real power and wisdom lie? – with this servant-messiah, or with those who crucified him? The unconverted Saul of Tarsus was constrained to take the latter alternative: only thus could he express his zeal for 'the traditions of [the] fathers' against which the crucified one set a radical questionmark; hence the persecution mania – 'how I persecuted the church of God violently and tried to destroy it!' (Gal. 1.13). The alternative, firmly suppressed, was to affirm the crucified Messiah. That would be to affirm that God was in Christ, reconciling the world to himself, and that his call was to a ministry of reconciliation (2 Cor. 5.18–19). It would be to say, on the one hand, that the servant proceeded from God and expressed his 'mind', and, on the other, to believe that God did not reject but rather vindicated the crucified Messiah. Thus, if we are to 'find' a signal of divine transcendence within the parameters of human existence, it is located in Jesus' obedient service, the very authenticity of which represented a power which the authorities saw as a threat and which they had to destroy: hence he 'became obedient unto death, even death on a cross' (Phil. 2.8). The final hymnic section expresses the divine vindication of the crucified Messiah: God's exalting of him, even to the point of bestowing on him the highest possible 'name' – *Kyrios*,[19] Lord of all: once more, no title to rival God the Father, but rather to work to his glory.

Several points relevant to our discussion emerge from these

considerations. The first is the extent to which 'resurrection' can be swallowed up in 'exaltation': God's vindication of his servant. The second is the virtual impossibility of isolating the resurrection as an independent element in the divine action. Hence, as we have already noted, when Paul 'saw' the risen Christ, he saw the complete 'Christ event'. To this he bears witness: not to Jesus' survival, nor even to his life beyond death. God's raising of Jesus is the final act in the divine drama, the divine vindication of the whole event, and therefore meaningful only in relation to the whole. To 'see the Lord' is to be made a participant in the Christ event itself. If the fulfilment of God's purpose is 'that at the name of Jesus every knee should bow...' (Phil. 2.10), then there is a commission to 'preach him among the Gentiles' (Gal. 1.16). To participate in the event was, for Paul, to accept this commission. And if Christ ministered in the form of a *doulos* (servant/slave, Phil. 2.7), then Paul must be not only the *apostolos* but also the *doulos* of Christ (Rom. 1.1).[20]

3 THE LANGUAGE AND CONCEPT OF RESURRECTION

In the attempt to articulate the reality which had overwhelmed him, it is evident that Paul had to struggle to find appropriate language or terminology. Consider the following:

'Paul an apostle...through Jesus Christ and God the Father, who *raised* [*egeirein*] him from the dead' (Gal. 1.1).

'Designated Son of God in power according to the Spirit of holiness by his *resurrection* [*anastasis*] from the dead, Jesus Christ our Lord' (Rom. 1.4).

'When he who had set me apart before I was born, and had called me through his grace, was pleased to *reveal* [*apokalypsai*] his Son [*in*] *me* [*en emoi*]...' (Gal. 1.15–16).

'Have I not *seen* [*heoraka*] Jesus our Lord?' (1 Cor. 9.1).

'Last of all...he *appeared* [*ophthesthai*] also to me' 1 Cor. 15.8).

Some of these are formula words: 'raised up' and 'appeared' suggest God's action and Christ's manifestation of his living reality. '*Anastasis*' is the regular word for resurrection, not always comprehensible in a Greek environment. '*Apokalypsai*' suggests the unveiling of a divine mystery. When speaking in personal terms, Paul simply uses the term 'to see' or 'perceive' Christ. Discernment is part of witness.

It is only fair to recognize that imparting the 'secret and hidden wisdom of God' revealed by God's Spirit requires words not taught by human wisdom but taught by the Spirit himself (cf. 1 Cor. 2.7–13); yet if they are to communicate, the words used must be comprehensible and intelligently selected (cf. 1 Cor. 14. 6–19). Here, the equipment to hand was clearly shabby and prone to deteriorate amid general imprecision. Undoubtedly, the language of resurrection – of raising up and appearing – already existed in the Church before Paul put pen to paper. Yet this language derives from a variety of sources, including apocalyptic usage in Judaism, where resurrection figures as 'a rather small part of larger scenarios of judgment'.[21] Here is found the language of awaking, exaltation, rising up, transformation, restoration or refashioning, coming to light again, etc.[22] And pressing in on Judaism was a pervasive Hellenism, bearing seductive gifts such as the immortality and incorruptibility of the soul. Paul's task, however, was far from synthesizing such language and concepts for the Christian cause. It was rather to select and apply such language as was serviceable to the articulation of the fundamental faith and experience of the Church, to clarify meaning and to build up understanding. In the process, he had to strain his linguistic resources and exploit their metaphorical possibilities to the limit; and sometimes he had to retrace his steps to recover ground lost in the misapplication of metaphor or the mis-interpretation of method. Illustrations of both procedures are given below.

Paul's struggle with the linguistic and conceptual complexity of 'resurrection' can be illustrated from the axes on which it operates. There is the axis of Christ's life–death–resurrection: the exaltation of the Messiah. There is the axis of the believer's life and destiny: 'resurrection' relating to 'new life' in one's present existence as the ground of 'eternal life'. There is the all-important question of the interplay of the two axes: the extent to which one affects or is the ground of the other. Perhaps the most critical aspect of the problem is the necessity Paul recognized to incorporate the notion of *participating* in the resurrection of Christ. It is not simply a matter of confessing the mighty act of God in raising Jesus; nor is it only a question of 'Christianizing' the hope of general resurrection at the close of the age. There has to be the notion of rising with Christ here and now – in baptism within the faith community, perhaps in eucharistic action, certainly in moral living. Yet this resurrection here and now must cohere with the total pattern of faith and action – without exaggeration and without distortion. The 'deep things of God' (1 Cor. 2.10) must be 'spiritually discerned'. And no topic requires greater sensitivity than 'resurrection'.

(i) *The Dynamics of Resurrection Faith*

(a) Power and participation

Paul's interpretation of the cross-and-resurrection is distinctive – and distinctively Christian – in that he insists that we not only find here the core of Christian proclamation (1 Cor. 15.3–4) but also encounter the crucified-and-risen Christ as a power or dynamic in the lives of believers: 'the power of God and the wisdom of God' (1 Cor. 1.24). For Paul 'to know Christ' (Phil. 3.10) is to recognize the *dynamis* – the power, dynamic – of Christ's resurrection, and the *koinonia* – fellowship, participation, solidarity – in his sufferings. These two concepts – *dynamis* and *koinonia* – are focal to Paul's understanding of resurrection.

The third chapter of Philippians gives a résumé of a familiar theme (3.16). The *exordium*, in warning against the circumcision party, identifies the Church as the 'true circumcision', the fellowship or community of the new covenant.[23] The subsequent *narratio* demon-

33

strates Paul's identification with Israel, but explicitly rejects his circumcision and Israelite lineage as the basis of salvation (3.5–11). The story of God's dealings with mankind has moved on to new ground. The old membership qualifications are written off as mere *skybala* (3.8): 'dung', in Calvin's trenchant translation. 'Knowing Christ' – not merely in a cognitive sense, but through commitment and faith – is now the criterion of surpassing worth (3.8), unlocking as it does the 'righteousness' that has its source in God and depends on faith (3.9). This is itself a goal: Paul speaks of 'gaining' Christ (3.8) and 'being found in him' (3.9). It is to seek the solidarity with Christ which the new covenant presupposes: a solidarity that is essentially relational and, at least in some important respects, interactive, for in Pauline language if I am found 'in Christ', Christ is also found 'in me'.[24] Therefore, as my *koinonia* in Christ grows – as my being is radically re-centred in Christ – there develops in me a new *dynamis*: liberation ('Am I not free?', 1 Cor. 9.1), the recognition of a new goal that represents fulfilment (Phil. 3.12–14), and 'the power of his resurrection' (Phil. 3.10). This dynamic, which denies death the final say, is also the power to transcend all that works for death in life, and it has its *fons et origo* in the death-and-resurrection of Christ: 'Thanks be to God, who gives us the victory through our Lord Jesus Christ' (1 Cor. 15.57).

To affirm the dynamics of Christ's resurrection is to operate with the fundamental polarity of the powers of life and death. As the Didache puts it, 'There are two ways, one of life and one of death; and between the two ways there is a great difference' (Did. 1.1). The concept of resurrection is, however, inseparable on the one hand from the notion of prior death, in particular the death of Christ on the cross, and on the other hand from the notion of victory over death. Hence, to speak of the dynamic of resurrection is to suggest that, in fellowship with Christ, a 'dying' must be accomplished as the price of transcending the negative and winning through to the positive. The possibility of 'the resurrection from the dead' hereafter (*exanastasis*) presupposes not only our suffering and death but our sharing in the sufferings and death of Christ (Phil. 3.10–11). The way of 'life' here on earth – of love, joy, peace, the fruit of the Spirit (Gal. 5.22) – means crucifying 'the flesh with its passions and desires' (Gal. 5.24), that is, the elimination of the destructive powers in human experience, and the releasing thereby of the dynamic of Christ's love, which is the power of authentic life: 'that those who live might live no longer for themselves but for him who for their sake died and was raised' (2 Cor. 5.15).

But it is not only the impulses from within which can be destructive. External factors such as 'the Law' and the structures of authority in society, though set up for good ends, can become destructive in human hands. The Law – 'the oracles of God' (Rom. 3.2) – was the guardian of Israel until Christ came (Gal. 3.24), and a restraining force against evil (Gal. 3.23); yet by itself it not only lacks the power to give life (Gal. 3.21) but is a curse to humanity, with its judgement on human failure and, in the wrong hands, its proneness to legalistic malpractice. The powers that be, established by divine authority (cf. Rom. 13.1), can become oppressive and demonic. The forces that govern the universe (the *stoicheia* or 'elemental spirits', Col. 2.8), in their alienation from God, can set up a web of deception. The letter to the Colossians presents an imaginative theological response to the cosmic condition. The exalted Christ is head over all the cosmic powers (2.10). The security of believers comes from their solidarity with him: a solidarity given pointed expression in baptism in which 'you were buried with him...[and] you were also raised with him' (2.12).

Romans 6 gives fullest expression to this concept. It occurs in response to a suggestion that Paul's position – abandoning, as it does, a 'law' model of faith-understanding and substituting a 'grace' model – is necessarily antinomian: a suggestion which Paul totally rejects. He begins by taking the shared experience of baptism as the effective sign of our 'dying' and 'rising' with Christ. It is, to apply Austin's terminology, a 'performative event': an event which, through its performance, effects change in the situation of those involved. The change, signified by metaphors of baptism 'into his death', 'burial with him' or 'being crucified with him', is that our former mode of being ('our old humanity') is terminated. Specifically, our organic connection with the power of sin (the body – *soma* – of sin, 6.6) is broken – our 'enslavement' to sin is no more – therefore, practical expression can be given to the exhortation not to let sin hold sway (lit. 'rule') in our continuing mortal existence (6.12; cf. 6.15–23). But while the death of Christ speaks of something already accomplished, the ending of a bondage, the resurrection of Christ opens up new life-possibilities for those who participate in it: both present possibilities – 'that...we too might walk in newness of life' (6.4) – and future hope – 'we shall certainly be united with him in a resurrection like his' (6.5; cf. 6.8).

The change is 'from death to life' (6.13), from being 'under law' to being 'under grace' (6.14). Christ's work puts a radical question mark against humanity as it is: questioning its *dynamis*, the power that impels it, as well as the allegiances, addictions and goals that form its very being. But it also releases a power – an enabling power – which makes possible a radical re-centring of life and a well-spring of gratitude, of *eucharisteia*, for the gift. 'Thanks be to God that you who were once slaves of sin now give heartfelt allegiance to the pattern of teaching to which you stand committed' (6.17; my translation). The pattern or standard (*typos*) of teaching is not itself the ground of salvation (as it would be in the 'law' model), but the description of the way of life the new allegiance involves, complete with directional indicators and parameters. It is grounded in the tradition that came from Jesus: in specific 'words of the Lord' and in the 'ethic of transformation' outlined in Romans 12 and so evocative of the Sermon on the Mount. To enter this new kind of existence is to participate in Christ's resurrection. It is to become a new creature of God – 'the old has passed away, behold, the new has come' (2 Cor. 5.17). It is to share in a new kind of *koinonia*: 'one body in Christ, and individually members one of another' (Rom. 12.5). It is to experience a new dynamic, enabling one to 'overcome evil with good' (Rom. 12.21).

But from what source does Paul derive the material he uses in his account of the eschatological significance of Christ and what has he done with it?

(b) Eschatology and participation

Jewish eschatology, of which a full account cannot be rendered here, was engendered within a religious tradition aware of the contradiction between historical reality and the fulfilment of God's purposes for his people and for his creation. Strictly, eschatology concerns 'the last things', understood particularly as the final expression of God's work: the goal, completion or fulfilment of his relationship with his creation. Apocalypticism – the unveiling of what is hidden – fed upon a pessimistic reading of history: indeed, upon the temptation to despair, to find an escape clause in humanity's contract with history by projecting a panoramic dream-world peopled by a variety of figures, from the Messiah who in his several forms was probably more at home in eschatology to the Son of Man who was truly apocalyptic: a world in which the righteous were vindicated, the wicked vanquished, Israel restored, the elect of the Gentiles brought in, and sovereignty rightfully rendered to the Creator. The orientation was to a great cosmic event in the future, objective and inescapable, which sometimes cast its shadow before it in the cosmic struggle of good and evil, the sufferings of the righteous and even the anticipation of God's rule in the community of the faithful.[25]

When we recall Paul's treatment of the 'Christ event', with the implications of a new dynamic in human experience and participation in the cross-and-resurrection, it is evident that he presents a radically new understanding of eschatology. Jesus actually performed the messianic ministry in a given historical context. Its nature was essentially that of ministry 'unto death', an expression of divine self-giving. Here is that 'newness of life' which Christ summoned his followers to share at the invitation of the King of creation: a realm of being boldly outlined in his teaching, entry to which required a veritable death-and-resurrection on the part of the believer. Indeed, it might be said that if Christ lived out his ministry 'unto death', he lived it also in the power of resurrection. Paul does not say this in so many words: his interpretation of the historical Jesus is limited in the main to ancient formulae. But since the resurrection dynamic involves the transcending of the powers of death and destruction, Christ's power to be faithful 'unto death' is *also* the power of resurrection. Engagement with suffering and death in the power of the resurrection – combining messianic woe and messianic blessing – is demonstrated in authentic form in the one being in whom true humanity was found without qualification. To believe in Christ is to share this comprehensive dynamic. It is to share in his 'body': not simply in terms of belonging to his people, but as organically related to the life and power he represents. The reality for which the term 'eschatology' stands has been opened to us as participants. The dream has been 'realized' to the extent that it has been enacted in Christ and has been opened to those moved to respond. The events of cosmic restoration have become transforming events in the midst of history.

The foregoing paragraph must not be construed as indicating that the power of resurrection was expressed only or mainly in Christ's ministry. On such a view, the resurrection after physical death could simply be a projection of the dynamic of transcendence in his ministry. 'Extension' or 'completion' are better terms. The message is that the 'raising' of Christ is the final act by which the bounds of mortal life are transcended, the life of service 'unto death' finally vindicated, and the dynamic of life affirmed 'in Christ' for eternity. Clearly, for this part of his message Paul reaffirmed an ancient confession of the Church concerning Jesus:

> born of David's line – to speak in human terms:
> designated Son of God in Power – to speak of the work of
>   the Holy Spirit –
> through the resurrection of the dead:
> Jesus Christ our Lord (Rom. 1.3–4).   (my translation)

The word 'designated' suggests the centrality of Christ in the consummation which still lies in the future, though he is already marked out for the task. And the Holy Spirit operates through the resurrection of the dead. It is preferable not to translate as if Paul had written 'as the result of *his* resurrection from the dead' – there is no 'his' in the text.[26] The consummation takes place after the general resurrection of the dead, of which Christ is the first-fruits, the first stock of the harvest. Hence we have 'the light of the knowledge of the glory of God in the face of Christ' (2 Cor. 4.6) – although this treasure always comes 'in earthen vessels' (2 Cor. 4.7).

Indeed, this theme is strikingly developed in 2 Corinthians 4.6—5.10. Paul is aware of the tensions with which the believer must live in this world. In a series of paradoxes, he expresses the death-laden experiences of human life and the life-giving power that sustains the believer (4.8–12): 'always carrying in the body the death of Jesus, so that the life of Jesus may also be manifested in our bodies' (4.10). Paul's own awareness of death is acute (4.12); but equally strong is his conviction that the divine power manifested in the raising of Jesus also embraces himself and those he is addressing (4.14). Here we may 'sigh with anxiety', but finally we shall be 'swallowed up by life' (5.4). Meanwhile, the Spirit, the foretaste of eternity, strengthens faith (5.6–8) and sharpens awareness of ultimate goal (5.9–10). Put differently, Christ's love channels and transforms our living, which is henceforth directed to him whose death was 'for us' and whose resurrection is equally the assurance of life (cf. 5.14–17).

(c) The resurrection of the dead

It is not easy to present a consistent eschatological picture, especially where an event of epoch-making significance is believed to have taken place, breaking asunder the symbols of the hitherto accepted world-view, and straining language and cultural presuppositions almost beyond the point of viability. Something like this underlies the great final theme of disputation in 1 Corinthians, and its focus on the 'resurrection of the dead' (cf. 1 Cor. 15.12).

Much scholarly ink has been spilt in the cause of elucidating the precise position adopted by the Corinthian group which was arousing acute apostolic concern. The approach adopted here is in line with recent emphasis on the place of the reader in exegesis. We propose to engage with the world which opens out in front of the text of 1 Corinthians 15 and try to appreciate what the author-in-the-text is saying to the readers implied in the text. Only then can we assess what Paul may be saying to us.[27]

The initial address of writer to readers establishes the common ground which all parties share in the *kerygma* – with one proviso: 'if you hold it fast – unless you believed in vain' (15.2). Here, a broad hint is given that there may be a problem about the way some of his readers have responded to the basic message of salvation. It is not that they have rejected the kerygmatic statements that Christ 'was raised' and that 'he appeared' to many witnesses. It is, to the best of Paul's understanding, that they couple such beliefs with the affirmation 'that there is no resurrection of the dead [*anastasis nekron*]' (15.12).[28] Two points emerge: the first is that they have separated Christ's resurrection from that of 'the resurrection of the dead' in general and probably from the whole apocalyptic scenario that goes with it; and the second, that for them the resurrection hope has force 'in this life' only (15.19). What is the nature of the conflict that is emerging with such force within the world of the text?

From the noticeably personal way in which Paul introduced the topic (15.1), it is reasonable to conclude that the position in question is a misrepresentation of Paul's own message. One hesitates to say a 'misunderstanding' of Paul's position, for it is possible that they knew what his position was and rejected it. If so, they would hardly be impressed by Paul's attempt at a *reductio ad absurdum* in 1 Corinthians 15.13–19: if no general resurrection, then no resurrection of Christ – and a total collapse of all the gospel stands for. The nub of the issue is precisely the connection which Paul has taken as self-evident, namely, that the raising of Christ cannot be neatly extracted from its eschatological setting, which includes the resurrection of the dead (15.13). So far, Paul has merely asserted this point, without justifying it. Clearly, he and his aberrant readers are on different wavelengths.

The Corinthian deviants might well have justified their position *vis-à-vis* the *kerygma* by identifying 'he was raised' and 'he appeared'. If we accept that the collocation of 1 Corinthians 14 and 15 is not coincidental, then there are good grounds for affirming that the charismatic emphasis should apply also to the group in question in 1 Corinthians 15. Paul has moved on from their disorderly worship, which required correction (14.40), to their disordered belief, which was equally in need of being set right. For them, the *kerygma* led on to 'visions and revelations of the Lord' (2 Cor. 12.1) and to the experiencing of the risen power of Christ in this life (1 Cor. 15.19).[29] After all, had not Paul often emphasized precisely this dynamic? And did not the Corinthians know it through the irrefutable experience of spiritual exaltation? There is a case to answer.

Paul begins to come to terms with it in 1 Corinthians 15.20–8 when he introduces the idea of corporate existence. Mankind is a corporate concept, symbolized by Adam. All share his mortal limitations, of which sin and death are characteristic. Therefore, when we speak of Christ, whose work was precisely to break the bonds of slavery to sin and death and to give new life to all, we are also speaking of a corporate figure (15.22). If he brings new life to all – if he is the new Adam (Rom. 5.14–18; 1 Cor. 15.45) – his resurrection must be viewed not in isolation but as 'the first fruits of those who have fallen asleep' (15.20). On a purely individualistic interpretation, Christ's resurrection would have no meaning for 'those...who have fallen asleep in Christ' (15.18). In fact, Christ's victory over the powers of death has profound implications for all. Even now, Christ 'must [*dei*] reign until he has put all his enemies under his feet' (15.25; cf. Ps. 8.6; 110.1). Jesus Christ is Lord; we are his subjects; the messianic conflict continues, but the decisive victory has been won. Christ's exaltation leads on to his messianic reign. And Paul, in a surge of apocalyptic imagery, points to the outcome: the final resurrection when all who belong to the victorious Christ shall be raised (15.23), and the glorious *telos* when he delivers the Kingdom to God the Father (15.24–8). Here is the final solidarity – with God.

Three little arguments, possibly reflecting popular preaching, reinforce the necessity of believing in 'the resurrection of the dead': baptismal practice would otherwise be meaningless (15.29);[30] Paul's apostolic exertions – 'I die every day!' – would have no point (15.30–1); and ethics would descend into mere hedonism (15.32b). A quotation from Menander – 'Bad company ruins good morals' – suggests either that the aberrant group has been adversely affected by harmful cultural influences or that the rest of the Corinthians should not associate with them for fear of moral infection. The root of the problem is ignorance of God, rather than 'spiritual' knowledge of him which the deviants may have claimed with fervour; in fact, they have real cause for shame (15.34).

Paul then returns to substantial matters. In diatribal manner, he admits rhetorical questions to his discourse – as if to give his opponents their say, but in fact to demolish any remaining argument. In effect, he makes them say: 'This apocalyptic scenario is all very well, but how are the dead raised? Are you serious when you speak of the resurrection of *the body*?' (15.35). Modern commentators have tended to identify this point as the cultural root of the problem. To the Greek, it was self-evident – through cultural conditioning – that there was a total dualism between the material and the spiritual. Seneca spoke of 'this clogging burden of a body to which nature has chained me': death is either welcome annihilation or the removal of the burden.[31] To speak of the resurrection of the material body would have been self-evident folly. Hence the irony in Paul's rebuke, 'You foolish man!' (15.36). By well-developed analogy, he demonstrates both that life regularly arises from death (15.36), and that each form of existence has its own 'body': that is, its own organic being (15.37–41). 'So it is with the resurrection of the dead' (15.42). He demonstrates his point by a whole series of antitheses (15.42–9), which leads back to the fundamental antithesis between Adam and Christ, the 'man of dust' and the 'man of heaven' (15.49).[32] There is movement, growth through dying, from one to the other: from the physical to the spiritual. The movement is therefore one of transformation. 'If I must spell it out,' says Paul in effect, then 'flesh and blood cannot inherit the Kingdom of God, any more than the perishable can inherit the imperishable' (15.50). The weight of this statement must not be underestimated. At first sight, Paul has almost given away his case, but he is not in fact contending for 'the resurrection of the flesh'. The flesh dies, like the seed that is sown.[33] The body that is raised is the spiritual body, organically related to Christ, the life-giving Spirit (15.45). And in a final flourish of apocalyptic imagery, Paul celebrates the transformation to come, ending with a characteristic cry of thanksgiving: 'Thanks be to God, who gives us the victory through our Lord Jesus Christ' (15.57). If his argument is properly understood, therefore, he has not given anything away, but has affirmed the organic nature of our bond with Christ and ultimately with God. Hence, he has not been arguing against the 'immortality of the soul' as such (although that is not the view he advances). He is even prepared to say without hesitation that 'this mortal nature must put on immortality' (15.53b).

What Paul is arguing against is the radical individualism – that last infirmity of the Western mind – that tends to substitute in its religious manifestations some kind of individual spiritual exaltation, individual hopes of being 'caught up into Paradise' (2 Cor. 12.3), in place of corporate life in Christ. Those who indulge in *glossolalia* edify themselves rather than the community (cf. 1 Cor. 14.4). When Paul himself speaks, under duress (2 Cor. 12.11), about his own involvement in similar experiences, he finds himself adding the comment, 'whether in the body or out of the body I do not know, God knows', as if a devaluation of the body is implied by the realm of discourse itself. What is of fundamental importance, however, is to recognize that life is a bundle of solidarities: with nation, family, business, social setting, and, much more deeply, with humanity, mortality, sin and spirit. In that solidarity of spirit with Christ, there is the seed of new being, which can be experienced proleptically on earth but which will blossom in eternity – but only as part of that greater solidarity of the spirit with God in Christ. From the human point of view, there is the sleep that intervenes, but even that sleep is 'in Christ'. The eternal solidarity is the body of Christ. The deviant Corinthians have noticeably failed to discern their organic connection with Christ – to 'discern the body'. Instead, their individualism has led them into a superficial view of his exaltation, an inadequate view of his work, and possibly an unserviceable view of Christian *praxis*.

(d) The body of Christ

A key concept in Pauline thinking, 'the body of Christ' expresses precisely the solidarity in Christ which has emerged in our discussion as the primary description of Christian existence and as central to our understanding of 'resurrection' in Paul.

In this sense, 'body' (*soma*) denotes an organic structure.[34] It is used of our mortal existence in which the flesh (*sarx*), life (*psyche*) and spirit (*pneuma* – the transcendent factor) coexist – but not necessarily in harmony. The characteristic feature of humanity (Adam) is estrangement, alienation; sin and disobedience (cf. Rom. 5.12–21). Paul emphasizes the sin, rather than the original perfection, of Adam – the humanity in which all share.[35] The whole human organism as we know it is dominated by 'flesh', to the detriment of 'spirit'. 'Flesh', as J. A. T. Robinson demonstrated in a notable monograph, expresses humanity's 'distance and difference' from God in the solidarity of earthly existence.[36] 'Man as *sarx*, as part of the world, stands always in a relation of ambiguity to God, since the world to which he is bound in the flesh is a world fallen under sin and death'.[37] Hence, to live *kata sarka* ('according to the flesh') is to live in separation from God. By contrast, to live *kata pneuma* ('according to the Spirit') is to live in openness to the transcendent. Indeed, *pneuma* can denote the transcendent Spirit (cf. 1 Cor. 2.10–15) as well as the human spirit that is open to it: the Spirit itself (neuter in Greek) bears witness with our spirit that we are God's children (Rom. 8.16). Hence to live *kata pneuma* is to enter into a new solidarity with God. The 'natural man' (man viewed simply in terms of *psyche* or physical life) cannot receive the things of God, but the *pneumatikos* – the person who lives by the Spirit – does (1 Cor. 2.14–15). Here, then, is a new solidarity, a new bodily existence, in the fellowship of the Spirit. Here is a transformation of the basic character of human existence, the proleptic expression of the final cosmic transformation (cf. 1 Cor. 15.51). Henceforth, we live by the Spirit, by the Lord (cf. 2 Cor. 11.17), by love (Rom. 14.15), 'always and for everything giving thanks...' (Eph. 5.20). We are 'alive to God in Christ Jesus' (Rom. 6.11); we can therefore glorify God in our body, for it is the temple of the Holy Spirit within us (cf. 1 Cor. 6.19–20).

Body (*soma*) is used of the human life and ministry of Christ, 'born of a woman, born under law' (Gal. 4.4; NIV) 'in sinful flesh like ours' (Rom. 8.3; my translation). Yet this identification with humanity in its sinful plight is not a capitulation to the fallen human condition, but the expression within it of a liberating dynamic, which paradoxically can be brought about only through Christ's obedient servanthood (cf. Phil. 2.7–8). This liberating dynamic, however, cannot be discerned if we know Christ only 'according to the flesh' (2 Cor. 5.16): that would be 'to miss the whole truth of what God has wrought in His new act of creation'.[38] One must discern – 'according to the Spirit' – the new creation, the reconciliation which Christ effects for us (2 Cor. 5.17–21), so that the liberating dynamic may work in us. Once alienated and hostile, we are now reconciled 'in the body of his flesh through his death' (Col. 1.22; my literal translation – most versions paraphrase). Therefore, there is a common bond, a solidarity between Christ the liberator and us the liberated. It is to this body – and not to life 'according to the flesh' – that we must commit ourselves; just as the Lord also commits himself to this organic relationship: '...it is not true that the body is for lust; it is for the Lord – and the Lord for the body' (1 Cor. 6.13, NEB).

   Solidarity with the risen Christ is also a central theme: Robinson even coins the phrase 'the body of the resurrection' and speaks of 'the Christian's participation in the resurrection body of the Lord'.[39] The following passage is worth quoting in full:

> God not only raised the Lord but will also raise us up by his mighty power. Are you not also aware that your bodies are Christ's limbs? Shall I then take the limbs that belong to Christ and make them a harlot's? No way! Are you not aware that one who has relations with a harlot forms a bodily union with her? In the words of scripture, 'The two will be one flesh'. And one who has relations with the Lord forms a spiritual union (1 Cor. 6.14–17; my translation).

While participation in the resurrection has both a present and a future reference, the present relationship involves incorporation into a spiritual union: 'one spirit' (*pneuma*). It is an organic union which claims our whole being – including our physical body. There is no room for divided loyalties: one must not separate the flesh and the spirit into two different spheres. The spirit involves the whole being. To press the point home, Paul goes on to speak of the physical body as the temple of the Spirit. Indeed, our fellowship with the risen Christ may be imaged as a productive marriage: 'so that you may belong to another, to him who has been raised from the dead' and thus 'bear fruit for God' (Rom. 7.4).

   'Body' denotes an organic unity of human beings, a corporate fellowship, an interactive community. It is therefore not limited, even in a worldly application, to the special boundaries of individual human existence, but can be applied to a group united by a recognized community of interest, which thus engenders and is also sustained by a particular 'spirit' or ethos. Hence, as soon as one begins to experience 'bodily' existence of this kind, one is made open – to whatever extent – to one's neighbour: 'individually members one of another' (Rom. 12.5) – a significant step in self-transcendence. This openness can take the form of sensitivity to the needs of others (cf. Gal. 6.2), or to the diversity of contribution the members can make to the well-being of the whole (cf. Rom. 12.4). All have a variety of gifts, to be expressed in the service of the community (cf. Rom. 12.6–8; 1 Cor. 12.4–31).

   'Body of Christ', therefore, denotes the organic community of the faithful in Christ, the risen Lord: 'one body in Christ' (Rom. 12.5). While the community is diverse – many members, Jews or Greeks, slaves or free – the creative and sustaining power is that of the Spirit (cf. 1 Cor. 12.12–13). The Spirit – this dynamic power that works for openness and self-transcendence, and brings freedom and hope – is closely identified with the risen Lord: 'the Lord is the Spirit' (2 Cor.

3.17–18).[40] It is he who enables us to manifest the Spirit 'for the common good' (1 Cor. 12.7), in the deployment of gifts and talents (Rom. 12.6–8; 1 Cor. 12.4–11), in the exercise of office (1 Cor. 12.27–30) and in the quality of moral life (Rom. 12.9–21): 'to maintain the unity of the Spirit in the bond of peace' (Eph. 4.3). He therefore imparts a dynamic quality to the community, which is a living, growing, developing organism. 'And we all...are being changed into his likeness from one degree of glory to another; for this comes from the Lord who is the Spirit' (2 Cor. 3.18). The picture is therefore not only of diversity and variety of contribution, openness to others and personal development within the overarching unity of the organism; but also of participation in a transcendent, all-embracing unity in Christ.

Ephesians and Colossians give striking expression to Christ as the focus of this transcendent unity, the head of the body (Eph. 4.15; Col. 1.18). His 'ascent', like his descent 'into the lower parts of the earth', illustrates that he expresses the unity and fulfilment of the whole created order (Eph. 4.9–10). As the celebrated Colossian hymn (Col. 1.15–20) puts it:

> He is before all things
> and all things in him find their coherence.
> He is the head of the body (the church),
> for he is Beginning, the first-born from the dead,
> so that he might in all things take first place
>
> (1.17–18; my translation)

The perspective is cosmic. Ultimately, the body of Christ embraces the whole of creation. The ecclesial interpretation which emerges in the text (1.18) may well be secondary, but expresses the valid insight that within the Church where the kingship of Christ is recognized his cosmic rule is anticipated.[41] His resurrection is the clue to the cosmic leadership that is his. Meanwhile, the faithful must exercise their gifts in ministry and so grow towards maturity: that is, towards the fullness that Christ embodies (Eph. 4.13). 'Speaking the truth in love', the necessary ethos for such growth (Eph. 4.15), is therefore of cosmic significance. Christ is the source from which the whole organism, in all its articulated complexity, derives its organic development and builds itself up in love (Eph. 4.16).

All these meanings come together in the Eucharist. In 1 Corinthians 11, Paul enlarges upon some features of community life which are incompatible with the body of Christ. Self-assertion and selfish practice seem to underlie the fault he finds with the manner in which certain men and women are engaging in worship (11.2–16); but the full weight of his anger is directed at malpractices in relation to the common meal (11.17–22). The group dynamics they practice are counter-productive. They are sabotaging the body corporate by their social divisions, which may serve to show up those who are genuine from those who do not know what they are about, but which otherwise are wholly negative (11.18–19). They may *call* their table-fellowship 'the supper of the Lord', but it is far from being such. They do not 'discern the body' (cf. 11.29). There is self-indulgence and over-indulgence, to the disregard of the feelings and needs of the poorer members, and the whole event is a parody of a church gathering (11.21). Here indeed is a clear indication that there can be no automatic identity between the Church and the body of Christ. There is no discernment in such Corinthian practice, no participation in the Spirit: only the gratification of the flesh. The negativity rebounds on them in the form of judgement (11.29) – even if Paul adopts a peculiar way of reinforcing his point (11.30). The need is for proper discrimination and discernment (11.29, 31).[42]

'Discerning the body' is a useful approach to the interpretation of the Lord's Supper (11.23–6), which is grounded in the tradition of the Christian communities and sanctioned by the word of the Lord himself (11.23–4). The action, imitating that of Jesus with his disciples at the Last Supper, takes place within the context of thanksgiving (*eucharistesas*, 11.24) and recollection of Christ (*anamnesin*). The primary action is breaking, sharing and eating bread (11.24): the cup is taken 'in the same way'. The challenge is to *discern* the body of Christ, not so much in the elements of bread and wine as in the action-in-community. Other elements are important: the awareness of tradition, the thanksgiving, the memory – and therefore the story – of the Christ 'obedient unto death'. All cohere in the action which is not only intensely communal (that is, the realization of 'body' in the corporate sense) but is also characteristic of Jesus and of the kind of community he creates. The divisiveness and self-centredness of the Corinthian fellowship (11.18–22), as we have seen, make discernment impossible. Discerning the body requires the appropriate ethos and community spirit, as well as attentiveness to the meaning of the action. The action itself is a parabolic enactment of the mystery (cf. Mark 4.11) at the core of its fellowship: thus the community of Christ re-enacts his self-giving and celebrates his life-giving power. But the enactment also involves the community *in* the mystery: it is 'for your sake' (11.24; my translation). Hence the body of Christ is to be discerned not in a piece of bread as such, but in a sharing interactive community, celebrating its own interdependence and also its at-one-ness with Christ, crucified-and-risen: a community receiving his life into its very being – hence the symbolism of the cup, 'the new covenant in my blood' (11.25). The new covenant is itself a corporate concept:

> I will set my law within them and write it on their hearts; I will become their God and they shall become my people. No longer need they teach one another to know the Lord; all of them, high and low alike, shall know me, says the Lord, for I will forgive their wrongdoing and remember their sin no more (Jer. 31.33–4, NEB).

Indeed, the community through its eucharistic action proclaims – to the world – the meaning of the cross 'until he comes' (1 Cor. 11.26).

The body of Christ is therefore the community that operates by Christ's life-giving power. It is the community of the Spirit; the body of Christ's resurrection. It can never be *simply* identified with the Church, though it is identified with the faithful. By its very nature it points beyond itself – to the Christ who is its Head and who always transcends it, even though he dwells in it; and to the world, the object of Christ's love. The eucharistic community *proclaims* the cross, which is the power of salvation to all believers, Jew or Greek (1 Cor. 1.24). While the Acts may give the impression that in his conversion Paul encountered Christ through the Church he was trying to stamp out, Paul himself goes beyond this to the Christ whose saving work united Jew and Gentile in the people of God: hence his apostleship to the Gentiles. The body of Christ can encompass the nations. The proclamation of the eucharistic community is Christ's life-giving power for the world.

(e) Awakened to reality

How may we sum up the scope of resurrection language in Paul's writings? The key to the whole realm of discourse lies in the recognition that *one is involved in the resurrection of Jesus*. Though part of the earliest tradition (1 Cor. 15.1–8), it is meaningful only in so far as it becomes a known reality in the believing community and in believers themselves. Bultmann is right to divert our attention from attempting to use the apostolic witness as a 'proof' of the resurrection as an objective, historical 'fact' open to the kind of historical research that would establish 'what actually happened'. It is not that such an approach is inconceivable; it is rather that it is inconceivable that it would elucidate what is meant by the resurrection of Jesus. The apostolic witness, of course, points to the *reality* – one might dare to say the *objective reality* – of Jesus' resurrection; but it is at one and the same time a transcendent reality. It is always greater than we can know or grasp or think. It is encountered – *he* is encountered – by us, and we by him. The horizons of our life, the direction of our journey and the quality of our involvement with others are transformed in the encounter. To know him is to become a new creature…We might attempt a summing up, therefore, in a few brief propositions:

Jesus is himself the focus of the transcendent event of resurrection. The significance of his ministry, like the power he embodied, is not limited or curtailed – far less terminated – by his death. Indeed, the quest of the historical Jesus is productive only in so far as it identifies the transcendent element in his ministry and death. There is no profit in knowing Jesus 'in a fleshly way': nor, we may add, in pursuing the question of his resurrection 'in a fleshly way'. To scratch around in Palestinian debris in the hope of finding 'the bones of Jesus' – or establishing their absence – would be to misdirect our energy.[43] The recognition of Jesus' transcendent reality and power is of the Spirit. And his Spirit bears witness with our spirits, now awakened to reality, that the transcendent domain of God's love and salvation are opened to us through him (cf. Rom. 8.12–17). Hence the extravagant imagery that is applied to his exaltation, the taking of the seat 'at the right hand of God', the bestowal of 'the name that is above all names': all this is to establish Jesus as the focus of the transcendent event of resurrection. His power and significance are cosmic – for all, and therefore for us. The basic element in 'seeing Jesus' is the recognition of precisely this reality.

The resurrection affirms Jesus' transcendence of sin and death. To be awakened to the reality of the resurrection is to see the cross as an expression of Jesus' engagement with and ultimate victory over the powers of evil and death. It is to see life, like the author of the Didache, as a conflict between life and death: a conflict in which failure and powerlessness are transcended by a new, life-giving dynamic. The way of death is characterized by the powers of alienation and division, of fear and destruction. It works with the logic of domination and brutality, and leaves behind it shattered relationships and broken people – even extinction. Paul's characterization of the way of death – the obvious (*phanera*) 'works of the flesh' (Gal. 5.19) – tends to reflect the dimensions of interpersonal relations and sexual practice; but in his thinking the full scope of 'death' is cosmic and includes not only the exercise of brute power by 'the rulers of this world' but the demonic forces of evil which hold the whole of creation in thrall.[44] This pervasive dynamic of death requires that salvation is also cosmic: in its full form, it finally brings the dynamic of death to halt and, even in its proleptic manifestation here and now, imparts hope and strength. For the Christian, 'life' is thus always 'new life', the life of resurrection; by grace God has 'raised' us from the dominion of death.

In the twentieth century, there is little need to elaborate on the depersonalizing forces that so distort the human scene, or to explain how primary groups[45] – such as family, village, neighbourhood or other interpersonal groups – can so readily become the instruments of exploitation and oppression; how secondary groupings – such as nations, cities, trade unions or political parties – are caught up in the imprisoning game of power politics; or how a dynamic of evil can be built up that is far beyond the control of individual, group or even world power. Perhaps there is some need to underline the consequences: that we are all victims, disabled and damaged, and that we tread the way of death.

The salvation that brings life must therefore transcend the dimensions of our enslavement, both in relation to the release itself and to the *praxis* that flows from it. The Pauline emphasis on the cosmic Christ secures the scope of the release: there is no part of creation that can defy him; 'thanks be to God, who gives us the victory...' The problem is how to give expression to the cosmic victory in our present situation. In the West, identification with the Christian faith – whether through nurture or conversion – may represent a movement of the Spirit or a determination of the will which tends to be narrowly channelled into the private world of community devotion or congregational life. Less often does it have a full social, political or institutional expression: it is often argued that such an expression is impossible.[46] The result is that the logic of the depersonalizing forces continues unchecked, while Christian awareness is limited to the interstices of life. Hence the compromises with the arms race, coexistence through mutual fear of mutual annihilation, the violation of earth and space, assent to the great divide of rich and poor...because we have been unable to make a positive connection between the cosmic Christ and contemporary *praxis*.

In the Third World, various types of liberation theology have at least the merit of appreciating the dimensions of the problem, because they have begun with a radical questioning of the position in which human beings find themselves and have fostered a programme of growing awareness – 'conscientization'[47] – by which the intensely human problems and possible solutions are actively canvassed (in the light of Scripture, in Christian groups).[48] Thus are hopelessness and despair transcended and transformed into a new *praxis* of faith and expectation. The resurrection, in the words of Ronald Gregor Smith, 'is a way of affirming the forgiving purpose of God in the historical reality of the life of Christ'[49] – and, we may add, in the historical reality of our own existence-in-the-world.

The resurrection is the power of openness. It is the power that defeats death and breaks open the prison that constrains the sinner. It is the grace that overcomes captivity to self and the powers that find expression in self-centred existence, and it makes one open to others. It is thus the power that overcomes barriers and creates genuine community. It is a power that finds expression *par excellence* in corporate existence that embodies the Spirit of Christ, which is the power of love and healing. Thus the 'body' which gives primary expression to the Spirit of Christ on earth – 'the body of Christ' – is not a reconstituted corpse but a corporate fellowship, in which members learn a new interdependence on their neighbours and thus bring to expression a new humanity.

The risen Christ relates to this body both in terms of immanence and transcendence. In its several members and in its corporate nature, it is the shrine of his Spirit. He can be described variously as its head, which gives direction and sustains life, or as the inherent power which gives coherence and promotes the growth and development of the whole. The body is the mode by which he manifests himself in the world; yet it never possesses or controls him. In so far as the body is given an ecclesial interpretation, it does not represent the exclusive instrument of his presence on earth. He remains sovereign and transcendent; yet its destiny is 'hid with him in God'.

The supreme expression both of the body of Christ and of the openness which is its essence is found in the eucharistic community: both as the community of thanksgiving and as the sacramental community. The body of Christ is discerned in a community gathered round a table and sharing the gifts of God. It expresses its response to God-in-Christ in its thanksgiving. It expresses its corporate identity in Christ in the act of recollection and of sharing. In so doing, it expresses its openness to the transcendent order and to the neighbour who takes the same bread and wine. And the mystery – the *mysterion* – is that through this corporate action, God's gifts in Christ are received as life.[50] Here is the life-giving Spirit; here is the foretaste of heaven. At the same time, here is signified the new humanity, the new creation: the purpose God has for the world, transfigured and renewed.

The resurrection is life for the world. At the beginning of this chapter, we noted that, for Paul, encounter with the risen Christ coalesced with his commissioning as apostle to the nations. The link is organic, not accidental. The Gentiles had always been problematic candidates for salvation in a particularist religion such as that of ancient Israel. Yet certain strains within it were distinctly inclusive:

> I will give you as a light to the nations,
>   that my salvation may reach to the end of the earth (Isa. 49.6).

In Pauline discourse, Christ – the Messiah – is the exalted Lord; Paul, his servant, is commissioned to take the message of salvation to the nations. This involved a Copernican revolution not only in Paul's career but also in his thinking. In the course of his mission, he had to rethink the message of salvation not in the particularist tradition of Judaism but in the universalist tradition of salvation for the nations. Out went circumcision and Law, the marks of pre-messianic particularism. Into the centre came grace, gospel, faith, baptism in the Messiah's name, the fruit of the Spirit...

The extent of the revolution is seen not merely in confrontations with synagogues but in the strains and tensions between Paul's Gentile mission and Christian tendencies which kept nearer to the Jewish model. It emerged clearly in Paul's unyielding stance at Antioch. What was at stake was the truth of the gospel (Gal. 2.14): the good news of the grace of God in Christ as the focus of salvation. Here is the message of salvation in universal, global terms, and it follows from the recognition of Christ as risen Lord. The resurrection, breaking as it did the cosmic powers of sin and death, is cosmically and globally unitive. There is one Lord, one faith, one baptism, one God and Father of us all; at the name of Jesus, *every* knee shall bow.

It is a strange paradox that later formulations of this universalist faith evinced particularist features. The table-fellowship designed to express the unity of the body of Christ became a mark of division ('Is Christ divided?', 1 Cor. 1.13); 'catholic' Christianity evinced the dogmatism and exclusiveness of sectarianism; and the resurrection became an element in a credal formula. The rediscovery of the Pauline spirit reaffirms the cosmic reality of the resurrection. The risen Christ is the life of the world: that is the meaning of sacrament, Church and confession.

Here is certainly an invitation – perhaps a demand – that theology be approached in a radical way. Though its subject-matter is God, its approach to its subject-matter is through the life of humankind and the world: an 'anthropo-theocentric' approach, in the words of Ronald Gregor Smith.[51] Its leading edge is found in the resurrection of Jesus. Dark and defaced, the world is in the sleep of death. The resurrection is the awakening – and the enlightenment:

> Awake, O sleeper, and arise from the dead,
>   and Christ shall give you light   (Eph. 5.14).

1 A detailed discussion of this subject is found in Munck (1959), pp. 182–7 and Dunn (1975), pp. 101–2.
2 On the rhetorical approach to Galatians, the standard work is Betz (1979); cf. Hester (1986) and, on Paul's concern for a wider audience, Lategan (1988).

3 cf. the Excursus in Betz (1979), pp. 64–6.
4 Dunn (1975), pp. 143–4.
5 In Bartsch (1954), p. 39.
6 ibid., p. 72.
7 ibid., p. 112.
8 From O'Donoghue (1983).
9 This translation gives *harpagmos* its full weight: the ending *-mos* primarily denotes process, hence 'an act of plundering': cf. Lightfoot (1913), p. 111; also Moule (1970), pp. 266–8, 271. There is a danger in following theological preferences, rather than observing lexicographical accuracy, and translating as if the text had *harpagma*: such a translation is just feasible, but one wonders why the writer did not use this word if that is what he meant.
10 *Doulos* may be 'servant', as in the suffering servant of Isaiah, or 'slave' as in characteristic Pauline usage (cf. Rom. 8.15–21; Gal. 4.3–7); the servant/slave mode may stand in contrast to Adam (man), who did not humble himself in this way; Moule (1970), p. 268, suggests that it denotes 'the extreme in respect of deprivation of rights'.
11 Two dimensions are present in this line: identification with the general human lot, and manifestation as the new Adam (man).
12 For a neat review of the current debate on this passage – 'one of the most disputed passages in the history of New Testament interpretation' – see Hurst (1986); cf. also Wanamaker (1987). Cf. also the monograph by Martin (1967).
13 cf. Murphy-O'Connor (1976); Dunn (1977), pp. 134–6; Dunn (1980), pp 114–25.
14 See note 9 above.
15 cf. Lightfoot (1913), pp. 127–33 and many subsequent interpretations.
16 Casey (1987), p. 128.
17 Particularly notable is *b. Hagigah* 15a, where Metatron, seated in the heavenly court, gives Aher the impression that he is enthroned as an equivalent to God – and able to act independently of God – a heretical impression for which Metatron is punished! Cf. Segal (1977), pp. 60ff. Such Jewish material is, of course, directed against heretical tendencies, including apocalyptic messianism (cf. Segal, p. 59). The inhibiting factor is the premise of monotheism. Some such 'court of heaven' scenario is presupposed by the imagery of Phil. 2.5–11. In the poem, Christ receives the highest place in heaven after his cross and exaltation – but 'to the glory of God'. On the cosmic Christ, cf. also Col. 1.15–20. His primordial position is also exalted: it is equality with God which carries no hint of affront to the divine majesty. His ministry on earth is an extension and expression of his heavenly bearing.
18 For a succinct critique of the traditional view of *kenosis*, cf. Baillie (1948), pp. 94–8.
19 On *Kyrios*, it should be noted that although the term could be as mundane as 'sir' it could also stand for Yahweh, God of Israel: cf. the Aramaic *mar*, which also means 'Lord' in *maranatha* (1 Cor. 16.22; cf. Did. 10.6; Rev. 22.20). Its meaning could therefore, in certain contexts, 'slide upwards', as Casey suggests (1987), p. 126.
20 It may be added here for clarification that the interpretation of Phil. 2.5–11 given above is holistic, not diachronic. It does not presuppose that Paul's mature theology came to him complete and ready-packaged in a flash of inspiration on the Damascus road. It is much more likely that the implications of Paul's calling unfolded over a period: cf. Räisänen (1987). Indeed, the Philippian hymn – so often cited as pre-Pauline – might possibly

be post-Pauline: a later reflection on Pauline understanding celebrated in the Christian communities. Even if this part of Philippians did not come directly from Paul's pen, it remains a meaningful exposition – almost celebration – of his thought.

21 Perkins (1984), p. 47.

22 cf. the examples cited in Perkins, (1984), pp. 37–56.

23 Some commentators have suspected a new letter here, following its own rhetorical pattern: cf. Collange (1979), pp. 3–5, pp. 122–4. Cf. also Räisänen (1987), pp. 408–10.

24 A useful discussion of this is found in Ziesler (1983), pp. 47–50.

25 For further illustration, cf. the discussion in chapter 1.

26 cf. Allison (1985), pp. 67–8.

27 For an account of reader-oriented interpretation, cf. Suleiman in Suleiman and Grossman (1980), pp. 3–45; Fowler (1985); Petersen (1980).

28 In recent discussion, this Corinthian slogan has been related to the Hellenistic wisdom tradition by Horsley (1978); and to Cynic/Stoic preaching, by Wedderburn (1981). Neither proposal, though suggestive, is of central importance to the reading of the text.

29 In the background is the shadow of Gnosticism: cf. Pearson (1973), passim. However, any application of the term 'Gnostic' to the Corinthian deviants must be attended with caution. 'The quest for a developed pre-Christian Gnosticism, even a Jewish one, which could be said to have influenced the Corinthians, or Paul himself, has not yet yielded results', Wilson (1982), p. 111. But Wilson agrees that something is in the wind in first-century Corinth which may be called 'a kind of *gnosis*'.

30 The interpretations of this sentence are manifold. For our present purpose, we can be guided only by the context and the general thrust of Paul's argument.

31 Seneca, *Epistles* 24.18. For further discussion, cf. chapter 1, pp. 13–15.

32 Christ is the *last* Adam: possibly an attempt by Paul 'to counter current speculations about a primeval Anthropos (Man) who was fragmented by a fall, parts of whom are therefore within human beings, but who will finally be restored and reconstituted', Ziesler (1983), p. 51. Paul emphasizes a new humanity, to which Christ is the key, being 'life-giving Spirit' – i.e. a source of life for others.

33 cf. Dunn (1975), p. 121.

34 *Soma* does have other meanings: e.g., 'corpse' or 'body' in the individual sense. Cf. the article on *soma* by Schweizer in TDNT VII.

35 cf. Ziesler (1983), pp. 52–4.

36 cf. Robinson (1952), pp. 17–26.

37 ibid., p. 22.

38 ibid., p. 23.

39 ibid., p. 49.

40 This is a notorious *crux interpretum*. The Spirit and the risen Christ are not to be formally identified (contra Lietzmann (1949), p. 1; cf. Héring (1967), p. 26). Héring emends to read, 'there where the Lord is, is the Spirit' (ibid., p. 27), but this remains speculative, as Héring admits. The best solution is to understand the phrase 'now the Lord is the Spirit' as Paul's exegesis of Exod. 34.34: in this text, 'the Lord' means 'the Spirit'; cf. Bruce (1971).

41 cf. Perkins (1984), pp. 238ff.

42 For a discussion of the social context of the Corinthian practice, cf. Theissen (1982), pp. 145–74. There is, however, considerable debate about the interpretation of 1 Cor. 10.11. On the basis of a consideration of the

pseudepigraphical *Joseph and Aseneth*, Burchard (1987) argues for more weight to be put on the *sacramentalia* (the bread and the cup) than on the meal itself. Nevertheless, the interpretation of the community as the body of Christ would seem to be more fundamental than either meal or elements in themselves.

43 However, cf. the carefully argued case by O'Neill (1972). See below, p. 143.
44 cf. Carr (1981); Wink (1984).
45 cf. Sprott (1958).
46 cf. Norman (1979).
47 cf. Freire (1972), p. 81.
48 cf. Cardenal (1977).
49 Smith (1966), p. 97.
50 cf. Forrester, McDonald, Tellini (1983), pp. 57–61.
51 Smith (1970), pp. 110–42.

3

The Mystery of the Resurrection
The Resurrection in the Gospel of Mark

To you has been given the mystery of the kingdom of God...

MARK 4.11

O Master, who hast sown, arise to reap.

CHRISTINA G. ROSSETTI, 'MARY MAGDALENE AND THE OTHER MARY'

At first sight it would seem that to turn from Paul to Mark is to enter a different world. The method of communication is certainly different. Paul is self-consciously apostolic; his theology emerges through his vocation, his apostolic *praxis*, and his letters to young churches. In his understanding of the resurrection, he combines respect for tradition with a deep sense of the presence and power of the transcendent Lord and Christ within contemporary church community and personal experience. Mark is no less concerned with this presence and power, but since his approach is designed to develop gospel perspectives from their sources (*arche*, 1.1), he is committed to narrative.

The story to be told presents the reader with an invitation to diachronic engagement with its substance. So, far from reading it with an eye to its meaning (like the riddle of a detective story) or distilling the 'essence' of Mark's message from the complexities of the material, Mark's reader is challenged to come step by step with him through the unfolding of the story of Jesus the Christ and to share in the perspectives and challenges which the story presents to his understanding. It is a challenge to discernment – and to belief. Nor could it be otherwise. A narrative presentation of the gospel is faced with the task of showing how the transcendent is signified – how it may be discerned and revealed – in the story of a historical ministry. The elements of that ministry – whether word or deed, preaching or parable, living or dying – contribute to a perception of reality which may be deeply disturbing or offensive, or confusing and disorientating, or frankly puzzling; but interpreted as Mark would have his reader interpret them, these elements are shot through with ultimate meaning. They comprise the good news of the presence and power of God at work in his creation through the ministry of his Son (1.1).

Mark, therefore, is no mere chronicler or anecdotalist. Rather, he presents the reader with a metaphoric story designed to indicate and articulate, so far as that is possible in human language and action, the working of the transcendent within the historical reality which it necessarily transcends. Hence for Mark, at the heart of the events he describes there is mystery: the *mysterion* of the performing of God's Kingdom in worlds and cultures deeply alienated from God. Not surprisingly, this *mysterion* encompasses the death of the Christ: the death of the King of the Jews (15.26). Yet, if we read Mark's Gospel aright, we will learn to see God's power operating through brokenness and death: we will recognize the reality of resurrection. Hence, the Gospel leaves us with an abiding sense of mystery: the *mysterion* of the death and resurrection of the Christ. Its product need not be an undermining sort of bewilderment (which may, indeed, be true of the women in the story, 16.8). To those well tutored by Mark, it conveys the assurance of the continued power and presence of God in human weakness, and therefore hope and expectation for the future (as in the young man's message, 16.6–7).

Lest we be accused of self-contradiction by focusing on the end of the story, let us turn – with Mark – to its beginning and allow it to shape our perceptions and understanding.

1 METAPHORIC STORY

Long overshadowed by its more imposing partners, Mark's Gospel has come into its own in recent criticism. While its style and editorial procedures are as open as ever to charges of clumsiness and infelicity,[1] the combination of story and parable, image and event, intercalation and interpretation, suggests a sophistication of structure which also claims recognition.[2] Since it is impossible to go into these matters in detail here, the cumulative results of recent investigations are assumed rather than justified in this chapter.

A striking characteristic of Mark's Gospel is the interaction within it of the rhetoric of direction and indirection. As R. M. Fowler puts it, 'the stable, coherent guidance in the Gospel provides the "direction" required by the reader if the reader is to handle successfully the "indirection" which is based upon it'.[3] From the 'beginning' (1.1), which seems to be an echo of the creation story, the Markan prologue directs attention to the prophetic word, to the phenomenon of the Baptist, to the 'coming' of Jesus from Nazareth to his baptism, and to the proclamation of the Kingdom (1.1–15). Indeed, so deeply nuanced is the language and so rich the imagery that readers would surely be overwhelmed unless they already had some awareness of the religious and cultural milieu of the narrative. Message and messenger, Spirit, Son and Kingdom, and even location (wilderness, River Jordan, and Galilee) are all central to his statement of the good news of salvation. An informed and inquiring readership, found doubtless in the Christian communities who were living through the disequilibrium of the Jewish world around AD 70, is assumed.[4] The Gospel, therefore, is designed not primarily to provide information but to lead the followers of Jesus, in their bewilderment and powerlessness, and amid the ambiguities of their position, to deeper insight into the mystery of the ways of God with his creation and to renewed hope and confidence in the risen Christ.

To achieve this end, Mark must both support his readers and also, when appropriate, leave them to face new challenges on their own, however disconcerting this procedure may be. Like any good teacher, he begins at the point his audience has reached. He affirms Jesus as the Christ, the Son of God, and his coming as the fulfilment of Scripture. The narrative of Jesus' baptism gives direction to the whole story. The opening of the heavens proclaims divine deliverance.[5] The descent of the Spirit is an act of divine appointment, of commissioning to a God-given task.[6] The voice from heaven, affirming divine Sonship and divine favour, provides assurance that Jesus is indeed the representative of the true Israel.[7] Thus far the reader is directed and reassured. However testing and conflictive Jesus' ministry is, the Spirit directs his ways and the angels minister to him (cf. 1.12–13). The note of conflict, however, suggests controversy, contested issues, heated exchanges, alienation and offence. When the commissioned servant of the true Israel confronts the powers of evil through flesh-and-blood encounter with the defenders of current practice in Israel, the issues are deep and far-reaching, questioning not only the faith and practice of Israel but also the authenticity of Jesus' ministry and authority. Caught in the midst of the storm, fearful and pitifully dependent on Jesus himself, are the disciples, who reflect many of the tensions the readers also feel. Here is deliberate indirection – questioning, ambiguity, metaphor, paradox and irony – which produces in the short term the lack of understanding that characterizes the disciples throughout the Gospel but which can also lead to new direction, insight and stability.

In articulating and giving performance to the Kingdom in Israel,[8] Jesus evinces in his ministry an effective power – an *exousia* – which is widely recognized (1.22, 27).[9] It is a trigger for ephemeral adulation and excessive dependence on the part of the crowds, and for deeper scrutiny and theological objections on the part of the scribes (cf. 2.6–7). Apart from the *exousia* – the powerful dynamic – of his preaching, teaching and healing, there is also the question of his chosen life-style, in which the disciples are implicated. Is this man who calls a tax-gatherer to be one of his intimate circle (2.13–14), who sits at table with tax-collectors and sinners (2.15), and who flouts the sacred traditions of Law and sabbath (2.23—3.6), to be counted as an agent of the Spirit or of the devil? It is a critical question: to blaspheme against the Spirit – to look on the work of God and ascribe it to Satan – is the one sin that cannot be forgiven (3.28–30).

Thus Mark's narrative suggests the paradox that when the Kingdom of God is given expression in Jesus' ministry, powerful sections of the religious establishment in Israel resist and resent it. Such was the alienation which he aroused in their midst that Norman Perrin is not being extravagant in making a connection between Jesus' table-fellowship and his subsequent death at the instigation of the Jewish authorities.[10] Indeed, against this background of popular acceptance and official criticism, Mark inserts four gnomic or parabolic sayings which throw light on this aspect of his ministry. Table-fellowship is related to Jesus' healing work by the adage of the physician who attends to the sick rather than the healthy (2.17). The non-ascetic life-style of Jesus and his disciples is illumined by the thought that this is a time of celebration when the bridegroom is with his guests, but the shadow of bitter times is already recognized (2.18–20). Two images – the new piece of cloth (2.21) and the new wine (2.22) – emphasize the radical novelty of the enterprise to which Jesus is called. He has not come to prop up existing conventions! The themes of conflict and alienation are continued later in the image of the binding of the strong man (3.27) and that of the true family of Jesus (3.34–5). Such radical novelty leads even his friends to question his sanity (3.21). How can even the most sympathetic be convinced that the performance of the Kingdom in Israel must necessarily take this course?

It is at this point that Mark introduces the Sower as a master parable (4.1–9).[11] Here, Mark implies, the reader can learn how to handle the puzzling elements of indirection that have emerged so quickly in the story. As Amos Wilder has made clear, the parable evinces a strongly delineated pattern, and the coherence of the story-image makes it resistant to change.[12] A specific action inaugurates the plot: 'A sower went out to sow ...' Prominence is given to the triple loss, caused by birds, rocky ground and thorns.[13] All this, however, serves to highlight the triple gain: thirtyfold, sixtyfold and a hundredfold. In this way, the parable rises to a dramatic crescendo,[14] an almost defiant announcement of the coming harvest as an immensely productive gift. The disciples could not have been particularly surprised at the general theme of this parable, which not only resonates with their environment but is common enough in apocalyptic teaching. 2 Esdras 4.27–32 provides a contemporary example, concluding: 'how vast a harvest there will be when good seeds beyond number have been sown!' (2 Esd. 4.32). Yet in most other respects, including logic and structure, the two parables are quite different, and it is clearly the special twists that Jesus has given to the theme which puzzle the disciples.[15] Puzzlement and disorientation, however, are part of a learning process made necessary by the nature of the subject-matter, the *mysterion* of the Kingdom. This is not to be confused with the incomprehension of 'those outside', for whom the parabolic presents no way forward and who invariably react negatively to a prophetic ministry (4.12).[16] In Mark 4, the disciples are viewed in a mainly positive light: ready to be helped through the problems of indirection that confront the most earnest inquirers into the transcendent.

Let us go to the heart of the problem that seems to have 'thrown' the disciples. The parable speaks of a God-given power, as fundamental as the power of physical life and growth. Why does Jesus choose to build his image-story of the Kingdom on the harsh realities of Galilean cultivation? It is certainly not a matter of local colour: the hard realities are basic.[17] If it is a kind of cipher of his ministry, what statement is thereby made about the mystery of the Kingdom? Let us note the images which Jesus tacitly rejects.

Broadly speaking, standard eschatological imagery is of two types. One is the parable of judgement, as in the song of the vineyard (Isa. 5.1–7): the crop is a disaster; Israel and Judah have failed to produce the results for which Yahweh looked; the oracle of judgement is therefore given; the owners lose their inheritance. The second relates to the oracle of salvation and employs images of luxuriant growth:

> For I will pour water on the thirsty land,
> and streams on the dry ground;
> I will pour my Spirit on your descendants [Heb. *zera*, lit. 'seed'],
> and my blessing on your offspring.
> They shall spring up like grass amid waters,
> like willows by flowing streams.
> This one will say, 'I am the Lord's,'
> another will call himself by the name of Jacob,
> and another will write on his hand, 'The Lord's,'
> and surname himself by the name of Israel   (Isa. 44.3–5).

In this luxuriant scenario, Israel is the seed that flourished by the grace of God and the work of his Spirit. Water is abundant and growth rampant: so Israel is renewed. In Mark's story, God's work has begun; the Spirit has come upon Jesus and effected mighty works: the waters of baptism suggest the conditions for growth; an abundant harvest is promised. The story-image thus incorporates the oracle of salvation. *But* the seed is sown on unexpectedly difficult terrain and loss ensues.

Elements have crept in from the judgement scenario. Jesus has minted a new kind of eschatological image: hence the bewilderment of the disciple-group – and perhaps the reader. The question now is: What is the significance of this new image?

The sowing of the seed is the first action – God's action. New power and potentiality have been released: the seed of the Kingdom is sown. But the apocalyptic scenario in 2 Esdras 4.27–32 presupposed that the harvest of evil would be reaped in full before there would be room for the good: then the tremendous harvest would come. In Mark, the Kingdom is not held back in this way – now is the time! – but neither does it have such a clear run. It comes in spite of obvious reverses, losses and disappointments. It struggles against continued opposition and adversity to produce in the end a surprisingly bountiful harvest. The God of apocalypticism is all-powerful. His foes may have their fling, but when he acts, victory is total. Yet in the Sower, Jesus seems to qualify this transcendental triumphalism. The scenario is historical, and because of that the conditions for continued growth are not always present. Only the conclusion is the same: the final harvest is ridiculously great.

A similar transposition of imagery, it may be noted, occurs in the parable of the mustard seed (4.31–2). The 'greatest of all shrubs' recalls grandiloquent or highly poetic Old Testament descriptions of the noble cedar as an image of Israel in prophetic and apocalyptic writings, where it is used as a symbol of impressive power and majesty (cf. Ezek. 17.23; 31.6; Dan. 4.10–12, 20–1). No such image for the Kingdom in Jesus' ministry! Instead, a mustard seed; and *per impossibile*, the laughable image of its foliage as 'the greatest of all shrubs' with 'large branches, so that the birds of the air can make nests in its shade'. It is as if the pain of ministry in Galilee found release in humour, itself a way of transcending depression or despair. The 'take-off' here bears some resemblance to the rejection or qualification of triumphalist or judgemental pictures of the coming Kingdom in the Sower. Wilder's phrase, 'a vision of fruition through miscarriage',[18] is peculiarly apt.

The disciples' confusion may well be not so much blank incomprehension as a dim and disturbing awareness of what Jesus is actually getting at: which coincided not at all with their own preconceptions. But Mark has not yet finished with them – nor with his readers. As a final commentary on the parable, he has Jesus present a more allegorical version, the language and setting of which suggests the early Church rather than that of the disciples.[19] It is presented, therefore, with the readers directly in view. J. Drury has underlined the fact that Mark is concerned to interpret the historical particularities of Jesus' ministry: 'The Gospel is history, not psychological generality'.[20] Hence, the birds represent Satan, who through Peter attacks the notion of the suffering Messiah (8.32–3). The shallow, rocky ground represents those who give way when things become really difficult: like the disciples who forsook Jesus and fled (14.50). Those choked by the desire for riches include the rich young man (10.17–22). Each item of the parable has its counterpart in the later narrative of the book – except for the final abundant crop. Here, Drury suggests, Mark 'would seem to be looking beyond his book, with its famously abrupt ending, to the life of his church; hoping for better things after the resurrection than happened before it'.[21]

Drury is certainly open to challenge on the last point. Both Mark and his readers know that the resurrection does not provide a 'happy ever after' ending, nor does it guarantee better things on earth. For the rest, Mark's interpretation clearly includes the features Drury indicates but also goes beyond them. The most obvious element is that the product – be it loss of harvest or abundant harvest – is interpreted in terms of people. Here is the rise of the new Israel on earth, accomplished by the power of God which is as fundamental as the power of creation and of life itself, but is in tension at all times with the powers of chaos and negation. Satan operates as the distorter and disabler of creation, as in the exorcism stories, as the opposer of the work of salvation. It is all too easy to adopt his role and slip into negation (cf. 8.32–3). Historical circumstances – such as tribulation (suffering on an apocalyptic scale!) and persecution – induce negative responses; while fascination with the ephemeral and the insatiable appetite for wealth and material profit lead to further losses. All this can be documented from the ministry of Jesus, and readers are free to interpret the parable in this way. Even more fundamentally, it is an exposition of how the Kingdom works. Jesus' ministry is essentially the Kingdom brought to performance in the world: and that performance is stamped both with power and vulnerability. Through the whole process, the new people of God is being established – an astonishing harvest.

What, then, can be said about the resurrection at this point? The complexity of the concept must be recognized: it is much more complex than Drury allows. It may be thought of as the power of God bringing the new Israel to life within the process of history and in defiance of inhibiting factors. It may be thought of as the power of God which brings new life to people otherwise in the grip of death, as the Gospel itself testifies. It may be thought of as the power of God in the ministry of Jesus, who not only expressed it in relation to others but embodied it in his own dying and rising. Hence there is a fascinating range of meaning in the concept of 'the word' which is sown at the outset. It may refer to Jesus' teaching of the Kingdom: the parable would then be a commentary on the results in his mission and that of the disciples. It may refer to church missionary preaching and its reception in the world. But Jesus' teaching and actions form a unity (cf. 1.27), and are inseparable from Jesus as a person (cf. 4.41). Hence, Mark may imply, Jesus himself is 'the word'; not part of the harvest, but its necessary condition. That is what the Gospel is about (1.1). Or, perhaps better, 'the word' can mean 'the story'. The story of Jesus encapsulates the whole mystery of the Kingdom: in all its power and dynamism, as well as in his vulnerability and in the rejection he suffered. It is the story of the life, death and resurrection of Jesus. The resurrection coheres not only with the concept of 'word' but also with the image of seed. In Pauline language, what is sown cannot come to life unless it dies (cf. 1 Cor. 15.36). As J. G. Williams has put it, 'the seed that is planted and the seed that grows are distinct but inseparable in the organic imagery of life, death and the new life'.[22]

The master parable has established the basic metaphor of Mark's Gospel.

2 POWER AND PRESENCE

If the parabolic concentration of Mark 4.1–34 is as central to the writer's purpose as the above discussion has suggested, the reader is in a better position to appreciate the kind of statement Mark is making. His leading theological concern is the power of God; but that power is depicted through the immanent processes of nature and human interaction with them. The divine power is all important: all creation – and all renewal of creation – rests upon it. The power operates through effective presence – above all, presence in community; yet there is an inescapable hiddenness about the divine operation which places a premium on discernment and sensitivity rather than unambiguous theophany. It follows, therefore, that the language and method of revelation are indirect and parabolic.

The consequences for Mark's rhetorical method are considerable. In his narrative, he must affirm the power and presence of God without suggesting that they ever come under human control. He must suggest their hiddenness, their challenge to human perception, their capacity to disorientate as well as to amaze. Even the adequacy of the readers' deepest convictions about Jesus' nature and mission – for example, that he is Christ and that the Kingdom is at hand – is subjected to challenge and scrutiny, for if revelation entails indirection and parable, then the narrative must be their instrument. Like the disciples, the reader is forced to ask again about the real nature of Jesus and the Kingdom, not only after some narrative manifestation of the power of God to still the tempest and raise the dead, but also in face of Jesus' powerlessness to confound the forces that brought him to his own death. Such a presentation is designed to elicit response from an audience which perhaps was all too aware of the hiddenness of God amid the disorientating conflicts and dislocations of the times and which found the power of resurrection and hope hard to discern. Hence, there is the deepest possible correlation between Mark's rhetorical method and his theological aims and understanding. On the basis of Mark 4.1–34, it may be suggested that he derived an awareness of this correlation from the practice of Jesus himself.

The section into which we now move (4.35–8.26) is an excellent example of Mark's rhetorical procedure. As with the Sower, he uses repetition to underline significant themes: narratives tend to be paired, or to appear in two or three different forms. The matching of narratives can lead to striking intercalations. And there is a core to the narrative cluster. It is found in the tale of the Baptist's death: not a piece of narrative padding to fill the gap between the departure of the disciples on their mission (6.6b–13) and their return (6.30–4), as Nineham and many other commentators have assumed,[23] but an indication of the shadow under which most of Jesus' ministry is lived out. The paradox of the divine power and powerlessness is kept in view throughout.

Mark begins with a narrative of power and presence (the storm at sea, 4.35–41), and reinforces it with a corresponding narrative in the second part of the cluster (walking on the sea, 6.45–51). Such narratives emphasize circumstance, but with a metaphoric twist: the disciples are all at sea, all in the same boat! Jesus is effectively removed from them, either by sleep (4.38) or physical absence (6.46). Though left in charge, the disciples are unable to cope with the emergency (4.37) – the second story seems deliberately contrived to make this point (6.48). The first story highlights the disciples' desperate dependence on Jesus – like afflicted people in some of the healing stories – rather than their faith (4.40). 'They have no root in themselves' (cf. 4.17). The story presents Jesus as the agent of the power of the transcendent God, who rules the raging of the sea (Ps. 89.9) and saves the faithful from the engulfing flood (Ps. 69.2).[24] Mark's point is that, whereas human perception of the power and presence of God is refracted through human experience and is open to interpretation, there is nothing ambivalent about the power of God itself. The disciples are left to question the adequacy of their own understanding of Jesus (4.41). In the second story, the focus of the symbol is the paradoxical presence of Jesus (6.48b, 50): 'it is I' (*ego eimi*, a most evocative statement).[25] The narrative is a kind of epiphany story, rather than a miracle story. The disciples once again misunderstand the event (6.49) and end up in total astonishment (6.51). The central problem, to which the narrative returns again and again, is how to understand the operation of transcendent power and presence in history, and in particular in the ministry of Jesus.

Healing stories – taken together rather than in isolation – contribute some elements to the scene. Mark interrelates three of them. The first is set abroad: on 'the other side of the sea' (5.1). It is an elaborate exorcism, the legion (evocative term!) being banished to the watery wastes (5.13). The power is that of the Most High God (5.7). Its effect on the demoniac is openly acknowledged, and the customary response of fear in face of the uncanny is evident once more (5.15). On this occasion, however, it is not the disciples who betray their unease but the general population, who request Jesus to leave (5.17). Even the power of healing is disconcerting, and they are not yet prepared to come to terms with it. The erstwhile demoniac is left to give personal witness to the mercy of God (5.19–20).

Two intercalated stories suggest the element of need within Israel. The request of Jairus, 'one of the rulers of the synagogue' (5.22), is for the healing presence of Jesus (5.23). Thereafter, attention is focused on two contrasting cases, both female, and their relation to Jesus. There is the exhausted and impoverished woman, drained by a twelve-year haemorrhage (5.25); Jesus, drained of energy (*dynamis*) by her demand (5.30); and Jairus' daughter, twelve years old (5.42), drained of life itself. There is the faith of Jairus (5.23), the faith of the woman (5.28, 34), and the faith demanded by Jesus (5.36). There is the privacy of the woman, finally shattered (5.27–33), and the private circle gathered round the dead child (5.40; cf. 5.37), finally overcome with amazement (5.42). And the power that casts out demons and heals the sick is the power that raises the dead from their slumber.

G. Rochais has made a detailed study of the development of the story of Jairus' daughter in terms of tradition history.[26] He found that it had its source in Aramaic tradition, first as a healing account and then as a resurrection story. It then acquired certain catechetical features, designed to reassure the community on the subject of the dead. There is no suggestion that the narrative owes its origin to reflection on an Old Testament source such as 2 Kings 4.18–37, nor to a church narrative such as Acts 9.36–43. Its locus is in the ministry of Jesus. How then should this tradition history be interpreted? In terms of the writer's purpose, the most significant point is not that the resurrection element is secondary to that of healing, but that Jesus' healing power is interpreted in terms of resurrection. It suggests on the one hand that all healing is life renewed and opened to new possibilities, and on the other hand that this possibility of renewal is not finally negated even by physical death. Jesus' presence therefore conveys the power of renewal and resurrection. Henceforth, the phrase *Talitha cumi* (5.41) will echo unchanged down the ages, proclaiming that the boundary of finite existence itself is transcended by the power of God operating in Jesus' name.

The people across the sea were not ready to receive Jesus. At home (6.1–3), the picture is little different. The power and wisdom of his ministry (6.2) are subordinated to a family stereotype and become a cause of offence (6.3), debilitating Jesus' ministry – he could heal only a few sick people there (6.5)! Unbelief, therefore, is akin to the closed mind ('hard of heart' is one of Mark's favourite descriptions of the disciples at their most obtuse). It is an unwillingness or inability to be open to the transcendent, to the moving of the Spirit of God in historical existence. Hence Jesus' advice to Jairus when he received ill-tidings: 'Do not fear, only believe' (5.36).

The core of this narrative cluster, as we have noted above, is the mission of the disciples (6.7–13, 30) and the story of the Baptist's death (6.14–29). The latter is no mere intrusion, like an interval in a dramatic presentation. It shows the death-dealing power of Herod: dynastic tyranny in all its irrationality and capriciousness, standing as a foil to the kind of power that is evident in Jesus' ministry. In this situation, it is Herod who feels threatened. In suggesting the inimical relationship between Herod and Jesus, Mark makes provocative use of a popular characterization of Jesus which he attributes also to Herod: Jesus is the resurrected John (6.14, 16). Clearly, Jesus is not being identified with John – or Elijah, or 'one of the prophets'[27] – in a visual or personal sense, but in terms of the presence of effective power: 'that is why these powers are at work in him' (6.14b). The grammar of resurrection here – the logic of the metaphor – is that power formerly invested in and manifested by one person is now invested in and manifested by another. If Jesus should die, as John did, at the hands of Herod, in whom would his power be reinvested? Who would embody his resurrection? The question is not raised specifically, nor is the popular Herodian interpretation endorsed by Mark: but neither is it dismissed. The questions are left to linger in the mind of the reader, and grim consequences of a collision between the two powers under discussion prompt yet another question: If Jesus suffers John's fate, with whom does true power lie – with the victor or the victim?

The birthday feast over which Herod presided was 'a banquet for his courtiers and officers and the leading men of Galilee' (6.21). The feeding of the multitudes, a repeated motif (6.30–44; 8.1–10, 14–21), was a celebration in the desert with the crowds who insisted on invading the privacy of Jesus and his disciples (cf. 6.31–4). Herod abused his power within a privileged group to indulge a spoilt young member of his dynasty. Jesus acts in compassion towards crowds of ordinary people, whose physical wants symbolize deeper needs. He is shepherd or pastor to them (6.34), thereby enacting the role of the biblical shepherd who sets them down in green pastures and refreshes their being (Ps. 23.1–2; cf. Mark 6.39). The word 'shepherd' (Heb. *to'eh*), as Carrington indicates, 'means one who finds food or pasture for his flock'.[28] Hence, if 'King Herod' (6.14) is taken as the leading foil, Jesus' enactment is that of the shepherd-king of Israel, giving real content to the symbol of the messianic banquet. In fact, a variety of foils is provided: in particular, that of Elisha, who fed a hundred men with twenty barley loaves and had some left over (2 Kings 4.42–4). If this analogy were pressed, it might suggest ecstatic performance in the prophetic tradition.[29] It would certainly appear to have provided the general pattern of the enactment. The Mosaic image of the manna in the wilderness is obliquely suggested by the setting, the three days in the wilderness (8.2), and the curious phrase, 'a prophet, like one of the prophets of old' (6.15).[30] The most important feature, however, is that the action portrays the power of Jesus as a resource adequate for human need and capable of realization in a sharing community.

The focal action is, of course, overtly liturgical: the invoking of heaven, blessing (6.41) or thanksgiving (*eucharistesas*, 8.6), the breaking and giving. R. M. Fowler is certainly correct to raise the problem of eucharistic interpretation here.[31] However, it is not so much a matter of a first non-eucharistic reading and a second eucharistic reading of the Gospel, as he tends to suggest.[32] As we have seen, Mark presupposes a measure of knowledge on the part of his readers: without it, much of his narrative would be even more strange than it is! Hence, eucharistic overtones are not excluded, even in the first reading. Where Fowler is undoubtedly correct is in his insistence that the crowd stories provide an introduction to the Last Supper, rather than vice versa. 'To read casually the former story in the light of the latter is simply to overturn the gospel'.[33] In fact, the feeding stories are extensions of Jesus' table-fellowship with his disciples, as Mark's elaborate introduction makes clear (6.30–4). In a sense, they stand as a mid-point between the intimate but open fellowship of disciples in 2.15–17 and the intimate but tense Last Supper community.

Indeed, there is a persistent tension between Jesus and his disciples throughout Mark's accounts of the feedings. In the Old Testament paradigm, Elisha's servant protests against the unreasonable prophetic demand (2 Kings 4.43). In Mark, there is a sharp exchange between the disciples and Jesus on the same issue (6.35–7; 8.4). In the first, more discursive version, the disciples seem to be protesting about the cost of such a level of provision (6.37): self-help is a much better option – the people should be sent away to buy their own bread (6.36). Fowler connects this dispute with the disciples' failure to carry out the terms of Jesus' commission to them: 'no bread, no bag, no money in their belts' (6.8). Jesus knows that they do carry bread – 'How many loaves have you?' (6.38; 8.5). In the third and final discussion of the issue, they have in fact no bread – but this is an oversight! (8.14, 16–17). The disciples have persisted in taking prudent measures for their upkeep during their mission, and in so doing have missed the point of their commission. In an evocation of the discussion that surrounded the Sower, Jesus rebukes them for their lack of perception and understanding (8.17–18). He recalls his paradigmatic actions with the five thousand and the four thousand, in each case observing the biblical injunction to 'eat and have some left' – for others (2 Kings 4.43–4; Mark 7.24–30). 'Do you not yet...understand?' Jesus asks, almost despairingly. The disciples must not be diverted by the leaven of the Pharisees (8.15) or by anxieties about mere subsistence (8.17), for the harvest which fulfils Old Testament expectation does not come by the Law as currently expounded and practised (7.1–23; 8.11–13, 15), and persistence in anxious care of material resourcing will prove unfruitful (4.19). The enactment at the heart of the feeding stories emphasizes the transcendent source and divine resource which sustain the disciple's life. The harvest is the gift of God: broken, shared, satisfying – and inclusive.

In spite of all disappointments, Jesus' work makes some advance. To the deaf, he gives the command 'Ephphatha' ('be opened', 7.34): his plea to the deaf of the world. The new openness gives new speech, new utterance (7.37). And the blind begin to acquire sight (8.22–6), though there is a long way yet to go before disciples and readers can say that they see everything clearly.

3 POWER AND POWERLESSNESS

'Who do you say that I am?' (8.29). The complex story of direction and indirection that comprises Mark's Gospel to this point issues in this direct question.[34] Peter, replying on behalf of the disciples, is uncompromisingly messianic: 'You are the Christ' – a positive, direct, unequivocal declaration, connoting sovereignty, power and triumphant victory. Jesus' response is neither positive nor negative, but severely qualifies the suggested role, for his way to glory lies through his passion, just as the way of discipleship lies in the *praxis* of the cross (8.34). The power of the Messiah is paradoxically expressed in powerlessness; the disorientation of the disciples is complete (8.32).

The material of the passion predictions merits attention. In the first, the subject is the Son of Man (see pp. 20–23) who 'must suffer' (8.31): the constraint is that of obedience to his commission (cf. 1.9–11), faithfulness to the will of God and integrity in his ministry (8.33). Until the truth unfolds in the event itself and the disciples come to terms with its shocking reality, silence is the order of the day (8.30).

The prediction centres on suffering, rejection by the religious authorities, death and resurrection (8.31).[35] The protest of Peter (8.32) indicates that Jesus has touched a nerve-cell in the disciples' 'hardness of heart'; their failure to understand (9.32) repeats their response to parabolic mystery. The parable, however, is now being enacted in the particular course which Jesus' ministry is taking. It demands that the disciples come to terms with his suffering and death, and with his resurrection 'after three days'. It appears that if they were alienated by the former, they were genuinely puzzled by the latter: 'questioning what the rising from the dead meant' (9.10). Yet Mark emphasizes that this is the programme set out by Jesus: 'he said this plainly'; (8.32); that is, not in parable. The perspective of the resurrection affords an understanding of Jesus' ministry which is not available in any other way (9.9). It does so – as we might deduce from Mark's narrative as a whole – precisely because the dynamic of his ministry has been that of resurrection or renewal – the power that makes whole. Yet it was costly to himself. Now the whole process is being internalized or enacted in what happens to Jesus himself. He is now embodying the forces which his ministry expressed: forces which require him to be not only exponent but victim. Hence the motif of death-and-resurrection, hinted at in the Sower master-parable and suggested more boldly in the healing ministry, gains definitive expression in Jesus' own ministry. It is precisely in this context that the 'glory' of Jesus is discerned and divinely attested, as in the epiphany story of the transfiguration (9.2–8): a glory that cannot be preserved or commemorated in merely cultic fashion (cf. 9.5) but requires the response of obedience (9.7) and faith (9.19), even in the face of failure (cf.9.17–19).

The introduction of the story of the disciples' failure (9.14–29) cannot be without significance. The disciples were dealing as best they could with scribal criticism, given point by their evident failure to exorcise a particularly deeply entrenched demon (9.14–18, 20–22). The underlying condition, affecting all present, is lack of faith: the symbol of the present generation in Israel (9.19; cf. 9.23–4). In the denouement, there is a twin spotlight: on Jesus and on the disciples. In the context of submitting to death and to powerlessness in the face of his enemies, Jesus evinces the power of faith, even to accomplish resurrection (9.26–7). Carrington writes:

> It is hard to resist the argument of Dr. Farrer that this tale is so told in order to present an image of Resurrection, like the story of the daughter of Jair. Perhaps sickness, sin, lunacy, and other perturbations of the human frame may all be regarded as instalments of death, which have to be overcome by an access of spiritual power as well as by medical attention. They may be aspects of that principle in our fallen human nature which St. Paul calls *phthora*, the element of decay in our human nature; our mortality.[36]

The story also highlights the dilemma of the disciples: so willing to be loyal, yet so helpless (9.28). The exorcist must learn to rely, as V. Taylor puts it, 'not on his own powers but on the power of God'.[37] But this means losing one's life in order to save it (8.35); it entails one's own dying and rising again – committing oneself to personal powerlessness in order to discover the power of God.

The second major prediction (9.31 – discounting the somewhat specialized prediction in 9.12) makes Jesus the victim of human action. Nevertheless, the underlying motif is unchanged: 'handing over', death, resurrection. Subsequent discourse is concerned precisely with the reorientation required by the 'internalizing' of Jesus' teaching: the servant motif (9.33–5); accepting the 'little ones' (9.36–7, 42; 10.13–16); recognizing the work of others (9.38–41); discerning the true intent of the Law (10.1–12); and giving up wealth, at least in so far as it is a distraction from discipleship (10.21; cf. 10.28). The unifying theme is the 'transvaluation' of worldly values, which makes the first last and the last first (9.35; 10.31); the archetypal transvaluation being the death-and-resurrection of the Son of Man.

The third prediction takes full account of the Jerusalem setting (cf. 10.32–3). There are more detailed references to the betrayal and trial, the sentence of death at the hands of Gentiles, the mocking, spitting and scourging prior to his death, and his resurrection after three days (10.33–4). Now the emphasis is on the inner meaning of the death of the Son of Man. It is not the cue for a dream-world scenario in which the disciples will have prestige and glory (10.35–45). The lesson of the 'transvaluation' has to be completely learnt. What lies in store for the disciples is identification with the fate of Jesus: the taking of his cup and the acceptance of his baptism (10.38–9). The 'fate' of Jesus is to follow out his commission to the end: to act not with the brute power of political dominance (10.42–3) but in the spirit of self-giving love and service (10.43–5a). A new quality of life, a new dynamic, is emerging from within a deranged and misguided people. For its full expression, it requires the death of Jesus – the ultimate self-giving – as the *lutron anti pollon* ('ransom for many'), the price for fulfilling God's purpose.[38] The background of the phrase 'to give his life as a ransom for many' is much wider than Isaiah 53.[39] The meaning is not 'sacrifice for sin', nor is it substitutionary.[40] The metaphor is rather that of delivering Israel from bondage: breaking the shackles of oppression, in a deeper sense than even the Maccabees had been able to do by their martyrdoms.[41] Through the action of Jesus, God is able to restore Israel, to bring about the new Israel – indeed, to raise Israel from the dead.[42] Well might the disciples question what rising from the dead meant (9.10). It is not a simple concept: not one that can be appreciated without renewed vision (cf. 10.46–52).

4 'A TEMPLE NOT MADE WITH HANDS'

The target of Jesus' final pilgrimage to Jerusalem is clearly the Temple. In the first and third predictions, the forces to be encountered are 'the chief priests and the scribes' (10.33; cf. 8.31): the religious power group at the centre of the Jerusalem establishment. The narrative of the entry (11.1–10), which suggests that Jesus is the true representative of the transcendent King of Israel (cf. 11.9–10; Zech. 9.9), leads immediately to an inspection of the Temple (11.11) and subsequently to his prophetic protest at its current operations (11.15–19). The criticisms in Mark are directed against its materialism (11.15), its secularization (11.16), its exclusivism and lack of spirituality (11.17). Jesus' action is seen as a challenge to the Temple power group, which takes steps to eliminate the threat (11.18). It is a prophetic condemnation of the barrenness of the existing order, expressed in (acted?) parable (11.12–14, 20) as well as in oracle of judgement (13.1–2). It is also an assertion of an alternative order of things, based on faith in God (11.22): an alternative dynamic, effective in operation even against seemingly overwhelming odds (11.23), sustained by divine grace (11.24) and characterized by forgiveness shown to others (11.25).

By what authority can Jesus issue such a challenge? The question, when applied to a prophetic ministry, does not admit of a simple answer (11.27–33). Jesus was not merely being polemical when he raised the question of the validity of 'the baptism of John' (11.30), for his own commissioning for ministry emerged from it. If his questioners could not make a response to this prior question, they were unable to make a valid assessment of Jesus' ministry. Authenticity, whether of word,

65

ministry or person, has to be discerned – like the question of the true Israel. Parables may be used as a stimulus to discernment (12.12), and operate accordingly even when 'textualized' in a written gospel.[43] A complex adaptation of Isaiah's song of the vineyard (Isa. 5.1–7; Mark 12.1–8) suggests not only that Jesus' authority is that of the beloved son killed by the wicked tenants and ejected from the vineyard (the Temple?) which is his by right, but also that the wicked tenants are destroyed and the vineyard given to others.[44] A crisis of discernment has occurred in the affairs of Israel. Is the current religious establishment the rightful heir to Israel's heritage of faith and practice? – a question which many dissenters in Israel would have answered in the negative.[45] Where then are we to find the rightful heir? Parabolic images undermine the present order and suggest the beloved son rejected by the wicked tenants, or the rejected stone which becomes the corner-stone of the new edifice (12.10; Ps. 118.22). In this way, we are to discern 'the Lord's doing' (12.11; Ps. 118.23).

The tension between old and new is expressed in dissension and disputation. The representatives of the old, probing the ambiguities of faith-existence in the world, test Jesus in the matter of loyalty to God – and to Caesar (12.13–17) – and attempt to find out where he stands in the hoary debate about the resurrection of the dead (12.18–27); while Jesus is represented as out-arguing the scribes on the subject of the Davidic Messiah (12.35–7), and concerning the ostentation of the scribes (12.38–40). On the other hand, people of real piety in the old order respond to the new: the scribe who recognizes the overriding priority of love to God and neighbour – 'much more than all whole burnt offerings and sacrifices' (12.33) – knows the reality of the Kingdom of God (12.34);[46] and the devotion of the poor woman whose tiny offering represented all that she had is commended by Jesus above all other contributions (12.44). The new community places a premium on people, on faith and devotion, on insight and obedience, rather than on cultic performance or institutional loyalty. The central concern is not wonderful stones and buildings, which are subject to destruction and will be destroyed when the foundations of the world are shaken (13.1–2). 'When will this be?' is an obvious question, raising matters of eschatological interpretation to which Mark devotes a whole block of assorted teaching (13.3–37). But while Mark's readers can take the hint about 'the desolating sacrilege set up where it ought not to be' (13.14) and maintain a proper watchfulness (13.32–7),[47] they must remember that the new order is brought into being not by the fall of the Temple as such but by the positive work of Jesus. The fig tree that represents the Temple has incurred the judgement of God and is barren for ever (11.14, 20). Another fig tree has a different message (13.28).[48]

As the disciples gather to celebrate the Last Supper with Jesus, tension reaches breaking-point. The transcending of the Passover motif signifies the break with the old Israel. Though set in the Passover season (14.1) and meticulously prepared (14.12, 14, 16), the meal redirects the significance of the elements (the bread, the cup, the dish – 14.20), and the details of accepted Passover observance are passed by. More significantly, the motifs of the impending arrest of Jesus (14.1–2), the anointing of his body for burial (14.8) and betrayal by Judas (14.10–11, 17–21) provide the effective context for the observance. Even at table, Jesus announces that one of the group will 'deliver him up' (14.18, 20), and immediately afterwards he tells them, 'you will all fall away...' (14.27). It is as if the tensions and misunderstandings that arose in relation to the earlier meals in Mark reach their fullest expression here – in sorrow (14.19), denial (14.30) and betrayal (14.18, 20–1). 'This', writes R. M. Fowler, 'is the true import of the Last Supper narrative for the evangelist Mark'.[49] 'For Mark, the Last Supper is the last of many meals in which the disciples have failed to grasp the significance of Jesus and his ministry.'[50] The disciples are shown to remain in the old Israel rather than the new.

The observance of the Last Supper is one of promise rather than fulfilment. It looks to a future fellowship in which the meaning of table-fellowship with Jesus will be realized. The actions are familiar from previous celebrations – taking bread, blessing, breaking and giving (14.22a). The interpretation is specific: 'this is my body' (14.22b). The parabolic action-in-community *embodies* Jesus. In the Aramaic which Jesus presumably spoke, the phrase was either *bisri* ('my flesh') or *guphi* ('myself'). In either case, the meaning is 'myself', 'my whole being'.[51] Jesus' physical presence is about to be removed from the disciples (14.3–9). Instead, when they meet in table-fellowship – the most characteristic and evocative form of their association with Jesus – the action they perform in taking and sharing the bread will effectively establish the living presence of Jesus in their midst. Here then is the final form of the *mysterion*: as the mystery of the Kingdom (cf. 14.25) acquired reality in the parabolic words and actions of Jesus' ministry, so now it is effectively enacted at the core of the disciples' fellowship. Jesus, the parabler, has become the parabled: and the parable is the mystery of how, through death and resurrection (14.27–8), he gives himself to his disciple-community. The giving and taking of the cup reinforces the parable. It is a vow of dedication – 'Are you able to drink the cup that I drink?' (10.38) – and the gift of life, for the whole community ('for many', 14.24). It is the symbolic re-enactment of God's covenant with his people.[52] The fig tree is putting forth its leaves: summer is near. The new Temple is about to emerge, painfully, from the wreck of the old.

Pain dominates Gethsemane: Jesus finding support and assurance neither in his disciples nor in God (14.32–42). He is left with 'the cup of staggering' (Isa. 51.17, 22), his unanswered prayer 'the beginning of Jesus' real passion – his agony at his forsakenness by the Father'.[53]

Two further images advance our understanding. In 14.27–8, the image of the shepherd, previously applied to Jesus in his compassionate concern for the crowds (6.34), becomes the stricken shepherd of Zechariah 13.7, unable to protect the scattered sheep against the final judgement of God. In the eschatological oracle of Zechariah, the shepherd being rendered helpless, two thirds of the nation perish; one third survives, a refined and tested remnant, in renewed covenant with God (Zech. 13.9). In the messianic woes now being recounted in Mark, the disciples join the rest of Israel in turning their backs on Jesus (14.27). But the pastoral work of Jesus will continue 'after I am raised up' (14.28a). As the shepherd going before his sheep, he will lead them forward into Galilee (14.28; cf. 16.7).[54] Resurrection language thus includes a pastoral note and relates to the renewal of the disciple-group in their homeland as the purified remnant of Israel.

The second image takes us back to the Temple and to a persistently cited saying of Jesus to the effect that he would 'destroy this temple that is made with hands' and in three days 'build another, not made with hands' (14.58). Mark suggests that it was part of the 'false witness' against Jesus, possibly because it was cited out of context and falsely construed. It coheres with Jesus' prophetic judgement on the Temple (11.15–19; cf. 13.2); it is eschatological in tone; the phrase 'in three days' suggests a code for resurrection; and it appears to relate to the emergence of a new, holy people by the act of God through Jesus. Clearly the disciples, pathetic though they appear at this juncture, have a key role in the divine economy, 'as a new Israel called by God to obedience'.[55]

The final drama is played out by *dramatis personae* who represent or embody the two opposing powers. The protagonist on the establishment side is the high priest, aghast that one so evidently opposed to the Temple over which he presided should have the temerity to speak as God's Messiah. His opponent, arraigned before him in utter powerlessness, dares to use the evocative *ego eimi* ('I am', cf. Exod. 3.14) and to identify with the final denouement of the Son of Man (14.62). The plot moves apparently at the behest of the powerful temple party, who have sufficient influence to secure political endorsement for their decision to condemn Jesus to death (14.64; cf. 15.1–15). Jesus is the helpless victim, abandoned by his disciples – even Peter (14.66–72) – and mocked as a kind of clown-king (15.16–20, 29–32). His helplessness is underlined by the cry of dereliction on the cross (15.34). Yet the irony is that the one who is mocked as king, and who dies under the inscription 'The King of the Jews' (15.26), is – in the deepest sense – precisely what he claims to be. As he breathed his last, 'the curtain of the temple was torn in two, from top to bottom' (15.38): a symbol of the fact that the glory of God is to be discerned not in this doomed building but outside in the world on the cross. The scene closes with the final endorsement of a Gentile, the centurion who witnessed the death (15.39).

5 THE TOMB – AND BEYOND

The final part of Mark's narrative is compounded of several distinctive elements: the devotion, watchfulness and ultimate astonishment of the women who followed Jesus (15.40–1, 47; 16.1–5, 8); the pious act of Joseph of Arimathea in affording Jesus' body proper burial (15.42–6); the witness to the fact that Jesus was indeed dead (15.44–5); and the attention paid to details: the linen shroud (15.46) and the stone rolled against the door of the rock tomb (15.46; 16.3–4).

At the heart of the narrative is the tremendously unexpected: the women find the tomb empty, the large stone rolled aside; and within, 'they saw a young man sitting on the right side, dressed in a white robe' (16.5). As the women are overcome with amazement[56] – they have no more to offer – the reader is left with this last interpretative challenge: What is the secret of the open tomb? Who is the young man of good omen, clad in white array, and what is his significance?

Answers are hard to find, but one can be given with assurance. The young man – whose personal identity is a fascinating riddle with which Mark teases his readers[57] – is a messenger who attempts, vainly it would seem, to jog the women out of their stupefaction and to redirect their quest. They will not find Jesus in the tomb. 'He has risen, he is not here; see the place where they laid him' (16.6). There is no suggestion of the argument or deduction that since the tomb is empty, Jesus must have risen from the dead. The message is proclamatory: 'He has risen'; *therefore*, 'he is not here'.[58] With these words, the messenger suggests not only that the women were looking for him where they could no longer find him, but that their devotional intention to anoint his dead body was misplaced. Judaism of this period developed an elaborate cult of the tomb.[59] There was a possibility that Christian devotion could have created a shrine out of Joseph's tomb. It could have become a pilgrimage centre, with veneration of such relics or effects as could be plausibly identified. To all such developments the Markan narrative gives a straight negative. Here is the place where they laid him, says the messenger, but his disciples must look in a completely different direction: not to this place but to Galilee; not to a tomb but to a living reality. His resurrection denotes a dynamic power, an opening up of the future: 'he is going before you to Galilee'. There is the promise of encounter and witness: 'there you will see him, as he told you' (16.7).

At this point, a possibility of closure presents itself to the author: the message neatly picks up 14.28. Readers, ancient and modern, are projected forwards to another dimension of Jesus' relationship with his followers. But the closure takes in a further puzzling aspect. The women were told to deliver the given message to 'his disciples and Peter' (16.7); yet they fled from the tomb with 'trembling and astonishment' and 'said nothing to any one' (16.8). W. H. Kelber has taken this as 'the final and decisive breakdown of oral transmission':[60] 'the text can be said to write its own cancellation of the contract with orality'.[61] It is true that, by fleeing from the tomb, the women reproduce the response of the disciples who forsook Jesus and fled (14.50); and Kelber has at least a *prima facie* case for arguing that Mark's narrative is distanced from the oral tradition that might derive from the disciples, the women, the family of Jesus or Peter. Certainly, since the women's story remains untold (as far as Mark's narrative is concerned), their experience at the tomb, their witness to the empty tomb and the message given to them are distanced from the Church's understanding of the ultimate destiny of Jesus. The women's story – they must, *pace* Mark, have told someone at some time! – is a kind of alternative oral witness to Jesus' resurrection, peripheral to the main resurrection witness (cf. 1 Cor. 15.3–8).

Mark accepts the story that the tomb was empty, but refuses to interpret the resurrection simply in such terms. For him, the empty tomb is a necessary but not a sufficient condition of the resurrection of Jesus. The main function of the story is to turn attention away from the locus of the tomb to the promised encounter of the disciples and the risen Jesus in Galilee: 'there you will see him'. But Mark does not record the subsequent event. It is important not to assume a final unambiguous meeting which would resolve all the disciples' problems. If one does so, then as Kelber observes, 'one has dulled the gospel's extravagance and trivialized its oddness. One has, in short, remained undisturbed by parabolic disorientation.'[62] The reader *knows* that the disciples and the Church recognized the reality of Jesus' resurrection and the new perspectives it afforded (cf. 9.9). Yet for Mark, this perception of reality could be achieved only through the recovery of fellowship with Jesus in the midst of the daunting circumstances of life. To present the reader with a happy ending to the story would have been to betray the understanding of Jesus' ministry – the understanding of life itself – which emerged in the Gospel. For the resurrection is devalued and the Gospel sentimentalized if it is regarded as a mere happy ending. It is the recovery of hope, the triumph of faith, and the affirmation of love. It is the power to transcend self and circumstance, the power that is never achieved but always given – in fellowship with Jesus. It is the realization – after the death of Jesus – of the effectiveness of the power that characterized his ministry.

The Gospel ends as abruptly as it began. In its introduction it showed openness to the past; in its conclusion, it shows openness to the future. Perhaps the absence of the 'appearances' tradition, evident as early as Paul (1 Cor. 15.3–8), suggests some reservation on Mark's part about focusing individual experiences. It is the disciples, corporately, who will see the risen Jesus in Galilee; and the ground of all Christian hope is the Church's corporate readiness to discern his presence. The promise that Jesus 'goes before' them may itself be a parable of transcendence: the future is in his hands. It may also be a parable of the good shepherd. Mark presumably stops his Gospel when he has accomplished his purpose, and his metaphoric story – 'the parable of Jesus' – has no conclusion.[63] This is because, as Kelber puts it, 'the parable, far from inviting us to settle for familiar, classical perspectives, shocks us out of them toward a new and unfamiliar logic'.[64] The mystery of the Kingdom, the focus of Jesus' parables, has become the mystery of Jesus and his resurrection.

6 RISING FROM THE DEAD

When the disciples questioned what 'rising from the dead' meant (9.10), they were registering a real difficulty. While their tradition provided them with certain models of resurrection, Jesus seemed in general to operate on a different wavelength. To be sure, in debate he refuted the Sadducean denial of resurrection (12.18–27) and implied a living fellowship between God and the patriarchs of Israel: 'He is not God of the dead, but of the living' (12.27). John Baillie's comment is worth noting in passing:

> The argument is unanswerable; and is indeed the only unanswerable argument for immortality that has ever been given, or ever can be given. It cannot be evaded except by a denial of the premises. If the individual can commune with God, then he must matter to God; and if he matters to God, he must share God's eternity. For if God really rules, He cannot be conceived as scrapping what is precious in his sight.[65]

In other words, there is an eternal communion between God and the fathers of Israel, and therefore with Israel itself. Hence, all who truly belong to Israel participate in this everlasting relationship. In this sense, the resurrection from the dead is affirmed by Jesus.

But when they came down from the mount of transfiguration, the disciples once again experienced disorientation. The epiphany or manifestation suggested that Jesus had affinity both with Moses and Elijah, both of whom, being 'alive in God', present models of resurrection.[66] Peter's foolish proposal was presumably to 'ground' all three on the mountain, as a point of access to the holy ones in glory (cf. 9.5). The divine voice, however, points to 'my beloved Son' as the point of access, and Jesus imposes a silent embargo on the disciples 'until the Son of man should have risen from the dead' (9.9). Coming as it does in sequence from Caesarea Philippi, the essential point of entry to resurrection discourse in Mark is the suffering, rejection and death of the Son of Man (8.31), in context with the disorientation and alienation of the disciples (8.32–3). Meanwhile, the disciple community has to learn what is often called 'the way of the cross' (cf. 8.34) but what might equally well be called 'the way of resurrection' (cf. 8.35) – the way of the new people of God, expressing the power of love rather than that of destruction.

In facing the problem of closure, Mark remains faithful to the story he has told. There is the sorry tale of betrayal, denial, rejection – by those who were close to him or who represented Israel: points emphasized not only because they fulfilled various scriptural ciphers (which weighed heavily with some), but because the disciple-church, from which Mark's readers came, had come under as heavy pressure as Jesus' disciples had, and their failure and disorientation could be as complete. The story portrays what the disciples themselves – as part of the Church – came to appreciate, that Jesus' dying was part of the ministry he undertook for others ('for many'), but that it meant for him the full sense of forsakenness and the full measure of alienation which J. Moltmann has interpreted so powerfully.[67] Hence the readers, in the dismaying situation of their own Church, are invited to make common cause with Jesus who so fully shared their sufferings. But is there any real hope in this horrifying spectacle? For some, the only hope rests in Elijah (15.35): they interpret the scene in terms of a conventional model, which is mocked by others (15.36). But when the centurion at the cross breathes the words 'Son of God' (15.39), he has recognized in Jesus' dying a signal of transcendence: an indication that there was more here than the pathetic end of an unjustly condemned man, more to his dying than mere death. There was a dimension of human being and authority incomparably richer than the level of humanity evident in the other *dramatis personae* of the crucifixion scene. In Mark's story, this is a confession of the true nature of Jesus: Son of God.

Mark's story is almost complete at this point. In his own way, he has presented what Paul would have called 'the gospel of Christ crucified' – viz., that Jesus died for others, to release them from bondage to the powers that crucified him, and that the cross was 'theonomous' (that is, of transcendent concern).[68] The language of resurrection is used typically to denote transcendence: 'He has risen; he is not here' (16.6). Jesus' effective power and presence are not located in the tomb but in continuing experience, in the ongoing life of the disciple-group in Galilee. There, his power and presence, his personal being, will be discerned.

What then is the concept of resurrection that emerges in Mark? It is characterized by promise, as in the passion predictions to the disciples and the young man's message given to the women. At the end of Mark, there is a sense in which the resurrection has already taken place – the tomb is empty; and a sense in which it is not yet realized – 'there you will see him'. In a curious way, it is not about what happened to Jesus: it is about what will happen to the disciples in renewed fellowship with Jesus. Beyond that point Mark does not take his readers. Yet perhaps he has already said enough in his Gospel to enable us to present a consistent Markan theology of the resurrection.

To return to the first master symbol: 'The sower sows the word' (4.14). The word is now seen to be the story of Jesus, the gospel of Jesus Christ (1.1). As a seed cannot come to life unless it dies (1 Cor. 15.36), the word itself presents Jesus' dying-and-rising as the creative act of God, to realize the new Israel. As the passion predictions put it, Jesus rises 'after three days'. No one in Mark's Gospel is witness to this aspect of the resurrection. It takes place secretly, like the new life of the germinating seed. Hence, when the messenger announces 'he has risen', he indicates that the life of the new age has already begun. But unlike the apocalyptic scenario to which resurrection discourse frequently relates,[69] the harvest is brought forth amid losses and reverses. The new life is not depicted by Mark in triumphalist terms. The parallel between the disciples and the churches is too cogent to be set aside at a stroke. Parabolic disorientation, arising out of the refraction of the transcendent in historical experience, remains a growth point. Mark sees the resurrection as the birth of the new people of God, vibrant with the power discerned in Jesus' ministry yet uncompromisingly historical and humanly vulnerable (4.15–19). Yet the power of God 'is made perfect in weakness' (cf. 2 Cor. 12.9). Hence, in spite of all indications, the harvest is marvellous and assured: here is the eschatology of promise (4.20).

The audience presupposed by Mark's Gospel is one that needs to be reassured of the promise in the face of adverse circumstances. When the world is collapsing around you (cf. 13.14–20), disappointments foster impatient longings for an end to the present lot and encourage people to activate various escape routes from historical reality (cf. 13.4–6, 21–2). Apocalyptic extravagance has a field day, and the faithful become refugees from history. For all his astringency, Mark is not uninfluenced by the immediacy of such apocalyptic expectation, which is undoubtedly a deep-set strand in the Christian world-view (cf. 9.1; 13.30). But his message is basically one of counsel against such excess, combined with a strong exhortation to watchfulness (13.33–7), for the faithful are living in a period of woes through which the claim of the transcendent presses upon them. Yet the strongest signal of transcendence comes not from the menacing events around them but from community celebration.

The second master story was the feeding of the multitudes (in its various forms): the taking, blessing, breaking and the sharing of that which comes as God's gift. This master symbol reaches fullest expression in the Last Supper. Surrounded by a disintegrating world and itself party to the disintegration, the group receives Jesus' final gift in table-fellowship. The gift is identified as 'my body'. Henceforth, having learnt the hard way about losing one's life and saving it (8.35), or having undergone 'dying' and 'rising' as Paul might have said, the sharing fellowship of disciples will embody the presence of Jesus: not in an unambiguous way, as if its members could guarantee or control it, but obliquely, in blessing and thanksgiving, in bread and wine, in mutual acceptance and forgiveness. In celebrating the way of resurrection, the group encounters the risen Jesus. The transcendent Lord is immanent in 'the body' of his followers. Here is the alternative Temple, built in three days and not by human hands. Here is the everlasting fellowship with God which resurrection language affirms.

Such an understanding of the resurrection body of Jesus, prompted as it is by the Markan account, is the reverse of reductionist. It does not reduce the risen Jesus to an immanent force, a sacramental presence, a moral influence or a message of preaching. The main thrust of Mark's treatment of the subject is that he is transcendent. His 'rising from the dead' means that he 'goes before you': even, 'leads you on'. He is the shepherd who takes his disciples into the future and who is encountered in their history. The fellowship of 'his body' is open to the transcendent – and therefore always liable to be confounded by it, as the *mysterion* comes in new parables. The promise is firm; the harvest is great. Yet the last glimpse we catch of his followers in Mark's Gospel concerns a young man in a white robe, charged with an unambiguous message, and a small group of women – devoted to the end – who apparently cannot take it in and who flee in fear, as the disciples had done before them. Thus Mark maintains to the end his thesis that, in the presence of an act or word of God, no human being can be other than disconcerted.

POSTSCRIPT: ATTEMPTED FURTHER CONCLUSIONS TO MARK'S GOSPEL

(a) It has sometimes been thought that 16.8 is much too abrupt and inconclusive to serve as a credible ending to Mark's Gospel. Many such views are highly subjective and reflect latter-day presuppositions about how a Gospel should end. The case would deserve more serious attention if it could be established that the statement 'for they were afraid' is linguistically untenable as an ending. Recent research has shown beyond reasonable doubt that this is not so.[70] In addition, literary perspectives on Mark's Gospel have tended to underline the inherent power and consistency of Mark's work when 16.8 is taken as the intended conclusion.[71]

(b) Little need be said about the 'shorter ending'. Its manuscript attestation is weak,[72] and it can lay claim to no Markan characteristics. Its bland content is remarkable only in so far as it reflects the leadership of Peter in the disciple group.

(c) The 'longer ending' (16.9–20) is not attested by the best manuscripts:[73] one critic states trenchantly, 'no one who knows anything of textual criticism can deny that Mark ended at 16.8'.[74] This, however, need not mean that the material it contains is without significance. While it testifies to a tendency in the early Church both to summarize and to co-ordinate the tradition of resurrection appearances, it also allows us to draw some tentative conclusions.

Mark 16.9–11 presents a summary of the Magdalene tradition reflected in John 20.1–18 (and also Luke 8.2).[75] Its most significant contribution is to underline the original non-acceptance by the apostles of the tradition of female witness to the resurrection. It may therefore reflect an earlier stage of tradition than John 20.1–18, which substantiates Mary's discovery of the empty tomb and formally records the appearance of Jesus to her. In a similar fashion, 16.12–13 gives a bare summary of the Emmaus Road tradition but emphasizes the unbelief of the disciple group. Again, one wonders whether this reflects an earlier ending which accords with Luke's treatment of the women's discovery of the tomb[76] but which has not survived in his account of the Emmaus story with its evidently edited conclusion.

In 16.14, the 'longer ending' affirms the encounter of the eleven disciples with the risen Jesus in the context of table-fellowship. The 'eleven' is a pointed reference to the removal of Judas from the 'twelve' (14.17). At the Last Supper, considerable attention was directed to the imminent betrayal (14.18–21). Here, their encounter with Jesus overturns the tendency of the disciples in this Gospel to 'unbelief and hardness of heart' (see above, pp. 60–61). It also brings them to accept the witness of others to the resurrection. In view of the fact that this verse contains the most Markan elements in the 'longer ending', it is interesting to note its implication that for the core group of the apostolic community, the real presence of the risen Jesus came to be visualized within its common life in table-fellowship.

The remaining verses record the apostolic commission (16.15), with an emphasis on baptism and on 'signs' which recalls the life of the early communities in Acts (16.16–18). It concludes with a twofold emphasis: on the ascension of Jesus as Lord, and on the apostolic mission to the world (16.19–20).[77]

1 cf. Meagher (1979).
2 On Mark's Gospel as written parable, cf. Kelber (1983), pp. 90–139. On intercalation, cf. Kee (1977), pp. 54–6; Kermode (1979), pp. 49–73. For a structuralist view, cf. Malbon (1980), pp. 97–129.
3 Fowler (1983), p. 53. The term 'rhetoric of indirection' was applied to Mark's Gospel by Thompson (1978), pp. 223–31 (cited by Fowler).
4 Anderson (1976), p. 25 states: 'As things stand, the majority view that Mark was written within the period A.D. 65–70 has still much to commend it'. Taking Mark 13 as the key chapter and Mark 13.14 as the critical verse, Anderson prefers the earlier end of this spectrum, 'just around the outbreak of the Jewish War' (p. 26); cf. E. Schweizer (1971), p. 25. The Jewish War is certainly indicated as the relevant scenario, but when one considers not only Mark 13 but the extent of the disorientation of Jesus' followers reflected throughout the Gospel (above all in the disciples and in the parables), a date such as AD 71 (Brandon, 1967, pp. 227–9) or even slightly later (Johnson, 1960, p. 20) is by no means ruled out. Nineham (1968), p. 42, 'is inclined on balance to favour a date in the latter part of the decade from 65 to 75'. On the other hand, the ambivalence of the evidence and the fragility of hypothesizing about date of writing give credibility to bids for a much earlier date: cf. Robinson (1975), pp. 86–117. An element of circularity occurs in almost all arguments. The position taken here is that the deep alienation experienced by the disciples and predicated of church communities suggests a time of deep conflict centred on Jerusalem: hence, a date around AD 70 is adjudged the most tenable hypothesis.
5 cf. Isa. 64.1; less directly Pss. 18.9 and 144.5; Hooker (1959), p. 68.
6 cf. Tannehill (1980), pp. 60–1.
7 cf. the detailed discussion in Hooker (1959), pp. 68–73.
8 For a full discussion, cf. Chilton and McDonald (1987) *passim*.
9 However, its source becomes a matter of contention: cf. 1.27 and 3.22.
10 Perrin (1967), pp. 102–3.
11 cf. Williams (1985), p. 41.
12 Wilder (1971), p. 82.
13 cf. Wilder (1974), p. 139.
14 cf. Williams (1985), p. 43.
15 In 2 Esdras, the crop of evil is sown and reaped. Afterwards, there is room for good seeds. The apocalyptic separation of good and evil is total, though if the evil seeds produce such a great crop of godlessness, a correspondingly great harvest can be anticipated from the good seeds. In the Sower, the seed is good but the threatening environment greatly affects the outcome.
16 cf. the treatment of Mark 4.12 in Kermode (1979), pp. 2, 28–33.
17 Dodd (1936), questions whether the 'eschatological' (*sic*) school keeps close enough to the environmental data. It is evident that Jeremias (1954), does not (cf. p. 92). But Dodd himself is also culpable. He takes such data as 'part of the dramatic machinery of the story', but gives no real weight to it.
18 Wilder (1974), p. 134.
19 cf. Jeremias (1954), pp. 61–3.
20 Drury (1985), p. 51.
21 ibid., p. 52.

22 Williams (1985), p. 46. Cf. John 12.24–5.

23 Nineham (1968), p. 172.

24 ibid., pp. 146–8.

25 Literally 'I am', it recalls the Mosaic account of the nature and power of Yahweh (Exod. 3.13–14). The phrase 'he meant to pass by them' is most plausibly explained in terms of Exod. 33.18–23 and 1 Kings 19.11–14 – the language of epiphany.

26 Rochais (1981), pp. 54–73.

27 There was a strong popular expectation that Elijah would return to herald messianic times: cf. Mal. 3.1–2; 4.5–6; cf. Sirach 48.10f.; see above, p. 16.

28 Carrington (1960), pp. 134–6.

29 Lindblom (1962), pp. 50–1.

30 Conceivably a reference to 'a prophet like me from among you', Deut. 18.15; cf. 34.10–12.

31 Fowler (1981), p. 140.

32 ibid., pp. 145–6.

33 ibid., p. 140.

34 Under review are the popular responses that have already emerged (6.14–15); but John the Baptist was superseded by Jesus at the beginning of his ministry (1.14); cf. also the statement attributed to Jesus in 9.11–13.

35 This may be regarded as the 'core' prediction. It is not preoccupied with a particular issue (as in 9.12–13): it is neither over-generalized (cf. 9.31) nor over-particularized (cf. 10.33–4).

36 Carrington (1960), p. 200.

37 Taylor (1966), p. 401.

38 The term *lutron* means 'purchase money' in the LXX – 'the price that has to be paid' – and is not a sacrificial term. Metaphorically, it refers to God's deliverance of his people from Egypt. In a general sense only, it is picked up in the servant songs of Isaiah. Cf. Hooker (1959), pp. 74–9.

39 cf. Barrett (1959), pp. 1–18.

40 In view of the above discussion, it is disconcerting to find Williams (1985), pp. 45–6, locating the key to Mark 10.45 in Isa. 53 – without any refutation of the case against.

41 The common factor was deliverance from foreign oppression, which can be linked with the idea of atonement (but using *antipsychon*, not *lutron*); cf. 4 Macc. 6.27–9; 17.20–2.

42 The rebirth of Israel as a servant people is effected by the self-giving of Jesus; cf. the meaning of the Sower.

43 cf. Kelber (1983), pp. 105–16.

44 Apart from the question of sources, it is interesting that a parable of judgement is succeeded in Mark by the keystone image, which frequently occurs as an Easter text: cf. Acts 4.11; Rom. 9.33; Eph. 2.20; 1 Pet. 2.6–8. Cf. Anderson (1976), p. 271.

45 cf. the Teacher of Righteousness and anti-Sadducean movement at Qumran.

46 cf. Chilton and McDonald (1987), pp. 1, 93, 95, 108n., 128.

47 cf. note 4 above.

48 Withering of fig trees is a standard image for judgement in Israel; fruitful trees are the symbol of blessing. 'The temple mount may be removed and the temple itself be destroyed, but a new worshipping community will emerge, built on the risen Lord', Hooker (1983), p. 84; cf. Telford (1980), pp. 95–204.

49 Fowler (1981), p. 135.

50 ibid., p. 137.

51 cf. Anderson (1976), p. 313; Cranfield (1959), p. 426.
52 cf. Hooker (1959), pp. 81–2.
53 Moltmann (1981), p. 76.
54 cf. Carrington (1960), pp. 316–8.
55 cf. Schweizer (1971), pp. 329–31; Kee (1977), pp. 107–16.
56 *phobos* and *phobeisthai* do not distinguish between 'fear' and 'awe' as Rudolf Otto did in *The Idea of the Holy*. Human response to theophany and subjective perturbation are described by the same terms. When associated with verbs such as 'fleeing', the latter would appear to be the dominant connotation.
57 From Farrer (1951), pp. 141, 174, 334 (cf. 1948, pp. 143–5) to Kermode (1979), pp. 55–7, Gourges (1981), and Derrett (1982), pp. 60–7.
58 Note that the emphasis is no longer on the dead body but on the absence/presence of Jesus.
59 cf. the Talpioth ossuaries: on which, see Sukenik, (1947), Gustafsson (1956), and an imaginative discussion in Derrett (1982), pp. 124–8.
60 Kelber (1983), p. 104.
61 ibid., p. 105.
62 ibid., p. 129.
63 ibid., pp. 128–9; cf. Funk (1966), p. 196.
64 Kelber (1983), p. 129.
65 Baillie (1934), p. 107.
66 Moses, whose burial-place is unknown and who therefore has no shrine on earth, has an immanent expression in Torah, 'the books of Moses' (or, more widely, 'the Scriptures'). Elijah, translated to heaven and therefore without a resting-place on earth, embodies the resurrection hope of the faithful in Israel.
67 Moltmann (1981), pp. 21–60; also (1974).
68 This terminology is, of course, borrowed from Tillich (1948), p. 36; cf. Smith (1956), pp. 50–2.
69 cf. Perkins (1984), pp. 22ff.
70 cf. Boomershine and Bartholomew (1981), pp. 220–1.
71 e.g., Kermode (1979), pp. 66–8; Petersen (1980), pp. 160–6; Via (1985), pp. 50–7.
72 cf. Nestle-Aland (1979), *crit. appart. in loc.*
73 ibid. The textual history is complex, but it is not early.
74 Derrett (1982), p. 135.
75 See chapter 6.
76 See chapter 5.
77 These themes are discussed in the two following chapters.

4

Power and Presence
The Resurrection in the Gospel of Matthew

What we call the beginning is often the end
And to make an end is to make a beginning.
The end is where we start from.[1]

---

1 MATTHEW 28.16–20: THE KEY TO THE GOSPEL?

Is the resurrection beginning or end? Is it starting-point or climax? Is it inception or goal? It is not difficult to discern both aspects in it. The final resurrection narrative in Matthew comes as the climax to the Gospel. It offers 'a compendium of important Matthean themes', and is said to provide 'the key to the understanding of the whole book'.[2] The final piece has been placed in the puzzle and the whole picture emerges with clarity and conviction. But this same Matthean passage is about the commissioning of a ministry to the whole world. Here is, apparently, a new beginning, a new era.

The passage in question runs as follows:

> There has been given to me all authority [*exousia*] in heaven and on the earth. Go forth, therefore, and make disciples of all nations. Baptize them in the name of the Father and of the Son and of the Holy Spirit. Teach them to keep all that I have commanded you. And lo, I am with you at all times [lit. 'all the days'] until the close of the age (Matt. 28.18–20; my translation).

Since this passage has attracted considerable attention in recent debate, it may be helpful to begin with a review of three leading approaches to it.

The first is represented by O. Michel (1950) and J. Jeremias (1956), though in fact it has a long pedigree.[3] Both agree that Matthew 28.18–20 represents a royal enthronement or 'a triple-action coronation text'.[4] It comprises the assumption of 'all power' by the risen Jesus (28.18); the missionary charge to proclaim his message to all nations (28.19–20a); and the assurance of divine protection for his messengers (28.20b). Michel interprets the whole passage as a christological reshaping of Daniel 7.13–14, with its emphasis on the given 'authority', on 'all the nations' and on 'everlasting dominion': a royal enthronement passage not unlike Philippians 2.5–11.[5] Jeremias attempts to trace the threefold motif to ancient Egyptian coronation ritual, consisting of the elevation or assumption of power, the proclamation to heaven and earth, and the enthronement of the new king: a pattern he discerns in 1 Timothy 3.16; Philippians 2.9–11, and Hebrews 1.5–14, as well as in Matthew

28.18–20. Both scholars emphasize the eschatological implications of the passage. For Jeremias, 'the eschatological hour has arrived'. The consequence of this invasion of history by ultimate power is that 'God no longer limits his saving grace to Israel, but turns in mercy to the whole Gentile world'.[6] Michel takes it as the revelation of the theological premise of the whole Gospel. 'In a way the conclusion goes back to the start and teaches us to understand the whole Gospel, the story of Jesus, "from behind".'[7]

This type of criticism emerges from a period of scholarship when interest in Christology and dogmatic formulae (not to mention hymns and confessions) tended to dominate both theology and exegesis. It cannot be denied, however, that our passage carries both christological and exegetical import, and one would expect the study of a text concerning the risen Jesus to throw some light on the nature of the language and concepts used. Implied in the language of authority, for example, is the notion of sovereignty, and in that of presence there is the assurance of divine succour – not to mention the implications of the unexpected occurrence of the threefold name in the text. Yet while Matthew 28.18–20 is inescapably christological and theological, it is important that its integrity is recognized in exegesis. Its most distinctive feature is that, in strong contrast to hymns or confessions of the community such as Philippians 2.9–11, 1 Timothy 3.16 or Hebrews 1.5–14, the risen Lord addresses his disciples. It recounts the commission he gives his followers to make disciples of all nations, and it closes with an assurance of his constant and supportive presence with them on their mission. All this is somewhat removed from the concerns of the Egyptian coronation sequence which Jeremias took as his basic model. Michel's treatment of the passage is more sound, if less adventurous. His hermeneutical observations also have point. Although one would be more aware today of the oddness of reading a document 'from behind', there is nevertheless a reflexive element in interpretation, and Ricoeur's distinction between a first and second reading could accommodate both the primary encounter with the text and the subsequent re-reading 'from behind'.[8]

The second distinctive approach is represented by B. J. Hubbard (1974), who built on previous form-critical work by C. H. Dodd (1955) and W. Trilling (1964) in particular. On the basis of a comparison with twenty-seven commissioning stories in the Old Testament, he identified the model on which the passage is based as that of the commissioning *Gattung* (lit. 'type' or 'species') with five parts:

Introduction (28.16): the mountain of revelation.

Confrontation (28.17a, 18): the risen Christ appears to the disciples and approaches them; the declaration of cosmic authority is similar to the 'divine self-asservation' in the Old Testament and reflects the influence of Daniel 7.14 (LXX).

Reaction (28.17b): worship, as of a divine being, and doubt among the disciples.

Commission (28.19–20a): 'go' is typical commissioning language; the commission is to make disciples of all nations, initiating them into the community by baptism and teaching them 'all that I have commanded you' (another characteristic of commission).

Reassurance (28.20b): the assurance of divine presence is frequently found in Old Testament commissioning formulae; here, the assurance is in terms of the supportive, enduring presence of the risen Jesus.[9]

By means of a comparison of this passage with other Gospel commissionings, Hubbard posited a 'primitive apostolic commissioning' or 'proto-commissioning' narrative which – even more speculatively – he took to be only one step removed from first-hand testimony by one of the eleven, and subsequently relayed to the evangelist by a Gentile missionary. Matthew's expansion of the material brought it into line with the Old Testament commissioning form and effectively encapsulated within it leading themes of the Gospel.

From his form-critical perspective, Hubbard demonstrated the primacy of the commissioning element in Matthew 28.16–20 and justified his preference for it rather than the enthronement motif.[10] By its nature, commissioning turns attention to future tasks and suggests a beginning rather than an ending. He made allowance, however, for the strands, themes or trajectories which run through the Gospel to this climactic encounter with the risen Jesus. But in spite of the recognition of this Janus-like quality in the passage in question, Hubbard's preoccupation with commissioning and his relegation of the enthronement motif led him to bypass important christological questions which his methodology ignores but which are inherent in the passage itself. This may account for the apparent naiveté which characterizes his view not so much of the 'proto-commissioning' (although there is something of the lowest common denominator about it) as of the origin of the story in an account of a specific experience given by one of the eleven. What kind of experience was this? What kind of reality underlies the narrative? If the setting is symbolic (the mountain of revelation), was the experience something that occurred at a particular place and time? What is meant by the 'appearance' or 'approach' of the risen Jesus, not to speak of the gift of 'all authority'? Few indications of answers to such questions emerge from Hubbard's approach.

The third approach, which related Matthew 28.18–20 to prophetic discourse, is represented by M. E. Boring (1982) and G. Friedrich (1983). Rejecting the two previous views set out above, Friedrich interpreted the threefold structure of Matthew 28.18–20 as self-revelation, request and promise, and explained it as prophetic 'revelation discourse' expressing the will of God. Boring similarly underlined the fact that the Old Testament schema reflected in the commissioning formula of Matthew 28.18–20 was concerned with prophetic calling and the prophet's description of his vocation. Among the passage's prophetic features, Boring noted the fact that the risen Jesus takes the role of Yahweh (cf. Rev. 1.12–20); the chain of command 'from God the Father through the risen Jesus and his prophet to the church and the world';[11] the authority assumed by the speaker; and the re-presentation of Scripture (cf. Dan. 7.14) as the word of the risen Jesus. Other characteristics include eschatological concern and the way in which a 'word of the Lord' validates a contentious issue such as universal mission.

This kind of study takes the discussion on to a different plain. One is no longer concerned simply with the source of the imagery or the form of the pericope, but with the nature of the material. Prophecy is certainly concerned with revelation, which is communicated or proclaimed in appropriate ways and may launch ministry and mission. Central to Christian prophecy is the apprehension of the will of the exalted Christ and the reception of divine revelation through the prophet's openness and sensitivity to the mind of Christ.[12]

The passage in question suggests a group experience of the transcendent sovereignty and authority of the risen Jesus. It is located on 'the mountain to which Jesus had directed them' (28.16b). Apart from Galilee as a general indication, no geographical location is particularly relevant. An experience 'on the mountain' is one which unveils the secrets of Sinai or Carmel, the glory of transfiguration or the wisdom of divine counsel. The disciples 'saw' Jesus as Isaiah 'saw Yahweh' in all his kingliness (Isa. 6.1) or as Daniel 'saw in the night visions' of the heavenly court (Dan. 7.13–14).

Although the central concern is divine revelation, human perception – the heightened perception of spiritual discernment – is also involved. Consequently, the group as a whole is moved to respond in worship – 'lost in wonder, love and praise' – yet some members are beset by doubt (28.17b): a feature which serves to emphasize the extraordinary nature of the experience, which placed a premium on faith, discernment, obedience and receptivity. The doubts are apparently resolved by Jesus' approach to them and by the words he speaks. His self-revelation to them is not in terms of a figure 'sitting upon a throne, high and lifted up' (Isa. 6.1), nor even 'seated at the right hand of God', but one on whom authority over the cosmos has already been bestowed by divine gift and who relates to them in a divine–human encounter which is itself the extension and completion of his previous encounters with them.

Out of this culminating encounter in its cosmic setting comes the commission – 'request' is much too weak – to universal mission, itself the completion and transformation of the commission previously given to the disciples to 'go...to the lost sheep of the house of Israel' (10.6). All the world is now to be baptized as Jesus was baptized and to be taught as the disciples had been taught. Thus will the Gentiles come to know not only the God of Israel but the God who, through the divine presence in Jesus (cf. 1.23), is named as Father, Son and Holy Spirit.[13] Finally, there is the promise to be 'with you', a common feature in commissioning narratives, suggesting active help and resource for the given task. The time-scale in question is 'from now to eternity'.

It has often been remarked that the language of the passage is thoroughly Matthean. He has contextualized his materials not only within the language and conceptuality of his Gospel but within its structure also. In so doing, he has presented us with what we may call the resurrection oracle *par excellence*: a revelation discourse in which the risen Christ appears as cosmic, divine and authoritative, and encounters his followers and commissions them, with appropriate promises, to the work of discipleship among the nations. The whole statement draws upon biblical forms and images, whether the court of heaven as in Daniel or the not uncommon form of the divine commission in the Old Testament. The commissioning element, however, is contextualized within the prophetic realm of discourse, which is essential to the understanding of the peculiar nature of the divine–human encounter which forms the substance of the passage. And the briefest of comparisons with 'one like a son of man' in Daniel 7 is sufficient to illustrate how different is the treatment given to the risen Jesus in Matthew.

Yet the underlying logic of the apocalyptic world-view[14] retains its importance for the understanding of this Gospel. If Matthew 28.16–20 is the key,[15] then the story of Jesus the Messiah (cf. 1.1), whose mission to Israel (cf. 2.6) fulfilled through suffering and death (cf. 12.18–21) forms the substance of the book, concludes not with death and burial but with the assumption of divine authority 'in heaven and on earth' (28.18). It is thus the story of a divine act – the 'Christ event' – which decisively alters the position of humankind in relation to God. Hence, the Son of Man motif in Daniel and related literature is given performance in the story of Jesus. In it are to be found the commissioning of God's agent and the bringing of the faithful into God's eternal Kingdom. The Messiah now stands in a new relationship to creation. Complete sovereignty is his by divine gift. Hence, the scenario of royal enthronement is particularly appropriate in the light of the apocalyptic world-view which informs it.

But it is not a matter of repeating the established features of the apocalyptic scenario. Matthew 28.16–20 is not even modelled in any obvious way on Daniel 7. The divine action has moved on. By his suffering the Messiah has brought hope to the Gentiles (12.21). By his death, the veil of the Temple is rent asunder (27.51) and the power of resurrection made effective (27.52–3). Hence, in prophetic epiphany, Jesus the Messiah – risen and sovereign – commissions and validates the continuing task of world mission. The dream-world of apocalyptic has been actualized in messianic – and now in apostolic – ministry. The dream-figure of 'that Son of man'[16] has been given real expression by Jesus the Messiah – and now by those to whom his commission is given. Apocalyptic is no longer the primary mode for expressing the fulfilling of God's purposes. History is now the scene in which his purposes are manifested.

Thus in Matthew 28.16–20, the reader is challenged to recognize in Christ a kind of immanent transcendence. Henceforth, the symbol of Christ in glory combines sovereign authority (it is in his name that Christian mission is carried out) with covenanted presence. The story of Jesus – from Old Testament expectation to the exaltation of the Messiah – has therefore a theonomous[17] quality. It is punctuated by signs or

signals of transcendence. To this story, Matthew 28.16–20 may be said
to operate as the theological key.[18] Its central presupposition is the
resurrection of Jesus.

The test of such an understanding of the Gospel lies in the reading of
the text. We begin by looking at its treatment of divine immanence or
covenanted presence.

2 DIVINE PRESENCE

The key passage occurs in Matthew's account of the conception and
birth of the Messiah: 'and his name shall be called Emmanuel', the
translation of which is 'God with us' (Matt. 1.23b). The passage is cited
from Isaiah 7.14 (LXX), for 'virgin' (*parthenos*) in 1.23a is dependent on
the Greek rather than the Hebrew text.[19] The Old Testament context is
the troubled political situation of the eighth century BC. Jerusalem and
Judah were in imminent danger of invasion from enemies to the north,
namely Syria and the alienated northern kingdom of Israel. King Ahaz,
insecure and fearful, was led to seek a sign from Yahweh, which was
given in the utterance reflected in Matthew: 'Behold, a young woman
shall conceive and bear a son, and shall call his name Immanuel ... Before
the child knows how to refuse the evil and choose the good, the land
before whose two kings you are in dread will be deserted' (Isa. 7.14, 16).
That is, before the child has left infancy behind, the threat will have
disappeared. The child's name, 'God is with us', is itself significant: a
powerful indication of the present activity of God in effecting
deliverance through the historical process.

For Matthew, as for the community to which he belonged, the child
whose birth was of decisive significance was Jesus, the Messiah. Hence,
although the text had no messianic connotation in its Old Testament
setting, early Christian interpretation found no difficulty in understanding Isaiah 7.14 in terms of the activity of the Holy Spirit in the
conception and birth of Jesus (cf. Matt. 1.20).[20] Even the name Jesus is
accorded special significance. The Hebrew meaning suggests the
promise of salvation, 'for he will save his people from their sins' (1.21).
By interpreting this statement in the light of Isaiah 7.14, Matthew is
suggesting not a miraculous infusion of the Spirit at conception but the
presence and activity of the Spirit – of God himself – both in the coming
of Jesus into the world and in his subsequent ministry. The historical
events with which Matthew is dealing are the events of the conception,
birth and ministry of Jesus. The emphasis in 'Emmanuel' – like that of
the name Jesus – is inseparable from ministry. It is here that God's
presence is to be discerned as the divine power working for the salvation
of humankind.

Jesus' ministry may therefore rightly be termed 'theonomous'. It is
the living out of the effective presence of God in the human situation. It
is the mode of the divine work of salvation. It brings together the notion
of the saving purpose of the transcendent God and his immanent and

discernible presence in the particularities of historical encounter. The point will be illustrated below in the discussion of divine power in the ministry of Jesus.

3 POWER AND PRESENCE

If 'all *exousia* in heaven and on earth' came to be ascribed to the risen Jesus, something of that *exousia* was already discernible in his ministry. In Matthew, it is predicated of his teaching in particular – as is evident in Matthew's final comment on the Sermon on the Mount (7.28–9). In this context, *exousia* suggests inherent authority and authenticity. His teaching gives immediate access to the truth of things, in contrast to the elaborate casuistry of the scribes: 'You have heard that it was said ... But I say to you ...' Here is something akin to the prophetic 'word from beyond', in contrast to that mediated by tradition and argument. A channelling or embodying of divine *exousia* is presupposed in the notion that 'the Son of man has authority on earth to forgive sins' (9.6). Here, the perception is of a delegated *exousia* (9.8). Similarly, Jesus delegates to his disciples the *exousia* – in this case, something like 'effective power' – to exorcize and to heal (10.1). Finally, the critical question raised by the religious leaders in Jerusalem is, 'By what *exousia* are you doing these things, and who gave you this *exousia*?' (21.23): a debate which soon reaches impasse (21.24–7), because when the nature of authority transcends the merely institutional and falls within the prophetic realm, its validity is a matter of discernment and decision rather than of formal accreditation. The notion of *exousia* is thus complex and requires careful handling.

Some light is thrown on the matter by the story of the centurion's servant (8.5–13).[21] In Matthew's version, Jesus offers to go to the servant and heal him; power would thus be expressed, as so often, through physical presence. The centurion protests that he is unworthy of such honour: let Jesus simply give the word, and the servant will be healed. His plea is backed up by his awareness of how structures of authority operate. He himself is 'under authority', accustomed to give and receive commands which must be obeyed instantly. Here he stands under the authority of Jesus, requesting from Jesus the command that will transform the situation. The command is given and the healing effected.

A number of important issues emerge from the story. For example, the implications of such astonishing faith on the part of a Gentile, and the power of Jesus' spoken word to change a given situation. It also has implications for the notion of Jesus' presence. Jesus is present in the midst of Israel; he represents 'God with us'. He is accessible – even to the Gentile who seeks him out. His power, however, can have effects even when he is not physically present at the scene. Since it proceeds from God, it is not localized by the limitations of his physical being, for the power of God transcends the parameters of any human individual (cf. Matt. 9.8). In Jesus, it is made available to the questing and faithful suppliant.

A somewhat similar note is sounded in the 'walking on the water' narrative (Matt. 14.22–33), in which Matthew follows Mark, though with some modification of the material. The climax is the same: Jesus identifies his presence and power in the evocative phrase *ego eimi*, 'it is I'.[22] Here, the powerful presence is seen as resource; it is strength to deal with circumstances that threaten to overcome. Matthew adds a characteristic Petrine sequence (14.28–31), in which Peter represents the wavering and inadequate faith of the disciples – and the Church – longing to do what Jesus did, yet fearful and crying out in desperation to the Lord (14.30). The Christian community consists of those of little faith (14.31) who yet witness that they know Jesus to be Son of God (14.33), the one on whom the Spirit came at baptism (Matt. 3.16 par.).

At first sight, it is remarkable that Matthew makes such restrained use of the Spirit in his narrative of Jesus' ministry, in contrast to Mark's more popular practice.[23] As M. E. Isaacs has indicated, his restraint may have been prompted by the tendency of Hellenistic Jewish authors to reserve the word *pneuma* (spirit) for the action of God himself.[24] Inspiration on the day of trial is ascribed by Matthew to 'the Spirit of your Father speaking through you' (10.20). In general, Matthew differentiates carefully between the Spirit and Jesus himself. In Mark, the sin against the Holy Spirit is clearly a refusal to recognize the Spirit 'as the authenticating sign of Jesus' Messiahship'.[25] In Matthew, as in Luke, the connection between the Spirit and Jesus is much less direct. Blasphemy directed against the Son of Man may be forgiven, but not that directed at the Holy Spirit (Matt. 12.32; Luke 12.10).

But there is one significant passage in which Matthew seems to go out of his way to identify the Spirit of God as the source of Jesus' power. 'If it is by the Spirit of God that I cast out demons, then the kingdom of God has come upon you' (Matt. 12.28, a 'Q' saying). Luke's evocative phrase, 'by the finger of God' (Luke 11.20), is sometimes taken as the more authentic on the grounds of its scriptural connotation (cf. Exod. 8.19). If Matthew had known this version, it is argued, he would have found it so congenial that he would not have changed it. In fact, secondary features may be found in both. Luke's version may reflect hermeneutical discussion in church circles, while Matthew's version continues the interpretative tradition of the baptism narrative. In view of Matthew's general tendency, it looks as if he may have made a deliberate editorial decision to make reference to the Spirit here. Normally, as we have noted, he is reserved in his appeal to the Spirit: why, we need not speculate at this point. It is noteworthy that he has just quoted *in extenso* the servant passage from Isaiah 42.1–4 (Matt. 12.18–21), which contains an explicit reference to the Spirit: 'I will put my Spirit upon him'. In casting out demons, Jesus – so far from serving Beelzebul – fulfils the divine commission for which the Spirit was given and acts in the power of the Spirit. Moreover, in Matthew the crowds have just asked, 'Can this be the Son of David?' (12.23), a question which recalls the birth narrative (cf. 1.1), in which the Holy Spirit plays a key role (1.18, 20). Hence in Matthew the terminology of the Spirit is used in a controlled way to suggest the presence and activity of God, which receive dynamic expression in the ministry of Jesus as Son of David and Servant (Son) of God.

It now becomes apparent that the searching questions asked about the source of Jesus' *exousia* cannot be answered completely in terms of his endowment with the Spirit. The appeal to the Spirit – like the questions themselves – raises the problem of Jesus' own identity. 'What sort of man is this…?' (8.27). 'Where did this man get this wisdom…?' (13.54). The logic of Matthew's understanding propels him into Christology, and the riddle of the power and presence of Jesus is ultimately solved in these terms. The *locus classicus* is Matthew 11.27 – frequently described as the 'Johannine thunderbolt' (or words to that effect), but in fact Matthean and 'Q' tradition material rather than Johannine theology.[26]

Matthew 11.25–30 appears to combine two distinct but interrelated types of material. There is a devotional tradition (11.25–6), which includes the prayer-formula *Abba*, 'Father' – the heart of Jesus' devotional life, so far as one can deduce – linked with conventional acknowledgement of his sovereignty: 'Lord of heaven and earth'. Since the sovereign Lord of the universe – he who dwells in light inaccessible – relates to the faithful as *Abba*, divine Wisdom is imparted not to the established religious or scribal authorities but to 'babes': to the 'poor in spirit' and 'pure in heart', the children of God, who receive the Kingdom as divine gift. All of which is a matter of joyous thanksgiving (11.25a) and rests upon a particular perception of the 'gracious will' of God (11.26). This perception is in fact the bridge to the 'revelation' tradition which forms the second part of the logion. By embodying the devotional tradition, Jesus is afforded direct access to the divine will. 'All things have been delivered to me by my Father' is remarkably similar in general tendency to 'All *exousia* in heaven and on earth has been given to me' (28.18). Admittedly, 11.27 in its present context relates to the gift of wisdom rather than power, but the latter is implied in the former: 'all things' is a comprehensive formula! The divine gift – from the Father – and its cosmic setting are leading motifs. Thus is Jesus' Sonship realized. To recognize the Son is itself in the gift of the Father; while knowledge of the Father is mediated through the Son.

The whole realm of discourse probably reflects, as E. Schillebeeckx has observed, a 'Hellenistic Judaeo-Christian' background, 'completely at home in the Old Testament late Jewish, Chasidic heritage'.[27] It has close affinities with the wisdom tradition, the basic model being that of the messenger 'sent by Wisdom'. This model, however, is greatly enriched by the notions of interaction and intimate personal 'father–son' relationship. The most striking feature of all is that not only in Matthew but in the 'Q' tradition itself the terms 'Father' and 'Son' are used in an absolute sense. If one presses questions such as the source of Jesus' *exousia*, one ends up in such Christology. And if one presses questions about Christology one ends up not merely with 'the distinctive Wisdom christology of the Graeco-Jewish Q community' (in Schillebeeckx's phrase) but with the resurrection perspective of Matthew 28.18–20.

4 PRESENCE AND COMMUNITY

There is, however, another dimension to the presence of Jesus, not yet elucidated by our discussion. We have seen that, in certain circumstances, the power of Jesus operates in his physical absence. Much more paradoxical is the notion, now to be explored, that the 'presence' of Jesus can be known and realized in his physical 'absence'. If this proves to be the case, how are we to make sense of this paradoxical presence?

A case in point arises in connection with the settling of disputes within the community of faith. Several steps are outlined in Matthew. If one has suffered wrong at the hands of one's brother in the faith, one must try to resolve the matter on a personal basis (18.15). If this approach fails, one should bring the matter before one or two selected representatives of the community in accordance with Deuteronomic practice (Deut. 19.15) and in fulfilment of the scriptural obligation to reason with one's neighbour when a dispute arises (cf. Lev. 19.17). The next step is to bring the unresolved dispute before the church (*ekklesia*). If the offender refuses to respond or comply, 'Let him be to you as a Gentile and a tax collector' (18.17).[28] What is being affirmed is the necessity of peacemaking, in the tradition of Jesus' teaching; and, with it, the necessity of seeking mutual agreement, which may involve arbitration and compromise. In such delicate matters, the Church has the power to bind and loose 'in any business about which a claim arises'[29] (18.18). When two members reach agreement or accord in the way described, the blessing – indeed, the ratification – of heaven is assured on all such peacemaking (18.19).

The required condition is expressed in 18.20: 'For where two or three are gathered [i.e. brought together] in my name, there am I in the midst of them.' The binding and loosing operates only through the community convened in Jesus' name. The invoking of his name entails obedience to his commands and recognition of his authority. Matthew, however, speaks in this connection of the *presence* of Jesus. How is this presence to be understood? It is commonplace to point out, as J. D. M. Derrett has observed, that in Judaism God (or the 'Skekinah', the divine Presence) attends those who meet around the Torah, especially in the exercise of justice.[30] Psalm 82 depicts Yahweh himself in the divine council, while in the Sayings of the Fathers we read: 'If two sit together and the words of the Law [are spoken] between them, the divine Presence rests between them' (*Aboth* 3.2; cf. 3.6). It is attractive, therefore, to conclude that in the Christian communities, Christ takes the place of the Shekinah as divine presence. It is not suggested that Matthew is dependent on *Aboth*. The question of relative dating is, in fact, difficult. It may well be that they represent parallel but independent lines of thinking, each with its own frame of reference.

This assurance of the presence of Christ is in line with the climactic statement of the Gospel, 'I am with you always...' (28.20). This assuredly does not mean that the disciples in their missionary endeavours will continue to benefit from appearances of the risen Jesus. His presence is to be understood in different terms: for example, as support or resource, authorization or endorsement.[31] Yet in what sense does this amount to 'presence'? In the Old Testament, when Yahweh has commissioned his servant messenger, his promise 'to be with' his emissary is an assurance that, no matter what difficulties are encountered, divine presence encompasses the mere mortal, to inspire and sustain as required. A 'real presence' is involved, and operates as 'a very present help' as long as the human agent is faithful to his commission. In Matthew, the instructions to the disciples are not limited to the final commission. They are conveyed also in the teaching of Jesus, to which Matthew gives such prominence. Sometimes, under the influence of modern dialectical or kerygmatic theology, scholars have seemed to locate Jesus' presence in his commandments; for example, 'Jesus will be with his disciples *in this proclamation* until the end of the world'.[32] Well might J. A. Ziesler ask in what way this differs from saying that Jesus is absent but that his commandments are still with us.[33] The formulation is clearly inadequate. Rather, the presence of Jesus is sustaining reality for those who are united in Christian praxis. Hence, the community that is actively engaged in the work of peacemaking and reconciliation realizes the presence of Jesus in its midst. His presence can therefore be evoked through obedience to his teaching and commission: or, in Old Testament language, by 'keeping his covenant'.

A close connection between 'presence in community' and 'covenant' is evident in Matthew's account of the Last Supper (26.26–9). He follows the Markan tradition, 'this is my blood of the covenant, which is poured out for many', and adds 'for the forgiveness of sins' (26.28; cf. Mark 14.24). In the Old Testament, the phrase 'my covenant is with you' is virtually tantamount to 'I [Yahweh] am with you'. In Genesis 17.4, Yahweh says to Abram, 'Behold, my covenant is with you, and you shall be the father...' In Genesis 28.15, when the promise is repeated to Jacob, the assurance is, 'Behold, I am with you and will keep you...' The Old Testament passages speak of the promise and gift of God, presuppose responsive obedience and praxis, and imply or assert the help and support of Yahweh for the future. In the New Testament, it is no longer the old covenant that is celebrated, even in the context of the Passover (26.2). While Jesus is sharing the Last Supper with his disciples and giving thanks to God for the gifts of bread and cup, a new covenantal emphasis is emerging which will operate after Jesus' death and in his physical absence (cf. 26.29). His instructions to his followers to share these gifts – 'Take, eat'; 'Drink of it, all of you' – are instructions to re-establish *koinonia*, table-fellowship. In doing so, his followers participate not only in a human community but in 'my body'. *They* become the physical channel of his presence-in-absence, the corporate expression of his being-in-the-world. As they drink from the cup, they internalize 'the covenant' with Jesus for which his own blood was poured out (26.28) and enter into the new relationship with God which his self-giving made possible for them. Thus, in the celebration, 'my covenant is with you' (cf. Gen. 17.4); that is, 'I am with you' (cf. Gen. 28.15). In the evident absence of Jesus, the community evokes his presence in the shared praxis of the table, and is sustained by God's forgiveness, the ground and goal of the covenant in Christ.

5 THE SIGN OF RESURRECTION

As suggested above, the ministry of Jesus possessed a certain theonomous quality which afforded 'signals of transcendence' to the observant and sensitive participant; and such signals could also be received within the disciples' fellowship in so far as it allowed itself to be structured by Jesus. Signals – or 'signs', to use the New Testament word – enabled people to participate in the reality that was signified, whether that reality was described as the Kingdom of God, the power of the Spirit or the 'presence' of Jesus. Thus Jesus' community could discern 'the signs of the times' when his critics, though versed in a formal understanding of the ways of God with Israel, could not (cf. 16.3). No formal token of accreditation, such as the 'signs' Moses was required to give the people to demonstrate his divine authorization (Exod. 4.1–9), was available. In this sense, 'no sign shall be given to this generation' – a saying which probably belongs to historically the most 'authentic' layer of gospel tradition.

The one apparent exception is 'the sign of Jonah'. Brief reflection shows, however, that its exceptional nature is apparent rather than substantive. For example, the sign of Jonah does not provide a simple analogy between Jonah's preaching and that of Jesus, but between Jonah and the more complex Son of Man figure. Part of the reference is clearly to the reality signalled in Jesus' ministry: 'behold, something greater than [Jonah/Solomon] is here' (12.41–2; Luke 11.31–2). Jesus has already signalled the reality of the Kingdom[34] – again, a particularly authentic strand, characterized by 'christological reticence'. 'This generation' is therefore placed under the crisis of judgement, as the Ninevites were in their day. The latter repented. How inexcusable, then, is the hardheartedness of 'this generation'. The thought of the rejection of Jesus enlarges the sign of Jonah to encompass the image of the Son of Man in judgement, together with the Ninevites and 'the queen of the South' who will join in the condemnation of unrepentant Israel. As a 'sign', it is clearly ironical – a sign not identified. As such it coheres with an identifiable strand of Jesus' ministry.

Matthew exploits the image more fully. The development of the Jonah analogy in terms of the death and resurrection of Jesus,[35] though informed by a Christian perspective and to that extent secondary, need not be ascribed wholly to the creative imagination of Matthew[36] or to prophetic activity in the community he represents.[37] Responsibility to tradition involves progressive interpretation as well as transmission. Here, the critical factor is the connotation of 'Jonah', which Matthew explores.

The *kerygma* of Jonah (12.41) presupposes that 'Jonah was...in the belly of the whale'[38] three days and three nights (12.40). That is, Jonah himself, however imperfectly, represented renewed Israel, raised from 'the belly of Sheol' (Jonah 2.2). It was this Jonah, rather than the renegade fugitive of the first chapter, who called – albeit with comic reluctance – for the repentance of the Ninevites. The connotation of deliverance from death was thus an inescapable part of the Jonah symbol, as later Judaism recognized.[39] Matthew therefore finds in it the prototype of the Son of Man who, prior to his coming in judgement, will 'be three days and three nights in the heart of the earth' (12.40). Even if the christological reference is secondary, the imagery is nevertheless derived from the story of Jonah, not from that of Jesus. 'Three days and three nights' (Jonah 1.17) is not an accurate reflection of the resurrection story but is sufficiently evocative to provide an analogue. 'The heart of the earth' – that is, Sheol, the place of the dead (cf. Eph. 4.9; Sir. 51.5) – parallels 'the heart of the seas' (Jonah 2.3). In this figure, therefore, we find evidence, not of a rampant Christian prophetism,[40] but of a developing hermeneutical tradition aiming to elucidate the nuances of Jesus' teaching.

It could be claimed that the sign of Jonah is given such singular treatment because it is in effect an archetypal image of the gospel. On the one hand, it is bound up with the call to repentance (Heb. *shub*, to change direction) – addressed in Jonah's case to a foreign city, but in Jesus' ministry to Israel in the first instance, though ultimately to the nations (28.19). Even if the sign of Jonah is tied closely to proclamation, it involves Jonah as the prophet brought to fulfil his vocation through a remarkable deliverance from the depths, and it involves dying-and-rising as a repentance motif in the teaching of Jesus: taking up one's cross, and losing one's life in order to find it again (cf. 16.24–5, par.). On the other hand, the sign of Jonah embraces the fate of the Son of Man, identified in Matthew with Jesus as the Messiah (cf. 16.13, 16) who must go to Jerusalem to face death and be raised on the third day (16.21 par.; 17.22–3 par.; 20.18–19 par.), and also with the agent of divine judgement who 'is to come with his angels in the glory of his Father' (cf. 16.27 par.). Here we find echoes of the Danielic vision, also reflected in the final scene in Matthew (28.18–20).

The sign of Jonah is comprehensive in scope and profound in its implications. It represents the main thrust of Jesus' proclamation, the motif of his ministry, the destiny he fulfilled through his death, and the ministry that flowed from his resurrection. It is a signal of resurrection: the resurrection of the Son of Man and the resurrection of humankind. Truly, no other sign can be given.

6 RESURRECTION NARRATIVE

Matthew's resurrection narrative is a cosmic disclosure, conveyed in statements which move through a spectrum which has historical recollection at one end of the scale and theological statement at the other end, and is calibrated for apologetic and exhortatory purposes.

An example of his method is provided by his statement of the consequences of the death of Jesus: that is, following 27.50, where Jesus 'cried again with a loud voice and yielded up his spirit'. Following Mark, Matthew relates the rending of the Temple curtain (27.51). If our reading tends to the historical, we might be tempted by a rationalization such as that mentioned by Gundry: 'a sign of judgment visible to the general public, perhaps in the form of a sirocco wind tearing the outer curtain as well as bringing the darkness'.[41] But, as Gundry recognizes, the interest of Mark as well as Matthew is in the theological sector: 'from top to bottom' denotes the action of God. Matthew expands this interpretation by his narrative of the earthquake, which is like no other in that it releases the bodies of the saints from their tombs in resurrection (27.51b–52). The apocalyptic imagery reflects Ezekiel: 'Behold, I will open your graves, and raise you from your graves, O my people' (Ezek. 37.12); and Daniel: 'many of those who sleep in the dust shall awake...' (Dan. 12.2). Here is the language of cosmic event, to which – in Matthew – 'the centurion and those who were with him' bear witness (27.54).[42]

As do all the evangelists, Matthew finds in the burial story the essential link in the narrative chain between death and resurrection. Recounted in narrative sequence, death and resurrection are separate events. Interpreted in terms of cosmic significance, they are identified. Thus, the death of Jesus releases the faithful from their graves. Strangely, Matthew recounts the resurrection of the faithful before that of Jesus himself. The reason is that he proposes to treat the latter in narrative sequence. The burial of Jesus takes us to the sealing of the tomb with a 'great' stone: Matthew emphasizes its mass (27.60). Indeed, he moves round the spectrum towards apologetic in his inclusion of a passage, peculiar to this Gospel, in which 'the chief priests and the Pharisees' enlist Pilate's aid to make the sepulchre completely secure and so obviate the possibility that the disciples might remove the body and then proclaim the resurrection of Jesus! Thus Matthew turns anti-Christian propaganda ('the disciples stole the body') into Christian apologetic ('the tomb was sealed and guarded'): the common presupposition being, as has often been noted, that the tomb was discovered to be empty (27.62–6). This particular strand of apologetic is rounded off with the story of the bribing of the soldiers (28.11–15). There was to be quite a tradition of allegation and counter-allegation, not only 'spread among the Jews to this day' (28.15) but also evident in the Fathers.[43]

The narrative of the empty tomb is highly complex in Matthew. At one end of the spectrum are the two Marys, the constant witnesses to observable occurrences (28.1; cf. 27.56), who end up taking hold of the feet of their risen Lord in worship (28.9). At the other, there is 'a great earthquake', Matthew's code for an apocalyptic act of God, combined in this case with an angelophany (28.2–3). It is by angelic power rather than seismic force that the stone is rolled back and the guards neutralized (28.2, 4). The women then receive a kind of prophetic oracle through the angelic messenger (who replaces Mark's 'young man'). It takes the form of an oracle of salvation, with the conventional introduction, 'Fear not!'[44] There is then given the ground of salvation: the announcement of Jesus' resurrection, of which the emptiness of the tomb supplies an empirical indication. Finally, there is the specific commission which follows on the announcement: 'go quickly and tell his disciples...' (the locus of the disciples' encounter with Jesus is again Galilee).[45] 'Lo, I have told you': the divine message has been communicated (28.5–7). The ending of the narrative is in strong contrast to Mark's. The women's fear is tempered by 'great joy', and they run to deliver their message (28.8). However, Jesus himself encounters them. His greeting, *chairete*, echoes their note of joy, and his risen glory commands their worship (28.9). In Matthew, the women become the first Christian worshippers, anticipating the worship which the eleven disciples will give to Jesus (28.17). The divine message is now given directly to the women, the repetition of it serving to emphasize the great finale in Galilee (28.16–20).

7 THE CLIMAX

Matthew's narrative thus comes to the climax in Galilee: a climax that is both an end and a beginning. It confronts the reader with what is called, in modern jargon, 'eschatological event'. The *eschaton* or final age has been manifested in a particular human story that focuses on Jesus' ministry and his death on a cross. With this manifestation there is given the cosmic vision which provides a new faith-perspective on history. Sovereignty over the whole cosmos is given to Jesus, to whom worship is due. The disciples, prostrated in worship, are the prototype of a cosmos reconciled to the ground of its being. With worship goes discipleship – and the making of disciples: a mission to all nations. The eschatological vision, couched as it is in cosmic terms, is universal in scope. Truly, the veil of the Temple has been rent asunder.

Within the community of disciples, certain actions are sacramental: that is, they are actions through which, given faith and obedience, the divine effectively operates. Baptism in accordance with Jesus' commandment is an act which 'fulfils all righteousness', brings the gift of the Spirit, and inaugurates a life of Christian service. In Matthew's understanding of the gospel, the presence of the living Christ is realized in Christian praxis and, not least, in Christian table-fellowship. The transcendent reality of God, unveiled in the eschatological event, defies simple characterization in human language. In the story of Jesus, he is encountered as 'our Father'; the filial response of Jesus is so complete as to reveal his divine Sonship, itself the medium of revelation; and the Holy Spirit is encountered as dynamic power and presence in Jesus' ministry and in Christian service. Probably the threefold name was already invoked in the faith-community which Matthew knew. Here is a perspective on the divine that will fascinate and perplex the Church for centuries, yet remain the essential corrective to more limited views.

In the new eschatological perspective – from now to eternity – the teaching ministry is all-important for Matthew: the presupposition of the realization of Jesus' presence as resource and support. And so he ends – as he began – with the concept of 'God with us', though redefined and fulfilled.

With the drawing of this Love and the voice of this Calling
We shall not cease from exploration
And the end of all our exploring
Will be to arrive where we started
And know the place for the first time.[46]

1 T. S. Eliot (1888–1965), *Little Gidding*, V.
2 Gundry (1982), p. 593. In this chapter, Matthew is assumed to have emerged about a decade or so after Mark and to have used Mark as a source together with a collection or collections of mainly teaching material designated as 'Q'. For a consideration of 'the reader' of Matthew's Gospel, cf. J. D. Kingsbury (1988).
3 For Michel, cf. 'Der Abschluss des Matthäusevangeliums', in *Evangelische Theologie* 10 (1950); English translation in Stanton (1983), pp. 30–41 (references below are to the English version). For Jeremias, cf. Jeremias (1981).
4 cf. Stanton (1983), p. 36; Jeremias (1981), pp. 38–9.
5 cf. Stanton (1983), ibid.
6 Jeremias (1981), p. 39.
7 cf. Stanton (1983), p. 35.
8 Ricoeur's understanding of interpretation suggests a journey from 'first naivete', through critical engagement, to the 'post-critical moment' in which we stand in front of the text in a new way and find it conveying a revelation which gives new meaning to our existence. This understanding of interpretation offers a helpful description of how one engages with Matthew's Gospel. Encounter with the resurrection is central to the process. Cf. Ricoeur (1981), including the Introduction, pp. 1–37.
9 cf. Hubbard (1974), pp. 69–99.
10 ibid., pp. 101–36.
11 Boring (1982), pp. 150–2; cf. Revelation, the Fourth Gospel and Luke 10.22/Matt. 11.27 – a Q passage. See note 2 above.
12 For a general summary of the characteristics of the early Christian prophet, cf. Boring (1982), p. 136; and for Christian prophecy in Matthew, cf. ibid., pp. 204–18.
13 As Beare (1981), p. 545, observes, 'the triple formulation found here is not early, but it corresponds to the realities of Christian experience'. Noting that 'it is not, properly speaking, "trinitarian"', he goes on: 'there is no element of speculation about the divine essence or the relations between Father, Son, and Holy Spirit. It reflects the modes in which the divine is manifested in Christian faith'.
14 See chapter 1, pp. 9–22.
15 cf. Gundry (1982), p. 593.
16 cf. chapter 1, p. 15.
17 The term 'theonomous' indicates 'being governed by God' as distinct from 'heteronomous', 'being governed by another'. It is therefore compatible with the 'autonomy' of the person if it represents personal 'fulfilment'.
18 Emphasis should be placed on 'theological': it does not provide a structural key. Hence, we dissent from the kind of approach adopted by Brooks (1981), who took the two themes of authority and teaching as controlling the overall design of the book. In fact, ten important themes can be identified in Matt. 28.16–20: discipleship, Galilee, mountain, worship, authority, baptism, the name of God, teaching, 'I am with you always', and the close of the age.
19 The Hebrew is *ha'almah*, 'young woman'.

20 The subject is always taken up by commentators: cf. Beare (1981), pp. 71–2; Gundry (1982), pp. 24–5.
21 This is a 'Q' passage – see note 2; cf. Luke 7.1–10.
22 The phrase readily suggests the divine title I AM (cf. Exod. 3.14), especially in the context of walking on the water.
23 cf. Ziesler (1984), pp. 92–4. Matthew avoids speaking of the Spirit of Christ but speaks freely of the Spirit of God. Ziesler suspects that part of the reason lies in the evangelist's understanding of the monarchy of God, 'and that we may have here the inchoate beginnings of the sort of thinking that much later led to the Eastern rejection of the *filioque* clause' (p. 94).
24 cf. Isaacs (1976), p. 143 and *passim*.
25 ibid., p. 118.
26 See note 2 on 'Q'.
27 Schillebeeckx (1979), p. 265. For a discussion of Matt. 11.27 as a Q prophetic logion, cf. Boring (1982), pp. 150–2.
28 Derrett (1979), pp. 83–4 points out that the Church in Matthew's time did not discriminate in this way: Matthew is using a long-standing formula.
29 ibid., pp. 84–6.
30 ibid., p. 85.
31 Ziesler (1984), p. 60.
32 Marxsen (1970), p. 165. The italics are my addition.
33 Ziesler (1984), p. 61.
34 cf. Chilton and McDonald (1987), pp. 31, 70–6.
35 Justin (*Dial.* 107.1f.) omits reference to Matt. 12.40 but seems to assume it in his interpretation; cf. Gundry (1982), p. 245.
36 cf. Beare (1981), pp. 281–2.
37 cf. Boring (1982), p. 153. Boring, however, finds evidence of prophetic input in the secondary development in Matthew.
38 Or 'sea monster'. Matthew follows the LXX reading; the Hebrew has 'great fish'.
39 cf. Gundry (1982), p. 244.
40 *Contra* Boring (1982).
41 Gundry (1982), p. 575.
42 i.e., the dominion of Adam, like Israel itself, is being restored to proper form; cf. Smalley (1968–9), p. 283; Hooker (1967), pp. 24–30.
43 cf. Justin *Dial.* 108.
44 cf. McDonald (1980), pp. 13–14.
45 Gundry (1982), p. 594 emphasizes here the authoritative instructions of Jesus, and the possible connection with the mountain of the law (Matt. 5.1).
46 Eliot, *Little Gidding*, V.

5

The Glory of the Lord
The Resurrection in Luke/Acts

It happened, on a solemn eventide,
Soon after he that was our surety died,
Two bosom friends, each pensively inclined,
The scene of all those sorrows left behind,
Sought their own village, busied, as they went,
In musings worthy of the great event:
They spake of him they loved, of him whose life,
Though blameless, had incurred perpetual strife,
Whose deeds had left, in spite of hostile arts,
A deep memorial graven on their hearts.[1]

---

1 LIFE-GIVING MINISTRY

It has often been observed that the delightful Emmaus Road narrative comprises several distinctively Lucan motifs.[2] It is the story of a journey, and journeys are central to Luke's understanding of the ministry of Jesus and the mission of the Church.[3] The key that unlocks the mystery of the crucified Messiah is a particular biblical hermeneutic: the Scriptures hold a focal place in Luke's interpretation of the entire event of Christ.[4] The climax of the story is the recognition scene: the risen Jesus is known to the two disciples in the breaking of bread. In Luke's Gospel, table-fellowship is the recurrent context in which the truth of the gospel is revealed in social or interpersonal terms.[5] Besides, the recognition of the true nature of Jesus is the constant concern of the whole Gospel, from its literary prologue (1.1–4) to Christ's 'entering into glory' (24.26) and the final note of joy and praise (24.52). The Emmaus Road story not only brings together these elements with remarkable artistry but also shows that the historical Jesus and the risen Jesus cohere in a single framework of meaning which also embraces the life and mission of the Church.

A detailed study of the Emmaus Road narrative will be made later in this chapter. Meanwhile, Luke's method of presenting the Christ event merits closer examination. In particular, some reflection is needed on the significance of what we have called distinctively Lucan motifs.

Luke is no mere raconteur. He is a skilled interpreter of narrative. His method is to encapsulate a particular dimension of meaning in a memorable image or symbol, introduced into his narrative at strategic points. Care must be taken, therefore, in using such phrases as 'Luke the historian'. If he is not a mere chronicler, neither does he present a 'positive' or 'objective' view of history as nineteenth-century historians tried to do.[6] Though he makes reference in his prologue to his sources ('those who from the beginning were eyewitnesses and ministers of the word', 1.2), he has in fact 'no interest in the causal connection of events',[7] and the truth he would set before Theophilus far exceeds the bounds of anything we would call historical today. Perhaps Collingwood's celebrated distinction between the 'outside' and the 'inside' of an event provides a way of coming to terms with Luke's method.[8] For him, the 'outside' of an event – 'bodies and their movements', in Collingwood's phrase – is an essential part of story or recital: *diegesis* or 'narrative' is Luke's own term (1.1). But the *diegesis* must also point to or manifest an inner meaning which the reader is given help to discern but which may remain closed to many. This inner meaning is included with the 'assured truth' (*asphaleia*) of the narrative. The sources or 'eyewitnesses' (1.2) are to be trusted not only in relation to the 'outside' of events but also, as 'ministers [servants] of the word', in relation to the 'inside'. Luke is thus properly described as historian *and* theologian.[9]

The importance of the symbolic aspect of Luke's presentation is thus seen to lie in the illumination it gives to the 'inside' of events. Jesus' story in itself works with the raw material of alienation and forgiveness, brokenness and healing, and comprises the ambivalences of controversy, rejection and death. The symbolism of prophetic oracle suggests that, through all the complexity of historical experience, he is bringing light to the Gentiles and glory to his own people, Israel (2.32); yet he will also be an offence to many in Israel (2.34). The first two chapters of the Gospel have an intensely interpretative role. In similar fashion, the story of Jesus' death is interpreted as his exodus (9.31). The climax of the story is 'the days of his assumption' (9.51; my translation): his reception into glory. The 'firm truth' which Luke sets before his readers is that Jesus' ministry and death are of cosmic significance. The challenge to the reader is to discern his 'glory' in the midst of his pain and sorrow.

The characteristic Lucan motifs – the separate strands of the Gospel's symbolic meaning – express an aspect or aspects of the central mystery and cohere finally in the glorified Christ, whom Peter and the apostles in Acts confess as 'Leader and Saviour' (Acts 5.31). An appropriate approach to study is therefore to select several prominent motifs and allow them to demonstrate the coherence of Luke/Acts and the pivotal position of the glorified Christ within it. In this way, the degree to which a resurrection theology is implicit in the whole work should emerge clearly.

(i) The Nazareth manifesto

One such motif is provided by the characteristically Lucan passage often described as 'the rejection at Nazareth' but in fact constituting a kind of manifesto or declaration of the nature of Jesus' ministry (4.16–30). The Galilean mission has already begun (4.14–15). In the context of synagogue worship at Nazareth, where he had been brought up, Jesus allows prophetic Scripture (Isa. 61.1–2; cf. 58.6) to interpret the ministry on which he has embarked. Anointed of the Spirit, he is God's agent in liberation. He brings release to the poor, the captive, the blind and the oppressed. Power radiates from him to effect healing (6.19). Scripture is fulfilled; the time of salvation has arrived for God's people (cf. 4.18–19).

This is a fundamental gospel motif not only in Luke but in 'Q',[10] as Jesus' celebrated response to John the Baptist shows (cf. Matt. 11.2–6; Luke 7.18–23). In 'Q', the concern is with the basic question, 'Are you he who is to come, or shall we look for another?' and also with the kind of answer which Jesus' ministry gives to such an inquiry: an answer which can be seen to fulfil prophetic Scripture (cf. Isa. 29.18–19; 35.5–6; 61.1). Luke emphasizes the basic question by repeating it in dialogue (7.20) and adds a commentary of his own on the extent of Jesus' healing ministry (7.21).

This crucial response to the question, however, is placed in a highly suggestive context. The healing of the centurion's slave introduces the theme (7.1–10). The Jewish elders apologize for their request to Jesus on the grounds of the centurion's worthiness: 'for he loves our nation, and he built us our synagogue' (7.5). The centurion himself professes his own 'unworthiness' – he is well aware of how Jews regarded Gentiles; but he nevertheless has high expectations of Jesus' healing power. Jesus' response is significant: 'not even in Israel have I found such faith' (7.9). The man's worthiness rests on his faith rather than his good works for Israel – and he is a Gentile. While the reader is mulling over the implications of this act of healing and acceptance – perhaps 'a light for revelation to the Gentiles' as well as 'for glory to thy people Israel' (2.32) – Luke relates the narrative of the widow's son at Nain (7.11–17). Here is a story of the raising of the dead, on the model of the Elijah stories;[11] and the reader's response is guided by the reaction of the bystanders: 'A great prophet has arisen among us!' and 'God has visited his people!' (as in Zechariah's utterance about the birth of John, 1.68). A number of hares have now been set running. An important one is the question about the role Jesus is playing – and, in the reader's mind, the relationship between the roles of Jesus and John. Both are mighty prophets; both are like Elijah. A striking feature of Luke's presentation is that, by introducing the Q logion at this strategic point, he makes John ask that very question. The answer, as we have seen, lies in what Jesus is actually doing: that is, in his liberating and life-giving ministry which includes, even in Q, the claim that 'the dead are raised up' (7.22).

'Blessed is he who takes no offence at me' (7.23): blessed because thus the power of new life will find realization. Luke recounts Jesus' authentication of John as 'more than a prophet' (7.26): as the prophet of the last days (Mal. 3.1), the returning Elijah (Mal. 4.5), the greatest servant of God before the reign of God itself was given reality – by implication – in the ministry of Jesus (7.28). Yet the prophetic role of John, like the eschatological role of Jesus in giving performance to the reign of God, is a matter of perception and decision. In relation to John, the 'Pharisees and the lawyers' had already 'rejected the purpose of God for themselves' (7.30). The parable of the quarrelsome children suggests that John and Jesus, though very different figures, will suffer the same fate. Hence, the life-giving work of Jesus, like the prophetic work of John, is coupled with final rejection. Only 'the children of wisdom' (cf. 7.35) recognize that wisdom proves herself right and true in human experience. Yet the acts of the children of wisdom will often be misunderstood, even by well-disposed people if they lack sensitivity to where true wisdom lies. Luke illustrates this by means of the relatively complex narrative of the woman who anointed Jesus' feet (7.36–50). Here the emphasis is not explicitly on anointing in preparation for death, as in Matthew and Mark (Matt. 26.6–13; Mark 14.3–9), but on the devotion of a 'sinful' woman which showed depths of wisdom that eluded Simon, the Pharisee: the wisdom of love which was open – as Simon's right-doing conventionality was not – to the receiving and giving of forgiveness. Thus the perspectives of life and death alternate in curious ways.

Back now to the programmatic presentation at Nazareth. The initial response of Jesus' audience is very positive. God's favour has rested on one of their own number, 'Joseph's son' (4.22). It is this latter aspect of their perception that triggers the second – and negative – response. Jesus begins, 'Doubtless you will quote to me this proverb, "Physician, heal yourself"' (4.23). The language is that of the rhetoric of debate.[12] It appears that the response has turned into a demand for 'signs', leaving Jesus no alternative but to refuse. Yet surely Nazareth is more entitled to witness such things than Capernaum! The thought leads to a further development of the motif. The 'kith and kin' – or 'own country' (4.24) – perspective is to be rejected. God does not work like that! Nor can Jesus be manipulated in this way. Scriptural illustrations are provided from the stories of Elijah and Elisha (4.25–7). The emphasis is not explicitly on Gentiles but simply on the wider world beyond the confines of home territory. It is in 'the wider world' that Jesus' mission will be fulfilled. This suggestion is met with astonishing hostility (4.28–9). It was an intolerable rebuke to a much-prized insular chauvinism. The programmatic statement, which put so much store on the fulfilment of Scripture and which so vividly delineated a liberating and life-enhancing ministry, ends with a powerful image of death (4.29).

The Nazareth manifesto proclaims the eschatological nature of Jesus' ministry while registering problematical features of any such claim. The new age has burst upon the historical scene in the ministry of the one anointed by the Spirit at baptism. This is what the prophets have been pointing to; this is the fulfilment of Israel's religious heritage. Yet it does not cohere with Israel's actual expectations, and the paradox emerges that the agent of the new age, the bearer of the good news of liberation and healing, is himself seized and threatened with death. The manifesto and the narrative of its reception enshrine the notion that the life of the new age, already manifested in Jesus' ministry, involves not only wider horizons and new perspectives but also costly conflict with the entrenched power and presuppositions of the old order.

(ii) The disciples' mission

The second major motif in the narrative of Jesus' ministry is the miraculous catch of fish (5.1–11), which symbolizes the eschatological significance of the disciples' mission. It is not simply that this is an image appropriate to the environment and that it suggests the impact Jesus made on the men he called as disciples. The image of fishers occurs as an oracle of judgement in Jeremiah 16.16. As punishment for her iniquities, Israel is about to be hurled out of her land and into exile. 'Behold, I am sending for many fishers, says the Lord, and they shall catch them…' The vivid image of fishing is adapted by Jesus for the reverse purpose: namely, as an oracle of salvation. The disciples are called to the in-gathering of God's people – an eschatological notion, indicating once more that the time of fulfilment is at hand.

The same motif occurs in a resurrection setting in John 21.4–13. As R. H. Fuller has observed, 'in both Johannine and Lucan versions the draft of fish symbolizes the call to mission'.[13] There seems little point in trying to deduce which is 'original' and which derivative, as Fuller does. A number of strands are woven together. In John, the eucharistic strand is clear, but there is also emphasis on the reaction of Peter to Jesus and on his commissioning to the pastoral ministry. In Luke, where the focus is on the calling of the disciples, Peter's 'Depart from me, for I am a sinful man, O Lord' (5.8), might appear more congruent with events after his denial of Jesus. On the other hand, the theme of being 'fishers' or 'catchers' of men is firmly rooted in the setting of Jesus' ministry, and the image of the great catch fits well enough with it. Peter's protestation would then be the human feeling of unworthiness in the presence of the divine – like that of Isaiah's in the Temple (Isa. 6.5). The most significant feature is that the image of the great catch is equally at home in a pre- or post-resurrection context, for it is concerned with mission and is a further instance of the congruity of resurrection and pre-resurrection motifs.

What then is the reader to make of Luke's narrative of the calling of the first disciples? To rationalize the miraculous catch is to miss the point.[14] The story may well suggest Jesus' prophetic powers. It certainly conveys a sense of 'something transcendent, numinous, utterly compelling'.[15] But the modern wariness of allegorizing should not prevent the reader from reflecting on the significance of the contrast between the disciples' unsuccessful toil throughout the night and the great return achieved when they act in accordance with Jesus' commands. 'Henceforth, you will be catching men' (5.10).[16] Clearly, the great catch denotes the eschatological harvest – the harvest of the final age. It is to this task that the disciples are called. In its scope, it is immense, transcending anything that they have known before, for it is no mere human work but the work of God.

The motif of mission represents a trajectory that unites Luke/Acts. The twelve are sent to proclaim the reign of God in Israel: relying utterly on God and on the hospitality of their hosts on the way, but bringing also a message of judgement to those who reject them (9.1–6).

Indeed, the message to Israel is followed by clear indications of the rejection to come: foreshadowed in the death of the Baptist (9.7–9) and confirmed by Jesus himself in his prediction that the way of the Son of Man was that of suffering, death and resurrection (9.22). It is after Jesus has 'set his face to go to Jerusalem' (9.51) that he sends the seventy 'ahead of him' as his heralds: symbolizing the mission that lies ahead for the apostles and adumbrating something of the great harvest (10.1–20). The seventy return with joy (10.17), and Jesus is moved to see 'Satan fall like lightning from heaven' (10.18). The demons are defeated. Jesus' emissaries are inviolable (10.19) and, above all, their names are 'written in heaven': they are an assured part of the harvest (10.20). Blessed indeed are those who witness the new age which kings and prophets longed to see (10.23–4).

Yet the powerful images of fulfilment are starkly juxtaposed to the grim story of Jesus' immediate fate in Jerusalem. He will not 'finish his course' (13.32) on a wave of euphoria, but by taking on himself, so to speak, the full weight of the deep alienation from God which his ministry has brought to light even in God's people, Israel. Hence, the drama that is played out in the final part of Jesus' 'course' is not so much that of traditional Jewish eschatology as a reinterpreted eschatology in which the alienation is encompassed by the forgiveness of God. The dying Jesus cries, 'Father, forgive them; for they know not what they do' (23.34). This is the fully comprehended message of the Scriptures; this is the point of Jesus' sufferings. The post-Easter mission will have as its aim 'that repentance and forgiveness of sins should be preached in his name to all nations…' (24.47). Acts will tell the story of that mission, up to the fateful point at which Paul relates the call of Isaiah (once more) to the rejection of the gospel by 'this people' (Israel) and to the potentially fruitful field of the Gentile mission: 'they will listen' (Acts 28.28). The miraculous catch will surely be brought in.

(iii) Table-fellowship

In Luke, as in Mark and Matthew, table-fellowship is a focus of the disciple group around Jesus. It is open – even to tax-collectors and others like them: clearly outsiders as far as the conventionally religious are concerned. When the disciple group is interrogated on the matter by Pharisees and scribes, Jesus replies that it is the sick who need the services of a physician. His own services involve calling sinners 'to repentance' (5.32): probably a theological interpretation of the 'open table' which was so evidently a matter of offence.

What is the significance of Jesus' practice and the vigorous objection to it? Most obviously, the Pharisaic practice was based on the segregation of 'the holy and the common…the unclean and the clean' (Lev. 10.10).[17] Jesus' practice is 'salvation by association':[18] an association that effects repentance. Table-fellowship can be a celebration of such repentance, as well as a spreading of the net of association to enfold others. However, more is at stake than simply an alternative view of evangelism.

The table, the feast and the banquet were well known in biblical tradition. A place at table was in the king's gift, whether as an act of kindness or a reward for loyalty (cf. 1 Kings 2.7). It was a pledge of hospitality, acceptance, sustenance and security (cf. Ps. 23). The banquets of the Persian court are described in Esther (1.5–12; 5.4); a love feast is indicated in the Song of Solomon (2.4); and the excesses of the banquets of the rich are condemned by Amos (6.4–6). Yet Jesus preferred to celebrate than to be ascetic. The Q tradition records the carping criticism: 'a glutton and a drunkard, a friend of tax collectors and sinners!' (Luke 7.34; cf. Matt. 11.19). Celebration had a symbolic as well as a social value. Salvation is imaged as a banquet. People 'will come from east and west, and from north and south, and sit at table in the kingdom of God' (Luke 13.29; cf. Matt. 8.11). Hence, table-fellowship in the disciple group was a celebration and enactment of the family of God from which many of the household of Israel chose to exclude themselves (cf. Luke 13.28; Matt. 8.12).

This notion that table-fellowship was related to salvation probably explains the fact that, in Luke, the table – or a meal – is a particular setting in which important issues are faced. Dining at the house of a Pharisee (7.36) subsequently addressed as Simon (7.40), Jesus is approached from behind by 'a woman of the city, who was a sinner' (7.37) and treated with lavish devotion. The Pharisee's objections open up the whole issue of forgiveness. In discussion, Jesus shows that loving devotion relates well to forgiveness, but censorious rectitude finds little place for it. Jesus' fellowship with tax-collectors and sinners is a *cause célèbre* and occasions the parable of the lost sheep, the lost coin and, above all, the prodigal son and elder brother (15.1–32). In fact, Luke sets some of Jesus' most direct attacks on Pharisaic praxis in the context of a meal at which a Pharisee is host (11.37–52).

The dispute about healing on the sabbath has a similar setting (cf. 14.1–6), which also encompasses two subsequent parables. One is the parable of the marriage feast (14.7–11), which revolves around the issue of status-seeking and humility and is accompanied by advice on appropriate guests: not simply friends, kinsmen and well-off neighbours, but 'the poor, the maimed, the lame, the blind' (14.12–14). Here is a strong statement of the 'open table' policy characteristic of Jesus but not of the Pharisees, although they apparently invited him as a man of faith. The second parable – the great banquet – takes up a *bon mot* about 'eating bread in the kingdom of God' and suggests that, the invited guests having declined for various reasons, the messianic table is opened to 'the poor and maimed and blind and lame', not to mention those rounded up from the 'highways and hedges' (14.15–24).

In Luke, table-fellowship and passover celebration coalesce at the Last Supper (22.14–16). Luke has a distinctive approach to this narrative, especially if the tradition of the Western text is followed.[19] Several points stand out clearly. This is 'the hour' (22.14) not only of the feast but of the inception of the final stage of the ministry of the Son of Man (22.21–2). Around the table with Jesus is the apostolic group (22.14). The meal is expressly designated as 'this passover' (22.15), even though the apostles represented an irregular group in terms of passover celebration.[20] The passover context focuses on the exodus theme of deliverance or salvation through suffering. Jesus 'earnestly desires' to share the Passover with them 'before I suffer' (22.15). Hence, implicit in the symbolism of the supper is Jesus' impending 'exodus'. The apostolic table-fellowship is 'an anticipation of the great feast of the kingdom in which the Passover theme of redemption from bondage would receive its final fulfilment'.[21] For Jesus, the Last Supper marks the end of table-fellowship on earth until the Kingdom of God reaches its fullness (22.16, 18).

To the disciples he gives the cup, with orders to 'divide it among yourselves' (22.17). Why the focus on the cup in Luke? Here, the evangelist's understanding of symbolism may be at its most subtle. Is this the Messiah, offering them the Messiah's cup? If so, it is the suffering Messiah who does so: to share his cup is to share his sufferings. To be sure, the apostolic community has much to learn. As yet, it is immature both in its understanding and in its praxis (22.24–7). One of them, the betrayer, will never effect the change (22.21–3). Those who are faithful, who 'have continued with me in my trials' (22.28), will ultimately exercise not the authority of the Caesars and their kind but leadership in the new Israel. They will 'eat and drink at my table in my kingdom' (22.29–30). For the old Israel, it is the time of judgement (23.27–31); yet salvation is still offered to the repentant, as the story of the repentant thief makes clear (23.39–43).

The table-fellowship tradition in Luke reaches its highest point in the Emmaus Road narrative. The two disciples prevail upon their guest, expert as he is in the Christian interpretation of the Scriptures, to stay with them. At table, as he broke bread with them, 'their eyes were opened and they recognized him' (24.31). The tradition of table-fellowship has been, throughout the Gospel, the setting for important discoveries. None was more significant than that made by the two disciples. 'The Lord has risen indeed' (24.34). His *analempsis*[22] has been accomplished. It is not that they now know his whereabouts or can have any control over him. As soon as they recognized him, he disappeared! He belongs to the transcendent realm: the realm of God's sovereignty – he is 'Lord' – and the realm of the eternally alive. Table-fellowship is, from now on, a celebration of joy (Acts 2.46) and thanksgiving (Acts 27.35): a time for prayer and for the message of Jesus (Acts 2.42), especially on the first day of the week (Acts 20.7); a time for conversation, like the two disciples with the stranger on the Emmaus Road (Acts 20.11). It is a time to become open to others – and to the Other; and to discover that others – and the Other – are open to us. In short, it is a time to express and to enjoy the openness that was the hallmark of Jesus' fellowship with his disciples.

RESURRECTION

The presentation of the resurrection theme comes not as an appendix but as the climax of the Gospel. It is integrally related to what has gone before. The motifs which have supplied the dynamic and constituted distinctive trajectories in Luke's work come to full expression here; while the understanding of Jesus' ministry implicit from the beginning is now seen in its cosmic context.

(i) The prelude

Luke's narrative shows evidence of a carefully devised build-up to the climax of resurrection and ascension. The story of Joseph of Arimathea is deliberately given prominence. His role in the burial of Jesus springs from the most devout of motives: he was 'looking for the kingdom of God' (23.51). His 'rock-hewn tomb', which was to receive Jesus' body, was as yet unsullied by any corpse (23.53). The reverent entombment is observed by the women, who busy themselves with the preparation of the unguents (23.55–6). Throughout, there is a sense of irony. The pious expectations will find fulfilment in a totally unexpected way.[23]

Luke marks the resurrection event by phrases such as 'the first day of the week' (24.1) and 'the third day' (24.21). The women have an important role. It is they who discover the tomb to be empty and untenanted. It is to them that the truth of the resurrection is revealed in 'a vision of angels' (24.23; cf. 24.4–5). It is they who are made to face the radical question about the meaning of their conventional acts of devotion: 'Why do you seek the living among the dead?' (24.5). This is the sentence which conveys Luke's emphasis.[24]

The resurrection is not something that convention can take in its stride. It requires a revolution in thinking, for it comes as the fulfilment of a radically unconventional ministry. There must therefore be recollection of that ministry, and particularly of the expectation of the rejection, crucifixion and resurrection of the Son of Man (24.7). The angelic vision is the means by which the women 'remembered' Jesus' words. There dawns upon them the possibility of viewing Jesus' death in a different way. His death must be interpreted in the way that he himself indicated, as belonging within the scenario of dying and rising again. He is not to be located in the tomb. The empty tomb is not so much treated as a proof of Jesus' resurrection as an indication that he is not to be found among the dead or honoured as a sacred memory. He must be 'sought' among the living.

To this small band of women (cf. 24.10) is given the first perception of the truth of Jesus' resurrection: thereby bringing to completion the strand in Luke which recognizes the devotion and sensitivity of the women who followed Jesus (cf. 8.2–3). The story implies both revelation and response. The angelic messengers invite the women to 'remember' and then redirect their attention to the future. The women 'get the message' and act on it. They suffer the fate that has befallen many pioneers throughout history. Their report to 'the apostles' is received with incredulity and treated as an idle tale (24.11) – not because, as is so often said, they were but simple women whose status in a male-dominated world lent no support to their story[25] (their story clearly 'registers', at least in Luke; cf. 24.22–3), but because of the unprecedented content of their message. The apostles must undergo a similar learning experience before they could be expected to accept such a world-shattering view.

In Luke, the women's tale is part of the story of the recognition of the truth of the resurrection. It is clear that here we have to do with the world of story – the narrative means by which a cosmic disclosure is made. Narrative moves in sequence: from the burial to the discovery of the empty tomb and then to the awareness of the need for a new understanding; from the women's perception to the apostles' scepticism. And the narrator has the freedom to present the story in such a way as best achieves his purpose. A critical reading should therefore focus more on literary than on historical questions. It matters not at all that Luke has allegedly embroidered a basic tradition – introducing two men in dazzling apparel, for example, where Mark has only one.[26] His purpose is to reinforce the angelic message: to underline the fact that the new perspective now being advocated is suggested and endorsed by heaven. To be sure, Luke is alive to the fact that the human evidence is not without its importance. Some of the apostolic group visit the tomb and confirm the women's report, but are otherwise unable to make much of what might have happened (24.24).[27] The technique of the story-teller is to raise expectations of a denouement that has yet to be reached. The women, like the subsequent apostolic deputation, have not encountered Jesus himself: 'him they did not see' (24.24). The continued story will enable the reader to learn of moments at which Jesus himself was recognized within a living community and thus to place Jesus in the context of life rather than death.

(ii) The recognition

To appreciate the role of the Emmaus Road narrative in Luke, it is important to learn from the structure of the narrative itself. Without reviewing the intricacies of structuralist debate, we may find a useful starting-point in a study of this passage by Bas van Iersel.[28] His analysis of it may be summarized as follows:

A Departure (the two): 24.13–14
B Unrecognized Arrival (Jesus): 24.15–16
C Qualifying Test and Reaction (the two and Jesus): 24.17–27
D Main Test and Reaction (the two and Jesus): 24.28–9
Ć Glorifying Test and Identification (the two and Jesus): 24.30–1a
Ḃ Transfiguration (Jesus): 24.31b–32
Á Return (the two): 24.33

Such an analysis has the merit of identifying the boundaries of the story (A and Á), suggesting its development in terms of the three tests, pinpointing its turning-point (D), and revealing its chiastic structure. A provisional acceptance of it as an appropriate analysis does not rule out the option of amending it (for example, redefining B́) in the course of further exegetical study. Each motif in the structural pattern calls for examination.

A,Á. The opening of the story is readily identified (24.13). The time factor – 'that very day' – links it with 'the first day of the week' and the women's story. The destination, Emmaus, is also a significant marker. The final boundary (Á) is less precise, for it merges with the rise of the resurrection faith in the apostolic group at Jerusalem and the celebration of the appearance of the risen Lord to Simon. The Emmaus motif, however, is reasserted in 24.35, and it may be that this is the true end of the story. The starting-point (A) is the departure from Jerusalem, where the talk has been of idle tales and where there is disbelief in the resurrection; by implication, the two disciples talk in similar terms – at least, they have not yet come to a positive view. The return (Á) is of two believing disciples who find in Jerusalem a community which has meanwhile come to believe in the risen Lord.

A comment might be made here on the importance of journeys in biblical story. It is a commonplace of New Testament criticism that Luke develops the motif of the journey in his account of Jesus' ministry.[29] In doing so, he is using a pervasive motif of the Scriptures, from the patriarchal age onwards. For Jesus, the journey that matters takes him to Jerusalem, to complete his *exodus* ('departure') and his *analempsis* ('being received up'). The question is precisely whether he has, in some mysterious way, completed that task, or whether his work has ended in disappointed hopes (cf. 24.21). There is a need to recapitulate all that has happened, and a journey gives time and opportunity for this to take place. The initial conversation between the two disciples begins the process (24.14); their final conversation celebrates their discovery (24.32), articulates their witness (24.35) – and brings us back to Jerusalem.

B,B́. The arrival of Jesus in the *persona* of a pilgrim returning from the Passover at Jerusalem is a bold narrative feature. If 'their eyes were kept from recognising him' (24.16), it is simply because the moment of truth has not yet arrived. It comes as the 'peak experience',[30] not on initial acquaintance. The motif of the divine *incognito* – for example, in the guise of strangers to be given hospitality – is found in Genesis 18 and is a standard form of theophany.[31] The correlative in the chiasmus occurs in 24.31 when, their eyes being 'opened', the two disciples recognized the stranger as Jesus – 'and he vanished out of their sight' (24.31b).[32] Luke tells the story from the point of view of the beholders. It is a recognition story (24.31a). B́ should be redescribed as 'recognition' – the correlative of 'unrecognized arrival' – and be located in 24.31.

C,Ć. In terms of content, 'the fellowship of dialogue' would be the most appropriate description of C.[33] It is opened by a seemingly naive question from the stranger (24.17) – 'not without a touch of kindly humour', as A. B. Bruce once observed[34] – which serves to rivet attention on the theme of the disciples' discussion. The reader is aware of the irony in their reply (24.18). A further prompting from the stranger

(24.19a) elicits a recital of the story of the prophet Jesus up to his crucifixion (24.19b–20), together with a hint of their disappointed hopes (24.21), a note of the time ('now the third day') and a brief and inconclusive resumé of the empty tomb narrative (24.22–4). If this dialogue is in any sense a test of their discipleship or discernment, then they failed it! They are severely reproached by the stranger, now clearly speaking as Lord: 'Was it not necessary that the Christ should suffer these things and enter into his glory?' (24.26).

The traditions of biblical interpretation (which has been noted as fundamental to Luke[35]) and of the ministry of Jesus (of which the Gospel is itself an interpretation) coalesce in the suffering of the Messiah. The 'necessity' (24.26) is not defined. The Scriptures (unspecified, 24.27) adumbrated this pattern of ministry. The Christ who came not to be served but to serve is brought to the point of suffering and death as the logical outcome of his vocation. Suffering and death are necessitated by the encounter of the love of God with the resistance of humankind. They are part of the mystery of God's forgiveness of his alienated creatures and so the necessary prelude to glory.

The correlative to this passage is Ć (24.30, remembering that Ḃ has been redefined), where the stranger re-enacts the table-fellowship of Jesus' ministry. Table-fellowship with Jesus comes, therefore, as the climax to the discussion on the road. It is not so much the re-enactment of the Last Supper, where the cup was predominant, as that of the table-fellowship which had been a catalyst of meaning and insight for the disciples. The breaking of bread – the connotation of which is joy and celebration – is the effective condition of their recognition of Jesus. We are told nothing of the vision of glory – except that it was momentary. It was a moment of truth in which they realized not so much the identity of the stranger who fades from their view so dramatically as the identity of Jesus as the crucified and glorified Messiah. The Christ of glory – the risen Christ – is none other than the one who suffered. Their recognition of him presupposes an awareness of his sufferings as essential to the divine purposes (cf. C). Christ crucified is risen!

D. The pivot of the narrative is located in 24.28–9. The place is identified as 'the village'; that is, Emmaus. The stranger made to go further. There may be a hint here of the divine motif of 'passing by',[36] but the literary function of the move is clear: it enables the disciples to urge the stranger to accept their hospitality.[37] The theme of entertaining angels unawares is not far from the surface! The turning-point is therefore the invitation 'to stay with them'. Fellowship and hospitality provide the framework for the recognition of the glory of the crucified Christ:

> ...'The night', they said, 'is near,
> We must not now be parted, sojourn here.'
> The new acquaintance soon became a guest,
> And, made so welcome at their simple feast,
> He blessed the bread, but vanished at the word,
> And left them both exclaiming ''Twas the Lord!

106

Did not our hearts feel all he deigned to say,
Did they not burn within us by the way?'[38]

(iii) Reality and Recapitulation

The whole community of disciples receives the climactic Christophany
(24.36–49). The passage is apparently Luke's own composition, based
on some source material current in the churches (some material is
common to John 20.19–29, for example[39]) and designed as a fitting
climax to the Gospel. It also looks to the launching of Christian mission
and thus, directly or indirectly, to the story of Acts. Two aims are
apparent. One is to demonstrate the reality of the risen Christ. The other
is to recapitulate basic motifs of the Gospel: namely, the fulfilment of
Scripture in the suffering, death and resurrection of the Christ; and the
message of forgiveness for all nations.

Within the community of disciples, the close connection between
recognition of the risen Christ and table-fellowship has already been
noted. In Acts also, the apostolic preaching witnessed to the risen Jesus
eating and drinking with his disciples (Acts 10.36–43). But while Jesus
broke bread with the two disciples at Emmaus, in the climactic
Christophany the emphasis is on the fact that he asked for food and ate
the fish they were cooking for a meal. Attention has switched simply to
the reality of the risen figure. As G. B. Caird suggested, it was inevitable
that Luke should reflect the concreteness of imagery which Jewish
writers applied to eternal reality. He had to counter the suggestion that
the figure of the appearance was a ghost, 'not a living being, but a thin,
unsubstantial carbon-copy which had somehow escaped from the filing
system of death'.[40] Perhaps he was also countering early forms of heresy
such as docetism or Gnosticism.[41] Even if his methods may seem clumsy
to the modern reader, Luke was ruling out any truck with notions such
as subjective vision, psychic peculiarity or insubstantial shade to account
for the risen figure of Christ. Jesus is real and is found among the living:
in companies of disciples, especially at meals or in table-fellowship. He
is not a mere apparition: he is the Jesus-who-was, encountering the
disciples in a living relationship as the Jesus-who-is and the Jesus-who-
will-be.

The second theme demonstrates the critical importance of biblical
interpretation for Luke and his community. Effectively, he returns to
the theme of the Emmaus Road and to a kind of dominical hermeneutic.
The experience of the two disciples has to be appropriated by the whole
community. The focus of the problem is that the Messiah entered into
glory by way of suffering, and this in fulfilment of Scripture.

The starting-point may be described as a kind of 'first naivete', which
Paul Ricoeur identified as 'the condition of being in some sense
"called", but unable to distinguish the authentic message from the
reality-apprehensions of our culture and from the dogmatic and
ecclesiastical framework in which we hear it'.[42] This is clearly an
appropriate description of the initial position of the two disciples in the
Emmaus Road story, and it is now predicated of the whole community.

Their understanding of their 'calling' is promoted through scriptural interpretation initiated by Christ himself and therefore informed by his story (24.25–7). Thus, a 'new hermeneutic' is engendered: an 'inside' view of Scripture which liberates it from the inhibitions of dogmatic structures and cultural assumptions, makes possible a creative view of suffering and demonstrates the link between suffering and glory. Thus through criticism the community converts its naive faith into the register of hope.[43] In this way, the hermeneutical tradition first presented in Jesus' sermon at Nazareth[44] reaches full statement.

The 'opening of their minds to understand the scriptures' (24.45) is more than theoretical reflection. Their new understanding impels a new praxis: 'that repentance and forgiveness of sins should be preached in his name to all nations...' (24.47). Here is the effective launching of the mission to the world. It is not difficult to see the Emmaus Road story as the archetype or epitome of early Christian missionary work, with its suggestion of the itinerant missionary, scriptural discussion and Christian proclamation.[45] The story of Philip and the Ethiopian (Acts 8.26–40) presents an interesting comparison. Philip is the divine emissary, commissioned by an angel of the Lord to journey in a particular direction (8.26) and by the Spirit to encounter the Ethiopian traveller (8.29). The latter is already immersed in the prophet Isaiah but lacks the key to understanding (8.28–34). The central question is the identity of the 'sheep led to the slaughter' (8.32, 34).[46] As in the Emmaus Road story, the ensuing discussion is the crucible in which the testimony of Scripture to God's creative use of suffering is made to interact with the story of Jesus (8.35). The outcome in Acts is the Ethiopian's decision for baptism (8.36); in the Emmaus Road story, it is the recognition of the living Jesus in table-fellowship (Luke 24.30). In Acts the missionary, his work completed, is dramatically removed from the scene by the Spirit and the joyful eunuch sees him no more (8.39–40). In Luke Jesus, once recognized, vanishes from their sight (24.31).

At this point, the relevance of scriptural interpretation to missionary work is well illustrated. The meaning of the Scriptures is not self-evident. The fact of suffering – whether in the case of individuals such as Jeremiah or Job or the whole people of God or a faithful remnant – can be interpreted in various ways and is popularly taken as a sign of divine displeasure or rejection or failure. That it can have a positive or creative role in the outworking of God's purpose is implicit in some passages, but the notion may be relatively inert until activated by particular events. To some extent, this external activation had been supplied in Judaism by the sufferings of the martyrs, such as the Maccabees.[47] In Luke/Acts, it is materially supplied by the story of Jesus but perception and insight are required before the process of interpretation is effected. Deficiency in understanding may arise at different points. The Ethiopian needs to hear the story of Jesus (8.35) in order to activate the scriptural symbols. The two disciples on the Emmaus Road know Jesus' story, including accounts of the empty tomb and a vision of angels testifying that Jesus is alive (24.22–4), yet they fail to relate the narrative effectively to Scripture (cf. 24.25–7) and to find in it the fulfilment of their hopes (cf. 24.21).

The final coming together of the elements in insight and discernment is experienced as revelation, whether by Christ who 'opened to us the scriptures' (24.32) or by the Spirit, as the Acts narrative implies. It is accomplished through fellowship, through the interaction of speech and study. It leads on to a new praxis, a transformed way of life. For the disciples, this means returning to Jerusalem and rejoining the apostolic community (24.33). For the Ethiopian, the journey must be continued, but he goes on his way rejoicing (8.39) as a baptized Christian equipped for missionary work in the influential circles in which he moved (cf. 8.27). The story undoubtedly reflects Luke's conviction that explaining the Scriptures was a prime duty of the disciple community and an important element in missionary work.[48]

(iv) The Blessing

The Gospel concludes with Jesus finally parting from his disciples after bestowing his blessing upon them (24.50–3). The emphasis is on the blessing as much as on the parting, and the ascension into heaven is mentioned only in the inflated textual tradition (that is, the Western text). The Gospel effectively ends with the benediction. It is not necessarily a priestly act though, as Fitzmyer notes, 'lifting up his hands' could be taken as a hieratic blessing such as Aaron gave (Lev. 9.22) or the high priest Simon (Sir. 50. 20–1).[49] But even Fitzmyer agrees that Luke gives no place to Jesus as priest. Rather, Jesus is the sovereign Lord whose blessing[50] conveys *shalom* to his children. As usual, such a significant act involved a journey – this time to Bethany, on the mountain. The return of the disciples to Jerusalem pin-points the place from which the mission of the Church will begin. The Church is already in being in their acknowledgement of the Lordship of Christ in the context of joyful worship.

3 ESCHATOLOGICAL MINISTRY

Skilful writing ensures that the Acts of the Apostles provides an adequate sequel to the narrative of Luke's Gospel. Jesus' *analempsis* or ascension is the effective boundary (Acts 1.2, 11). But Luke has more to tell his readers before the narrative of Acts can get under way. The risen Christ gave his orders to his chosen apostles (through the Holy Spirit, 1.2); and the orders were to stay in Jerusalem until they themselves were 'baptized with the Holy Spirit' (1.5). To be sure, the appearances are now set within the framework of 'forty days' – a 'mountain top'[51] experience in which the mystery of God's sovereign ways was revealed to them (1.3). The agency of the Holy Spirit, however, is intriguing. If Jesus gave commands through the Holy Spirit, did he also appear to them 'through the Holy Spirit'? Luke does not say so in so many words, but the Spirit is the agent of mighty acts as well as prophetic commands.

Generally speaking, Luke has a preference for saying that 'God raised up Jesus'.[52]

The Spirit is the sign that 'the last days' have come (2.16–17). How, then, are Jesus' death and resurrection related to eschatology in Luke/Acts?

(i) Eschatology

'Lord, will you at this time restore the kingdom to Israel?' (1.6). In view of the abundance of eschatological signs – messianic woes, resurrection, ascension, Pentecost – the question is not unreasonable. The answer, however, is that 'times' and 'seasons' are in the Father's keeping. No eschatological *schema* is granted to mere mortals – not even apostolic mortals! The Spirit – the sign of 'the last days' – will in fact equip the apostles for a world mission that will transcend the divisions of mankind: Judaeans, Samaritans and Gentiles (1.8). Jesus' *analempsis* (ascension) may be *like* his parousia, or 'coming again', but it does not constitute it (1.11). The task for Jesus' followers is not speculation about the end but witness and mission.

Luke appears deliberately to adjust or correct popular eschatological perspectives. A corresponding adjustment is effected in Luke 19.11, where Jesus is said to have told the parable of the pounds 'because he was near to Jerusalem, and because they supposed that the kingdom of God was to appear immediately'. The parable is about the *departure* of the 'nobleman' and of the stewardship required of those left behind. Luke had to come to terms with the paradox that 'the last days' have come but the End has not. This looks not so much like a considered refutation of Gnostic views[53] as an attempt to reflect the process of rediscovery and adaptation which was part of the experience of the apostolic community.[54] A decisive shift of the ages has occurred. The penultimate age is upon us, when we must attend to the Lord's commands before he returns to examine our stewardship and pronounce judgement on his enemies (cf. Luke 19.14–15, 26–7).

Jesus' death, resurrection and saving work are held together in an indissoluble unity.[55] Jesus' death, the supreme manifestation of the power of darkness, was the 'hour' not only of his enemies' triumph but also of their judgement (Luke 22.53b). It was the time of cosmic darkness, when 'the curtain of the temple was torn in two' (23.45) and when judgement was thus pronounced on world and Temple alike. The darkness symbolizes the rejection of the 'light for revelation to the Gentiles, and for glory' to God's people Israel (2.32). But the hour of darkness, the triumph of evil, is also, paradoxically, the rebirth of hope and the reaffirmation of forgiveness. This positive side is realized gradually, as the sufferings of Jesus are found to resonate with prophetic understanding of the nature of God's engagement with his erring people and messianic sufferings are seen to be essential – 'necessary' (24.26) – to God's purpose. With this growing awareness there comes a rebirth of hope (cf. 24.21) and expectation (cf. 24.32), which are related to the recognition of Christ as risen (24.31). In other words, the power of renewal and forgiveness cannot be separated from the cross; just as the glorified Christ cannot be separated from the crucified Jesus.[56] 'God has made him both Lord and Christ, this Jesus whom you crucified' (Acts 2.36). Just as faith in the resurrection was not born without a positive understanding of the necessity of the Messiah's suffering (Luke 24.27, 45-6), so the suffering of the Messiah is the necessary condition of the mission of repentance and forgiveness to all nations (24.46-7). Hence, Luke's theology by no means lacks soteriological concern, even if he succeeds in avoiding some expressions of vicarious atonement with which Mark and Matthew have familiarized the reader (Mark 10.45b; Matt. 20.28b).[57] The passage of Scripture under scrutiny by the Ethiopian was in fact from a suffering servant poem (Acts 8.32-3; Isa. 53.7-8). In the sermons and controversies in Acts, the Lordship of Christ is never divorced from the fact that he hung 'on a tree' (5.30; 10.39; cf. 13.29) and that his Church was 'obtained with his own blood' (20.28): statements which suggest that his account is true to its sources. Thus Luke presents a view of the atonement that is at once primitive and profound.

If death, resurrection and the proclamation of forgiveness stand together, the same is true of the resurrection of the dead. Pharisees and Christians had in common a belief in the general resurrection of the dead (24.15, 21), while the Sadducees rejected it on the grounds that it was not found in the Torah (cf. 4.1-2). The Christians, however, proclaimed that it was through Jesus that one arrived at a properly grounded belief in the resurrection of the dead (4.2). Like Stephen, they could pray in extremity, 'Lord Jesus, receive my spirit' (7.59). Here is ample evidence that Jesus' death and resurrection were indeed 'the eschatological turning-point'.

(ii) Praxis

With his ascension, Jesus is parted from his disciples (Luke 24.51; Acts 1.9). He is Lord: sovereign. His sovereignty, however, has the strongest implications for his followers.

The picture with which Luke's Gospel closes is that of a joyous, worshipping community, in whom hope has been renewed. The locus was originally the Temple, although in Acts temple worship is supplemented by house groupings (2.46). The focal celebration is the breaking of bread (2.46; cf. 2.42) in a fellowship (*koinonia*) of close-knit groups that practised the community of goods (they held all things to be *koina*). This openness – a practical programme of love to neighbour – was informed by the apostles' teaching (*didache*) and punctuated by prayer. Hence, in story, instruction and worship, the community expressed its love to God. Other notes are mentioned: a sense of awe (*phobos*; literally, 'fear') at the manifestations of the power of the Spirit among them (2.43). Conversions and baptisms were by the proverbial thousands (2.41).

In the epiphenomena of a pneumatic or Spirit-endowed community, the realities to be underlined are the confession of Jesus as Lord and the powerful effects of this confession on the daily life of believers. The community element is strong. Luke emphasizes the fact that the disciples are together in the same place (cf. 2.1, 44). Awareness of transcendence creates community on earth. Community means sharing: whether goods or meals. And such table-fellowship – the breaking of bread – was immensely evocative of the disciple-fellowship in the Gospel: the open community centred on Jesus. Little wonder that it took a key position in the Emmaus Road story of the recognition of the risen Jesus. Little wonder that it was at the centre of the young church communities in which wonders worked by the Spirit were multiplied.

Luke's approach is 'charismatic' rather than sacramental. Even his account of the Last Supper is, of all the synoptic accounts, the one apparently least influenced by Christian sacramental practice. But there is much more to Luke's picture of early church life than the palpable exaggerations and devout distortions of hyper-excited or ecstatic communities. In their fellowship there is the sense of a divine initiative for salvation, accomplished in the 'Christ event'. There is a sense of the sovereignty of Christ: *Christos Kyrios*. And there is an experience of divine power which transforms life and creates hope. In all this, there is an awareness of vision: in the story of Christ's ministry, in his *analempsis* or ascension, in the gift of the Spirit, and in the foreshadowing of his *parousia* or coming again. At times, the vision may become intense: as when Stephen, 'full of the Holy Spirit, gazed into heaven and saw the glory of God, and Jesus standing at the right hand of God ...' (7.55); or when a light from heaven (a light to lighten the Gentiles?) flashed around Saul of Tarsus in his calling and commissioning (9.3; 22.6; 26.13). Inherent in all such epiphenomena is the interplay of the divine and the human, the transcendent and the immanent. In the intensity of their experiences, the communities abound in signals of transcendence; yet these signals are received, not as bodies from a strange world but as real-life happenings, within the network of human community, commensality and imagining.

The role of the apostles is to be witnesses to the world – near and far, fellow Jew or alien (1.8). To be a chosen witness is to be able to authenticate the story of Jesus from the days of 'the baptism of John' until his *analempsis* (1.22): it is, specifically, to be 'a witness to his resurrection'. There is a peculiarity about Luke's language here that gives pause for thought. How does one 'become with us a witness to his resurrection'? One might suppose that one either is a witness or is not: it depends on one's experience. Luke does recognize that point: personal experience of all 'the things concerning Jesus' is a prerequisite. But election as a witness to his resurrection suggests that the apostle in question will be able to share in the apostolic understanding of Jesus as the risen and ascended Lord. It is more than a personal account of 'the day I saw the risen Christ' – although such stories entered the tradition. It was to be able to interpret the signals of transcendence, to share in the apostles' *didache* (teaching), to open up the apostolic vision. Such testimony provided the framework and substance of the apostolic preaching as recorded in the sermons in Acts: the *kerygma* (proclamation), which might indeed be adapted to different situations (Paul at Athens is a case in point) but which never became idiosyncratic. And in the historic encounter of missionaries and world – in proclamation, debate, apology or conversation – signals of transcendence continued to be apparent: not least, in the notion of the ingathering of the Gentiles and of a world beginning to listen...(28.28).

Yet the strongest signals of all continued to occur in the fellowship of the worshipping people. Sometimes they might be prompted by the difficulties of the missionary situation – like Peter's vision at Joppa (Acts 10.9–16); but the setting of worship was itself creative. For here the community is itself brought together ('in one place', as Luke would say) and made open to the transcendent Lord. And here above all, the word of the Lord would be revealed. It may well be that visions of the transcendent realm and of transcendent action, such as the 'hymn' material in Philippians 2 and elsewhere, had their *Sitz im Leben* ('setting in life') precisely here. It was here too that the need for the ministry of the deacons was identified and met (Acts 6.1–6).

To what end these ruminations? Simply to underline the fact that to speak of the transcendent is simultaneously to speak of ourselves, the transcended; and that to maintain the distinction, as well as the interconnection, of the two is essential to interpreting Luke's theology. To confess Christ as Lord, risen and ascended, is to recognize his lordship here and now. It is to say with Peter and the apostles, when faced with unreasonable restrictions on their liberty of utterance, 'We must obey God rather than men' (5.29). It is to relativize every totalitarian pretence, every absolute claim that has a worldly source. It is to realize his lordship – not in an exhaustive nor a complete way, but yet really and truly – in the network of our lives. It is to believe that ultimately – though it is not for us to know the times or seasons – the signals will give way to the total reality and that Christ will come in like manner to his going.

It is also to begin to see the immensity of Luke's achievement. He has found a way of dealing with the transcendent aspect of the 'Christ event' so as to preserve the genuine humanity of Jesus' ministry and the authenticity of the apostolic ministry after his departure. He has found a way – perhaps at times risking caricature in the interest of bold relief – to relate the transcendent to history while preserving the integrity of both. Not for him the Gnostic sacrifice of the historical in the interests of the transcendent; nor the resort to the strait-jacket of *Heilsgeschichte* ('sacred history'), although he was alive to the place of recital. It may be true, as Helmut Flender has suggested, that he discovered 'a *via media* between the gnostic denial and the early catholic canonization of history...': a solution which involved giving 'simultaneous expression to the supernatural mystery and the earthly visibility of Christ and his history'.[58] But above all, he showed that the transcendent *matters* to human history and experience: that it signals its presence in Christian praxis – not least in the fellowship of the table when in the breaking of bread the glory of the risen Jesus is recognized.

Finally, Luke demonstrated that to recognize the sovereignty of the

113

risen Christ is to bring into question and eventually to transcend all the bounds and barriers which isolate and divide humankind: whether they are religious, social, economic, national or racial. The Christian mission, which appeared sectarian in origin, enshrined a universal perspective which sprang from the recognition of the one God who had acted in Christ for the salvation of the world. The narrative of Acts therefore closes on an appropriately open-ended note, with Paul, the hero of the mission, 'preaching the kingdom of God and teaching about the Lord Jesus Christ quite openly and unhindered' (28.31).

1 William Cowper (1731–1800), *The Walk to Emmaus.*
2 cf. Robinson (1984).
3 cf. Conzelmann (1969), p. 62.
4 The standard full-length study of the subject is probably Rese (1969). See now Bock (1987). Cf. Koet (1985); Delzant (1985).
5 See below, pp. 100–2.
6 One is thinking here particularly of Auguste Comte and the positivistic view of history. Others include von Ranke, Barthold Niebuhr and Lord Acton.
7 Flender (1967), p. 34.
8 cf. Macquarrie (1960), p. 83; Collingwood (1946), pp. 213–15.
9 cf. Marshall (1970a).
10 'Q' denotes a hypothetical collection of Jesus' sayings and related material, as in the commonly held models of source criticism. Cf. Isa. 29.18–19; 35.5–6; 61.1.
11 cf. Rochais (1981), pp. 32–5.
12 The synagogue could be the setting for heated debate. For a discussion of this passage cf. Flender (1967), pp. 152–7. Bock (1987), pp. 105–11 studies Luke 4.17–19.
13 Fuller (1972), p. 151.
14 e.g., that from his vantage-point Jesus was able to see a shoal of fish concealed from the fishermen!
15 Caird (1963), p. 90.
16 Lit. 'taking human beings alive': cf. Fitzmyer (1981), pp. 568–9.
17 cf. Manson (1948), p. 55. Cf. Caird (1963), p. 93; Fitzmyer (1981), pp. 580–1.
18 cf. Fitzmyer (1981), p. 589.
19 Codex D, some Old Latin mss and probably the old Syriac do not have 22.19b–20. There is a case for holding that they have been intruded from 1 Cor. 11.24–5 and Mark 14.24.
20 The issue has been much discussed: cf. Jeremias (1966), pp. 26–36; Dugmore (1965), pp. 1–18; see also my brief review of the subject in McDonald (1980), pp. 121–4.
21 Caird (1963), p. 238.
22 *analempsis* is the later form of the classical *analepsis* and is the preferred New Testament reading (cf. Nestle-Aland[8]1985 on Luke 9.51): it means 'being taken up', as in ascension.
23 George Herbert (1593–1633), expresses this paradox in his poem 'Easter'.
24 This question occurs only in Luke, and it suggests his emphasis even if we do not follow the Western text in omitting 'he is not here, but has been raised'. Luke emphasizes 'life': cf. Acts 1.3; Luke 24.23.
25 As Derrett (1982), p. 110, implies.
26 For the double testimony, cf. Deut. 19.15 and see above p. 87.

27 'Him they did not see': for Luke, the tomb is confirmed as empty, but belief in the resurrection does not flow from that fact.
28 van Iersel (1978), esp. pp. 309–15.
29 cf. Conzelmann (1969), p. 62.
30 The phrase is borrowed from the psychologist Maslow.
31 cf. Skinner (1910), pp. 302–3.
32 It is difficult to concur with van Iersel in describing 24.31b in terms of 'transfiguration' when the statement relates simply to Jesus' disappearance. Besides, the opening of their eyes, which van Iersel is forced to include with the 'glorifying test' to express reaction, is surely the proper correlative to 24.16. It is true that the longer ending of Mark paraphrases this narrative in terms of Jesus appearing 'in another form' (Mark 16.12). A possible correlative would therefore be a 'metamorphosis' or 'transfiguration'.
33 The oddness of the terminology used by van Iersel – Luke 24.17–27 is described as the 'qualifying test and reaction' – prompts the suspicion that he may be imposing an alien structure at this point. It is more helpful to focus on the fellowship which grows through perplexity and reaches its climax in the dramatic denouément at the table (Ĉ): cf. also Luke 24.32.
34 Bruce (1897), p. 646.
35 See above, note 4.
36 cf. 'my glory passes by', Exod. 33.22. But cf. Bruce's simple statement, 'Jesus wished to be invited to stay', (1897), p 648.
37 cf. Fitzmyer (1985), p. 1567.
38 cf. note 1, above.
39 cf. Fuller (1972), pp. 139–45.
40 Caird (1963), p. 261.
41 Ignatius, for example, interpreted this passge in an anti-docetic way, *Ep. Smyr.* 3.2 3; while the ghost of 'proto-Gnosticism' continues to haunt New Testament scholars!
42 cf. Ricoeur (1981), p. 23.
43 ibid., p. 28.
44 See above pp. 96–8.
45 cf. Legrand (1982).
46 'The primitive church did not feel the same inclination as later generations of Christians to apply this text to Jesus, but this was done in Philip's answer, when the Ethiopian asked the question which has been steadily repeated right up to our own time. Does the prophet in this passage speak of himself or of another? In Philip's answer this text, and probably the whole context, was explained as expressing the Gospel about Jesus', Munck (1967), p. 78. For a more technical discussion, cf. Bock (1987), pp. 225–30.
47 e.g., 2 Macc. 6—7, the earliest martyrologies, and 4 Macc.; cf. Hengel (1974), p. 98.
48 cf. Tyson (1987); Jervell (1984), pp. 122–37; also Jervell and Meeks (1977), pp. 87–106.
49 Fitzmyer (1985), p. 1590.
50 On blessing, cf. Pedersen (1926), pp. 182–90: also Pedersen (1959), p. 448.
51 Bethany was in fact 'on the mountain': the symbolism is implicit in Luke, explicit in Matthew.
52 Marshall (1970b), p. 103. Notice Marshall's critique of Wilckens.
53 cf. Talbert (1967). There is reason to be cautious about applying the term 'Gnostic' loosely to first-century belief.
54 Allison (1985), p. 78, inclines towards a dampening of 'over-realized eschatology', yet Luke's procedure could just as easily be described as an

adjustment of 'through-going eschatology' (ibid., p. 74). Indeed, if it is true to say, with Allison, that 'Luke refrained from interpreting the death and resurrection of Jesus as the eschatological turning point', it is so only in the sense that these events did not immediately bring in the Kingdom of God in its fullness. They *are*, however, the eschatological turning-point in that they inaugurate the ministry of 'the last days': the world mission of the apostles, energized by the Spirit; the bringing of the Gentiles into the family of God through the proclamation of divine forgiveness and the actions of repentance, baptism and the reception of the Spirit (cf. 2.38–9).

55 Almost as extraordinary as Allison's denial of Jesus' death and resurrection as the eschatological turning-point is the tendency of some scholars to assert that in Luke the death of Jesus has no saving significance and that Luke's theology lacks soteriological content: cf. Wilckens (1963), pp. 216–17. Even Howard Marshall seems to go along with the popular view that 'Luke does not make particularly strong links between the death of Jesus and the offer of salvation in the preaching of the gospel', Marshall (1970b), p. 103. The consequence of this view is to ground Luke's soteriology in Jesus as the exalted Lord who can exercise the divine prerogative to forgive sins. Thus, tacitly, a wedge is driven between the death and exaltation of Jesus in Luke.

56 Bock, in a useful note, identifies five themes in Luke's use of the Old Testament: '(1) The declaration that Jesus is the Messiah-Servant. (2) The declaration that Jesus performs the signs of the eschatological age. (3) The declarations surrounding rejection and the cross. (4) The declaration concerning his resurrection and exaltation. (5) The declarations promising his return'. Bock points out that the first two usages predominate in the Gospel until the last week of Jesus' life, when the other themes come into play, as in Acts. This reflects 'the progressive nature of Luke's christological use of the O.T. and the central role that the resurrection played in its development', Bock (1987), pp. 353–4. All this seems to me very much to the point. Bock also has an interesting discussion of the use of Psalm 16.8–11 in Acts 2.24–8 as a proof-text of the bodily resurrection of Jesus, ibid., pp. 171–81. We shall return to this theme at a later stage of this book.

57 In fact, Luke simply follows a different tradition at this point. He stays with the 'servant' image rather than introducing the 'ransom' idea, and this provides a telling comment on his understanding of power and powerlessness (cf. Luke 22.24–7).

58 Flender (1967), p. 167: the writer's concluding summation.

6

In Symbol and Story
The Resurrection in the Gospel of John

'Truly, truly, I say to you, the hour is coming, and now is, when the dead will hear the voice of the Son of God, and those who hear will live.'

JOHN 5.25

'I am the resurrection and the life; he who believes in me, though he die, yet shall he live, and whoever lives and believes in me shall never die. Do you believe this?'

11.25–6

In the Gospel of John, the word of Jesus is the word of resurrection. For some, he brings life; for some, judgement (cf. 5.25–9). His coming confronts the world with the Word from Beyond. In him the Beyond – the power of the new age, resurrection and judgement – becomes, in some sense, a present reality.

Such a programme makes a heavy demand on the writer. To fulfil it, he makes extended use of the potential of symbols, supported by narrative and dialogue. It is appropriate, therefore, to begin our study by relating his treatment of resurrection to the symbolic realm of discourse which provides its essential context.

1 THE RESURRECTION IN SYMBOLS

Symbols in the Fourth Gospel have a christological reference: Word, Lamb, Light, Bread, Vine, Resurrection and Life...They are also grounded in human experience. As far as communication is concerned, each one is a raid on the inarticulate, the ineffable, and so both reveals and obscures. Each one strikes home in a different way to different interpreters, yet contributes to the apprehension of reality. Each one prizes open a chink of meaning which may dazzle in its intensity but is the slimmest beam from an infinite source.

Yet the Gospel of John is far from being an array of symbolic oddments, unrelated to tradition or cosmic understanding. The basic symbols indicated above, cohering as they do in the figure of Jesus, coalesce with others more obviously derived from the Jewish messianic and apocalyptic traditions: Son, Son of God, Son of Man, Messiah...The compounding of the symbols makes for an extremely rich

117

statement of gospel meaning, yet it never dissolves into the thin air of cosmological speculation. It is earthed in the Word become flesh in Jesus. Its enfleshment ensures that the interpretation is always concerned with human existence and with the dimension of the human as the vehicle of God's salvation.

Certain symbols require closer scrutiny.

(i) Life

Of all the evangelists, John understands his message most explicitly as living reality. 'Life' is a leading symbol in the Fourth Gospel and denotes not so much 'existence' as 'reality'. To be sure, the created order is the product of the divine Logos (Word, John 1.1–18) and life does indeed comprehend existence; but by virtue of its constitution the created order contains a tension within itself. This tension may be described in many ways: light as opposed to darkness (cf. 1.5–9), trust as opposed to mistrust (cf. 1.10–13), grace and truth as opposed to Law (1.17), eternity as opposed to that which perishes (cf. 3.16). 'Existence' is characterized by the tension; 'life' affirms the positive.

Life is therefore the gift of God which is nourished and sustained by God (1.12–13). Human existence is grounded in the finite order, but is constitutionally capable of openness to the 'light', to the dynamic of the Spirit, and thus of transformation into life. Witness to the light, like signs of transcendent power, is therefore of prime significance in this Gospel, for it is life-giving. John the Baptist was such a witness (1.6–8). Jesus' words are 'spirit' and 'life' (6.63).[1]

Jesus is not merely witness to the light, he is its embodiment. He 'enfleshes' grace and truth, the 'glory as of the only Son from the Father' (1.14; cf. 5.26). To respond to Jesus in 'belief' (3.15) is to enter upon 'life' that is described as 'eternal'. The term denotes not an extension of life on earth but a transformation of life by the power of the eternal order. 'Eternal', as Macgregor put it long ago, 'is a qualitative and not merely a quantitative conception: it refers to the character and not merely to the duration of life'.[2] One may thus have 'life' that is 'eternal' here and now. The presupposition of the transformation is that one 'knows' God as 'the only true God' and Jesus Christ as his emissary (17.3). More, indeed, than an emissary in the formal sense: Jesus embodies a quality of life which in human terms can only be described as 'more abundant' (cf. 10.10), as fulfilling God-given human potential to the point where the boundaries of mortality merge into the limitlessness of eternity.

In human perspective, eternal life is life through death, and is therefore articulated as resurrection. In Jesus, resurrection and life cohere (11.25). As far as the person who is genuinely open to Jesus (that is, the believer) is concerned, the physical death which marks the end of mortal existence does not terminate the relationship with God in which an eternal quality is already manifest. When human existence takes on the transforming quality of life and faith, death itself is transcended (11.26). The focal pronouncement of Jesus in the story of Lazarus

(11.25–6) underlines the fact that the Christology with which John works does not, in spite of some impressions to the contrary, simply comprise a set of verbal propositions or an ideal system constructed of fixated perceptions or traditions.[3] It is a description of a living reality in which the believing community participated, by which it was transformed, and on which it grounded its life and hope.

(ii) The heavens opened

The significance of Jesus as the channel of 'abundant' and 'eternal' life is focal in the Fourth Gospel. He is at the heart of the mysterious interaction of the eternal and the finite orders. Nowhere does this receive more striking expression than in the 'Son of Man' tradition.

'Truly, truly, I say to you, you will see heaven opened, and the angels of God ascending and descending upon [?] the Son of man' (1.51).[4] Here is an important theme-statement for the whole Gospel. In the synoptic Gospels, Jesus 'saw the heavens opened' at baptism (cf. Mark 1.10 par.). In John, the solemn assurance ('Amen, amen' – rendered 'Truly, truly' by the RSV) is given to Nathanael that he (and, through him, the hearers and readers of this Gospel) will share the vision.

The content of the vision evokes Jacob's dream of a ladder from earth to heaven, on which the angels of God were ascending and descending (Gen. 28.12). Why Jacob's dream? And how does the concept of Son of Man relate to this scenario?

Jacob is, of course, Israel: not only the ancestor of the nation, but its embodiment. In John's narrative, Jesus has identified Nathanael as 'an Israelite indeed, in whom is no guile' (1.47). He had seen him 'under the fig tree' (1.48), a latter-day fulfilment of the prophetic figure in Hosea:

> Like grapes in the wilderness,
> I found Israel.
> Like the first fruit on the fig tree,
> in its first season,
> I saw your fathers (Hos. 9.10).[5]

In Nathanael, Jesus saw the first of the new Israel. Nathanael in turn saw Jesus as Son of God (Servant of God[6]) and King of Israel. The first title may well reflect the suffering servant: 'You are my servant, Israel, in whom I will be glorified' (Isa. 49.3). To say that Jesus is both Son/Servant of God and King of Israel is to affirm sovereignty or kingship through obedience unto death.[7] Jesus is thus seen by Nathanael as embodying the true Israel in himself and as the one who by his leadership would bring the whole body towards the fulfilment of its destiny.

It is this latter aspect which receives expression in the Jacob/Son of Man vision. The Son of Man has a corporate nature as well as manifestation in a particular being.[8] There is a hint of this in Psalm 80, where Israel is a vine planted by God (80.8, 14), deep-rooted but severely ravaged (80.12–13), and its restoration lies with 'the man of thy right hand, the son of man [*ben adam*] whom thou hast made strong for

119

thyself' (80.17).[9] In any case, the combination of the corporate and the particular is characteristic of the Son of Man tradition in Daniel, 1 Enoch and 4 Ezra (see pp. 15–17). What is distinctive here is the association of the image of Jacob's ladder with the Son of Man concept.

At first sight, it is tempting to apply the ladder image directly to the Son of Man figure. As the embodiment of the true Israel, he links earth and heaven, and the angels have free passage through him. There are, however, linguistic as well as conceptual difficulties in this attempted rendering.[10] In any case, since the Son of Man is fundamentally related to Jacob rather than to the ladder, it is better to think in terms of the access that Nathanael (true Israel) will have to the vision of a cosmos reunited by the work of the Son of Man. He will see the angels following the course which the Son of Man himself has taken.[11]

However this difficult logion is interpreted, its central presupposition is that Jesus, Son of Man and true Israel who shares his being with the faithful in heaven and on earth, has not only come from heaven but will also ascend to the right hand of God. Through him communication between heaven and earth is fully established. But the perspective of resurrection and glorification through suffering is essential to this whole realm of discourse and is made explicit in another logion: 'No one has ascended into heaven but he who descended from heaven, the Son of man. And as Moses lifted up the serpent in the wilderness, so must the Son of man be lifted up, that whoever believes in him may have eternal life' (3.14–15). The ascent and descent are clear: pre-existence, incarnation and ascension are neatly subsumed under the Son of Man figure.[12] 'Lifted up' is a key phrase (cf. 8.28), probably reflecting a Hebraic *mashal* or riddle-saying with the dual connotation of crucifixion and ascension (cf. 6.62; 12.23). The material reference is to Numbers 21.9 (cf. Wis. Sol. 16.6–7): as the snake-bitten Israelites had found healing by turning their eyes upwards to the brazen serpent on its pole,[13] so Israel will find healing and salvation by gazing in faith upon the Son of Man elevated on the cross and elevated to heaven. This double reference, so characteristic of the Johannine motif of suffering–vindication (12.34; 13.31), coheres once again with the suffering servant tradition (cf. Isa. 52.13). But the force of the purpose clause – 'that whoever believes in him may have eternal life' – should not be overlooked. The underlying concept is that of the believer's participation in the life of the Son of Man. As the Son of Man is 'lifted up', so also the believer is 'lifted up' to healing and eternal life.

The 'sending of the Son' carries similar weight in Johannine theology. John 3.16 ('God so loved the world...') provides the theological grounds for connecting resurrection and love (*agape*).[14] The effect of the concrete expression of divine love in the sending of the Son is to place the cosmos under judgement (*crisis*, 3.17–21). The Son is not sent to condemn; the world of darkness and unbelief effectively condemns itself (3.18–19). Yet judgement is part of the divine role of the Son of Man (cf. 5.27), and the historical enactment by Jesus of the role of the Son of Man means that he who above all is non-judgemental[15] inevitably conveys divine judgement.[16] This critical function, however, serves to identify those who do what is true and come to the light: those whose deeds are wrought in God. Living 'in God', they are part of the life of the Son of Man – for ever (cf. 5.25–9). Indeed, the Son of Man tradition is linked with an explicit model of the resurrection of the faithful to life and the resurrection of evil-doers to death (5.27–9). Thus the 'sending of the Son' and the 'lifting up of the Son of man' unite in expressing the *crisis* for all creation: they are the critical enactment of the Father's word for his creatures (cf. 8.28).

(*iii*) *Bread*

So far, we have spoken of life, eternal life, resurrection, light, love and judgement. The theme of 'bread' adds another factor – the receiving of divine resource: 'Truly, truly, I say to you, unless you eat the flesh of the Son of man and drink his blood, you have no life in you; he who eats my flesh and drinks my blood has eternal life, and I will raise him up at the last day' (6.53–4). Let us assume that these verses are part of a unified discourse, not a mere interpolation.[17] They stand at the climax of a discourse that began with the feeding of the multitudes (6.1–14). This was presented as a sign (6.14). The narrative has therefore something of the parabolic about it. It is an iconic representation of the meaning of the subsequent discourse,[18] on the manna or bread from heaven (6.31–5), and at the same time an introduction to it. The rhetorical practice of John ensures that, in the course of dialogue, the misunderstandings of the audience contribute to a clarification of meaning. Thus, to look to Jesus merely for the loaves he was distributing to them is to miss the 'sign'. What is 'significant' is not 'the food which perishes' but 'the food which endures to eternal life' (6.27). This is the gift which the Son of Man bestows. Properly understood, manna was a heavenly gift, not simply the gift of Moses (6.32). God – 'my Father' – is the source of the bread that gives life to the world (6.33).

So far, so good! Now the theme intensifies with its personalization in Jesus: 'I am the bread of life' (6.35). Jesus is both sign and substance. He is God's life-sustaining gift, to be received in faith (6.36). He has 'come down from heaven', to do the will of his Father; and the will of his Father is 'that I should lose nothing of all that he has given me, but raise it up at the last day' (6.39; cf. 6.40). Following John's rhetorical method, objection is made to his claim, partly at least on the grounds of Jesus' personal disqualifications (6.41–2). Jesus' reply emphasizes the need to be 'taught by God' (6.45). It is only through sensitivity to the Father's purpose (cf. 6.44–6) that one can perceive that Jesus is from the Father and offers the bread of life. Here, indeed, is the gift of eternity: not that 'the bread of life' is the 'medicine of immortality',[19] but rather that, by receiving God's gift – be it Jesus, or Jesus' teaching, or whatever Jesus offers by way of spiritual succour – one is kept by him and raised up at the last day (6.39–40). Jesus in fact offers all he has – his flesh – for the life of the world (6.51).

Objection is registered again (6.52): to 'give us his flesh to eat' is truly a hard saying. In the dialogue, Jesus reintroduces the Son of Man at this point (6.53). The statement now refers to eating the flesh of the Son of Man and drinking his blood – although the subsequent statement has 'my flesh' and 'my blood'. Nevertheless, as C. K. Barrett has emphasized, the Son of Man is cited here by design.[20] Why? It may be that John was familiar with traditions which connected the Son of Man and the Eucharist. Since the dialogue has now taken on strong eucharistic overtones, it was appropriate to make the Son of Man the focal point of reference.[21] Son of Man also most fittingly expresses the movements of 'descending' and 'ascending' which are essential to the narrative (cf. 3.13–15). Admittedly, the immediate context is concerned with the movement of descent (cf. 6.50): the gift of life from the Father to his people. But 'ascent' is also implied: it is the will of the Father that the faithful be raised up at the last day (6.40). Again, Son of Man, as we have seen above, is a corporate concept: the leading figure is the focus of the community of the saints. Hence, his descent enables the saints to receive his gifts into their beings; thus nurtured, they are raised by him through his ascent (cf. 6.62). Jesus, as Son of Man, is charged to 'lose nothing of all that he has given me' (6.39). Finally, the Son of Man – and Jesus as identified with him – gives himself utterly in his descent from heaven. His self-giving is total: his flesh and his blood. To 'eat and drink' of these is to identify totally with him, to receive his gifts into one's own being and participate in his being as the true Israel (see above p. 120). Through his self-giving and on the cross, the Son of Man is glorified (12.23), and in him God is glorified (13.31).

What then is the relationship between Eucharist and resurrection in John? It may be that the overloading of the symbolic discourse – for this can hardly be denied – stems from John's involvement in eucharistic controversy. The 'plain meal' notion is denied: the concern is not with 'the bread that perishes', but with that 'which endures to eternal life'. The danger is then the over-simplified identification of the Eucharist with 'the medicine of immortality', and the allusiveness and suggestiveness of John's language may be directed to countering this tendency (cf. 6.63). 'Simple' views of the Eucharist, whether in material or spiritual terms, are unacceptable, for the mystery that is celebrated is none other than the mystery of the divine action for the salvation of the *cosmos*. The Eucharist has therefore a transcendent meaning. The heavenly gift is not at the command of ecclesiastical authority or liturgical celebrant. The gift is the Son of Man through whose descent and ascent heaven and earth are reunited in the Kingdom, eternal and universal. The invitation is to 'come' to Jesus and to find security in him (6.37). The interpretation of the Eucharist must centre on the relationship of the believer and the transcendent one: Jesus, Son of Man. It is precisely at this point that the resurrection is essential to eucharistic meaning: 'what if you were to see the Son of man ascending where he was before?' (6.62). The bread Jesus offers is nourishment of the spirit. His words are 'spirit and life' both because they proceed from the Father and because they open the believer, through faith, to the transcendent one (6.63–4).

John has certainly avoided a 'simple'view of the Eucharist. In doing so he has stretched metaphorical discourse to its limits – perhaps even beyond them!

(*iv*) *The temple of his body*

Jesus' saying about the Temple (2.19) and the evangelist's comment on 'the temple of his body' (2.21) are prime examples of the intricate deployment of symbolism characteristic of this Gospel. No attempt can be made here to explore the many strands of what has been called 'one of the cruces of Johannine interpretation'.[22] Attention is focused single-mindedly on the allusiveness and suggestiveness of the images.

'Destroy *this* temple…' is an ironic invitation to his opponents to do precisely what they are in process of doing: 'destroy' suggesting 'invalidate', 'dissolve' or 'bring to an effective end', rather than denoting the physical destruction which, as John's readers knew, was the actual fate of the building in question. 'In three days' – the proverbial expression for a short interval – is evocative both of Scripture and of the resurrection story. The final statement – 'I will raise it up' – clearly refers no longer to the Temple *qua* building (as his incredulous audience supposed) but to its nature as the sanctuary of the divine presence. Hence, Jesus' words are an affirmation that the abolition of the divine presence is not in human hands. The divine power 'tabernacled' in Jesus will ensure that the presence of God is a reality on earth in spite of all human efforts to banish it. The prophetic 'I' indicates the identification of Jesus with this divine operation, not as one who is raised but as the one who embodies the power of resurrection. The thrust of the imagery is thus towards the renewal of the 'tabernacle' of God with humankind. To Jesus' opponents, this was an attack on the Temple itself – although Jesus' talk had been about *their* destruction of it.

Crucial commentary is offered in the statement, 'he spoke of the temple of his body' (2.21). At this point, the tendency of modern critics to cite possible Pauline parallels may obscure rather than illumine.[23] It is important to stay with the Johannine logic, which posits not simply a *double entendre* between Temple and body (as is often stated) but the intrinsic connection between the two. Both Temple and Jesus himself enshrine the presence of God, and both are tested to destruction by the sinfulness of humankind. But the power of God – which as the Logos has 'tabernacled' in the midst of humanity in Jesus and which gives life (cf. 1.4–5) – will bring about the radical renewal of worship (cf. 4.21–6) and the radical reaffirmation of life through death (cf. 11.25–6). The 'raising up' – the reconstitution and renewal – is thus characteristic of the power already evident in Jesus' ministry and manifested above all in the resurrection of Jesus himself (cf. 2.22). Hence, beyond the negative forces expressed in the corruption of the Temple and the death of Jesus, there is the new enshrining of the Spirit. The 'raised' Temple will find its transcendent horizon in God as Spirit (4.24) and in the risen Jesus as Lord (20.28). And the risen Jesus will always be the living testimony to the power which informed his own ministry and which turns death and despair into new life and fulfilment.

2 THE RESURRECTION AS NARRATIVE

The celebrated story of the raising of Lazarus develops the relation between resurrection and life by means of dramatic narrative treatment. The narrative method is designed to secure the participation of the readers, who are indeed addressed directly at certain points.[24] Through this narrative engagement, the readers' own life-concerns are brought into dialogue with the action of the story so that questions of self-understanding, life-stance and ultimate orientation are seen as live issues.[25]

Three perspectives concern us here: rhetorical form, narrative interpretation, and rhetorical function.

(i) Rhetorical form

For the sake of clarity, the basic structure of the story may be illustrated in the following way:

> (a) the problem defined (11.1–3)
> Jesus' first response (11.4–6)
> Jesus' second response (11.7–16)

> (b) the problem redefined (11.17–19)
> Jesus' response to Martha (11.20–27)
> Jesus' response to Mary (11.28–37)

> (c) the problem acutely defined (11.38)
> Jesus' first response (11.39–42)
> Jesus' final response (11.43–44)

(a) The problem defined

The problem comprises the circumstances which precipitate the dramatic action: 'a certain man was ill' (11.1). The place is identified (Bethany), and the *dramatis personae* quickly introduced. Lazarus is the victim. His sisters Martha and Mary are attached both to him and to Jesus; Mary's attachment to Jesus is specifically narrated (11.2). The sisters send an appeal to Jesus (11.3). They expect Jesus to perform the role of helper, presumably as healer. They also cast him in the role of friend by the manner in which they encode the message: 'he whom you love is ill'.

Jesus' first response is to surprise the reader by apparently denying the sisters' contention: 'This illness is not unto death' (11.4). In effect, he outlines an alternative project. The issue is not about securing Lazarus' recovery: it is to demonstrate the glory of God, in consequence of which the Son of God will also be glorified (11.4). Accordingly, he makes no move for two days – almost stretching the reader's credibility. For this reason, the reader is reassured about Jesus' love for the family (11.5). He is not acting out of indifference to them but from a higher motivation.

Jesus' second response is to propose to make the journey to Judaea (11.7): a proposal which triggers well-meant opposition from his disciples (11.8). The issue to which the reader has already been alerted is now re-explored with them. Jesus proceeds by the light of God (11.9–10); hence, he will not stumble in face of danger. In the same light, Lazarus but sleeps: Jesus' purpose is to 'awaken' him (11.11). The disciples' misunderstanding of this statement prompts an explanatory comment for the reader's benefit (11.13) and finally the plain assertion, 'Lazarus is dead' (11.14) – in striking contrast to his first statement, 'This illness is not unto death' (11.4). This paradox is maintained as Jesus affirms that his absence from the scene will in the long run stimulate belief in his disciples (11.15): a restatement of 'it is for the glory of God' (11.4). The disciples' failure to comprehend what Jesus was about serves as a foil to Jesus' action. Jesus speaks of the glory of God; Thomas speaks of all of them dying together (11.16) – the presumed fate of Lazarus will apply to the whole group!

(b) The problem redefined

The story returns to Bethany, but Lazarus is now dead and has been in the tomb four days (11.17). Mourners have come from nearby Jerusalem to console the sisters on their loss (11.19). The scene is one of deep grief.

Jesus' response to Martha. There is a hint of reproach in her statement, 'Lord, if you had been here, my brother would not have died' (11.21). But the reproach that Jesus had not come as healer is tempered by her continuing faith in Jesus and his power as helper (11.22). There is a neat little exchange in which Jesus speaks words of conventional assurance, though with a deeper purpose: 'Your brother will rise again' (11.23). Martha indicates that she accepts the widely held view of the final resurrection of the righteous, among whom her brother is numbered (11.24). But the implication is that Jesus can give more help than this. The clue lies in Martha's next response to Jesus (11.27). To believe in Jesus as Messiah is to accept that the powers of the new age are already at work in him, demonstrating the power of life over against the seeming finality of physical death and unveiling the reality of eternal life. 'I am the resurrection and the life...' (11.25). This is 'the word of resurrection' and Jesus is its bearer. Thus the role of Jesus, first raised in 11.3 (see p. 124), is clarified in 11.27.

Jesus' response to Mary. The second encounter – in this case between Jesus and Mary, together with those who followed her from the scene of mourning (11.28–31) – begins in similar fashion (11.32), and thus emphasizes the problem of Jesus' absence. Physical death has not been prevented. Emotions predominate and are reflected in the mourning and weeping: sorrow, distress, even a hint of anger or outrage on Jesus' part (11.33). Jesus participates in the human anguish (11.35) and thus fulfils the role of friend (11.36). The observers – 'the Jews' are like a chorus in a Greek play – comment on his evident love for Lazarus or suggest that he might have tried to prevent Lazarus' death (11.36).

This whole section stands in sharp contrast to 11.4, where the reader was assured that Lazarus' illness was not unto death (!) and that the glory of God would be demonstrated. But before the glory comes the anguish at the tomb (11.34–5). This element is not obviated in Christian perspective; but the expectation of an ultimate reversal or transformation of the situation is keen.

(c) The problem acutely defined

The action now takes place at the cave-tomb, sealed with a stone (11.38). Is there anything further to be said? There is a finality about the situation that is hard to deny.

Jesus' first response is to command that the stone be removed (11.39). Martha's consternation is great: after four days, decomposition would have set in. The natural process is irreversible. There is no hope of physical recovery. Jesus directs attention to the dimension of faith and to the glory of God: 'Did I not tell you that if you would believe you would see the glory of God?' (11.40). In the story, Jesus had not spoken in these terms to Martha: the words seemed addressed to the reader (11.4). Similarly, his reply to Martha is addressed to the reader also, who is thereby reminded of Jesus' original declaration. The stone is removed (11.41). The suspense increases as Jesus prays to the Father who has 'heard' him as always. The prayer centres attention on the power of God, on the Father–Son relation, and on the story as a sign or testimony prompting faith in Jesus' mission.

Jesus' final response is to utter the great command, 'Lazarus, come out' (11.43), like the voice of God on the day of judgement. Lazarus comes out, complete with bandages (*keiriai*) and face cloth (*soudarion*). 'Unbind him, and let him go' (11.44). There is no significant follow-up to the action of the story, no human-interest angle on Lazarus. The story itself is the sign.

The rhetorical form resembles a drama in three acts. The plot takes us from the situation of distress, through a period when most of the characters are bemused and when the human situation is one of deep grief, to the glorious outcome of faith in Jesus, who is himself the resurrection and the life. The story is thus a dramatic presentation of 'the word of resurrection' given by the Christ. It is to be received in faith, but faith does not sidestep the abyss of anxiety, grief, fear and anger which the death of a loved one involves. The narrative portrays such elements impressively, but the form also has its limitations.[26] To dramatize the raising of Lazarus takes the story into a bold but crude portrayal of resurrection. It could be misconstrued as the resuscitation of a corpse: untrue to human experience and a caricature of resurrection faith. If, however, it is taken as a dramatic enactment in narrative of the resurrection of the faithful in the end time (cf. 11.24–6), then it is – as it claims to be – a celebration of the glory of God and of messianic faith.

(ii) Narrative interpretation

Narratives are constructed to engage the hearer – or the reader, in the case of written narratives. They open up the situation and develop the action, or plot, in such a way that the hearer/reader is brought to participate in the narrative. Stories may be told simply for entertainment; perhaps, like the bedtime story, to create a pleasant, enchanting atmosphere in which the hearer may drop off to sleep. But stories may have a deeper significance (this may be true even of bedtime stories). They may, in effect, present a situation or an action which engages the hearer's life-concern. They may pose sharply questions of personal identity and being: for example, Who am I? How do I relate to others? How am I to face my present dilemma? How am I to deal with the threats to my own being – in short, with my own mortality? Narrative interpretation operates at the point where the story that is narrated intersects with the story of the hearer's own life and provokes change in the hearer's self-understanding and action.

The Lazarus narrative, being structured as we have seen in three parts, invites progressive interpretation in three stages.

First, there is the situation triggered by the illness of the victim and the appeal of his sisters for help. The human appeal is for the survival of the victim. It is a life-threatening situation, touching the roots of the human condition. Jesus' inaction is a surprise – the more so because of his love for the family – and suggests that the perspective in which the women see the problem at this stage is inadequate. The human longing for this-worldly survival leads finally to defeat. Life contains an element of threat: by going into Judaea, Jesus himself is at risk. Ultimately, the threat to life has to be accepted and seen in the perspective of the glory of God (11.4). The hearer is fascinated, for the theme strikes a chord in the depths of human existence. The healing that preserves mortal life is not guaranteed. Is there then an alternative to despair? How does one live and die in the perspective of God's glory?

Next, there is the double encounter at Bethany. Martha and Mary present the appeal of troubled faith, tinged with a suggestion of reproach or disappointment. Jesus had not brought about the healing they had hoped for. Their beloved brother was dead. Here is all the anguish of human loss, bewilderment, even resentment and criticism, which is expressed in cruder form by 'the Jews' (11.37). In this testing situation, one searches deeply for a faith that sustains. In Martha's case, there was a general belief in the final resurrection of the just and a particular trust in Jesus to help even in the present extremity (11.22–7). The reader has empathy with Martha in this 'limit situation': the point at which human resources are inadequate. One hears the word of Jesus, 'I am the resurrection and the life...'; and his question, 'Do you believe this?' (11.26).

Finally, there is the climactic narrative of the raising of Lazarus, which combines the crude horror of death – the realistic description of the cave-tomb (11.38–44); Martha's exclamation about the state of the body after four days (11.39) – with the graphic, unprecedented account of the raising of the corpse (11.43–4). The dilemma for readers lies in the tension between the crude realism of the story and its parabolic intent. The crudity underlines the reality of death, with which readers can readily identify. It is also clearly intended to demonstrate the reality of resurrection. Yet here readers, as has been suggested above, may find difficulty, not only with the unprecedented nature of the story, for which they have no analogue in experience, but also with the inherent contradiction in the crude imagery. The contradiction is seen in two statements attributed to Jesus: 'This illness is not unto death' (11.4) and 'Lazarus is dead' (11.14). In other words, 'death' has a double meaning. A crudely literal interpretation of the story – the level at which the disciples tend to operate, at least initially – ignores this factor and describes the resuscitation of a corpse. Lazarus is restored to human community (12.2), is something of a curiosity (12.9) or sensation (12.17), and is subject to death or to life-threatening hostility (12.10). Thereafter, we hear of him no more. The parable, however, relates to 'the glory of God' (11.40; cf. 11.4). It invites readers to discern in the story not the temporary resuscitation of a dead person but Jesus as 'the resurrection and the life' (11.25). Apart from its parabolic aspect, the story would not in the end impinge on the reader's existence. But parabolically it suggests the possibility of eternal life through faith. It suggests that though believers die yet shall they live. Eternal life is life, in faith and in God; not avoiding but transcending death, in fellowship with Jesus, to the glory of God. 'Do you believe this?' Jesus asks the reader. If the answer is positive, then one must live 'to the glory of God'. The narrative is transformative. It issues in transformed praxis. Faith and action interrelate. Indeed, the story explicitly focuses attention on the pivotal position of Jesus as Son of God (cf. 11.4, 41), and on the formation of a community of faith ('that you may believe', 11.15) to express and sustain praxis.

(iii) Rhetorical function

The story of Lazarus serves an important function in the Fourth Gospel. That function is expressed through its integration with the onward sweep of the story of Jesus' ministry. Lazarus is restored to table fellowship (12.2) and for a brief period is something of a celebrity (12.9, 17). He is a sign to some that the power manifested in Jesus will ultimately prevail (12.19); to others that he must be stopped at all costs, for an outbreak of religious fervour in the Judaean situation could have serious political consequences (11.48). But the main contribution of the story is at a deeper level.

Caiaphas unconsciously articulates its deeper significance. John shares with his readers the irony of a prophetic pronouncement from the high priest in office that Jesus should die for the nation and thus 'gather into one the children of God who are scattered abroad' (11.51–2). The irony does not lie solely in the high priest's utterance. It lies also in the fact that Jesus – 'the resurrection and the life' – must die. The helper must become victim. The raising of Lazarus has anticipated the resurrection of the faithful at the last day (cf. 11.24) through the performance which Jesus himself gives to the final age (cf. 11.25). That performance is complete only when Jesus has demonstrated the power of resurrection in his own person and through his own death. As it is through human suffering and death that the nature of existence is manifested (see above, pp. 6–7), so it is through suffering and death that the new age is born.

Hence the story of Lazarus is an encoding of the meaning of the Gospel. It is, however, important to identify what is encoded and what is not. A useful illustration – and a suggestive decoding – lies in its correlation with the resurrection narratives at the end of the Gospel.

The story of Lazarus focuses on a tomb (*mnemeion*, 11.38), as does the account of Jesus' burial (19.41; 20.1), and it is sealed with a stone (*lithos*, 11.38; 20.1). The high-point of the drama of the Lazarus story is the appearance of the figure bound hand and foot with grave-clothes (*keiriai*), his face wrapped in a napkin (*soudarion*, 11.44). The narrative of Jesus' entombment is not an exact replica. It describes in detail the services performed by Joseph and Nicodemus (19.38–42), including binding the body in linen cloths.[27] The napkin (*soudarion*) for the face is also specifically mentioned (20.7), but Jesus is not seen to emerge from the tomb. Deep grief is registered in both stories, especially by women (11.19) and particularly by Mary (11.31; 20.11,13,15). Other differences, however, are noteworthy. Jesus' tomb is new and unused (19.41) – suggesting an unsullied resting-place and also one where there was no possibility of being unable to identify the body. Mary's role is also different. In the Lazarus story, she laments the death of her brother (11.32–3). In the case of Jesus, her grief is focused on the fact that the corpse is not to be found: the last remaining vestige of her Lord has been taken away from her (20.2,13,15). The fact of the empty tomb, so far from being a comfort, is an outrage to her. Even to have his body in the tomb would have been a grain of comfort. Mary wants only to recover the body and take it away, presumably for reverential purposes. Here is the dilemma of Jesus' followers. They are faced with his total absence: a few linen cloths and a napkin, the pathetic relics of the living reality they had known.

The apparent absence of Jesus is a condition well known to readers. The continuing story therefore engages their interest all the more. By a kind of cumulative process, each stage marked by her pathetic search for Jesus (20.13,15), Mary rediscovers the living presence of Jesus: or, to put it more accurately, it is Jesus who encounters her (20.16). The element of surprise is total. Mary is not to repossess the beloved object (20.17). When she has recognized Jesus as a living presence – 'Rabboni' (20.16) – the empty tomb is no longer important: her attention is on the 'now' of the encounter. Nevertheless, she would touch him (20.17), longing to keep him within her grasp. But Jesus is about to ascend to heaven. The language of transcendence indicates that he transcends the tactile world and may not be detained within it. The absence of her beloved Lord is now to be thought of not as occasioned by his death but by his glory. She must learn to live as in the presence of Jesus, who has transformed her world by appearing to her. She has a joyful testimony to bear: 'I have seen the Lord' (20.18).

In spite of correspondences, it is the contrast between Lazarus and the risen Jesus that is striking. Lazarus was restored to human life: to table-fellowship and to discipleship. He was restored to *mortal* life and lived under the threat of death (12.10). His story may therefore be interpreted as an extension of the traditional healing model, as in the raising of

Jairus' daughter and the widow's son at Nain.[28] Its parabolic nature, however, prompts the reader to discern a deeper problem. The episode reveals the glory of God and of the Son (11.40). How is the glory of God to be revealed in the death of the Son himself? If Jesus is to be sacrificed (11.49–53), who will call him from the tomb? And to what kind of life will he be called? The implied answer is that he is raised by God but not to a resumption of mortal life. His resurrection is *not* a resuscitation, and if he is given back to his own he also transcends them. He stands among his disciples as crucified and risen, imparting his peace (*shalom*, 20.19,21,26), commissioning them (20.21) and conveying the Holy Spirit to them (20.22). The crucified one is thus a transcendent figure, not specifically delimited or hindered by physical barriers (20.19,26), but incontrovertibly *real*: as 'real' as the tactile world, yet not of it. Such, at any rate, is a reasonable deduction from the Thomas episode (20.24–8). Essentially, Jesus' reality is discerned by faith rather than sight (20.29).

The final chapter of John, which is readily identified as an appendix, does not add materially to what has already been said. It has to do with revelations of the risen Jesus to his disciples in connection with mission (21.1–3). The story of the miraculous catch, which partly reflects a tradition inserted by Luke in relation to the calling of the disciples (see above, pp. 99–100), is related here to the world mission of the Church. Apart from Jesus, the disciples will have no success. In fellowship with him, the harvest will be immense. The realization of the catch coincides with their recognition of Jesus (21.7). The climax of the episode is the renewal of table-fellowship by the lakeside in Galilee. The elements are bread and fish: doubtless, the mainstay of fellowship meals in the Galilean tradition.[29] But while this 'third' appearance – the editor likes to enumerate – is concerned with the launching or renewal of mission, it also suggests that fellowship with Jesus was recovered in the midst of the common life of the disciple group. It reasserted itself, according to this tradition, in the course of a half-hearted return to former routines. The work itself became a parable of their life-situation and, in the best tradition of Jesus' teaching, led to a disclosure of the new relationship between themselves and the Lord, as well as new possibilities of mission in his name.

Two traditions are appended to this 'third' appearance. One focuses on Peter: on his love for the Lord and on his pastoral ministry (21.15–17). It is accompanied by a logion which contrasts the wilfulness of his youth with the obedience unto death which will characterize his later years (13.18–19). Once more, the concentration is on the call to discipleship: 'Follow me'. The second relates to the fate of the beloved disciple (21.20–3). Here again, in spite of rumours current in the Christian community to the effect that this disciple would live until the return of Christ, the command was simply to concentrate on discipleship, leaving all else in the Lord's keeping.

In short, while the Lazarus narrative is designed as a special manifestation of the glory of God in the Son and anticipates the final resurrection of the faithful, the resurrection narratives relate to the divine act of God for the salvation of his creation. Henceforth, Christ is transcendent. The calling of the disciples is to serve the transcendent one in faith and obedience through suffering and death until the great harvest (12.24).

How are readers to respond to the appearance of the risen Jesus to the disciples? In so far as they identify with the Church, they can receive Jesus' blessing, share the gift of the Spirit and find reassurance through the forgiveness of sins (20.19,21–3). But the hub of the narrative is recognition (20.20), and it is this aspect which receives extended expression in the Thomas episode (20.24–9). The resolution of Thomas's uncertainty comes in the confession, 'My Lord and my God!' (20.28). Implicitly, the reader is challenged to make a similar response and is expressly included in the closing comment: 'Blessed are those who have not seen and yet believe' (20.29). The final resolution of the human predicament is found through faith in Jesus.

Faith, however, is fostered through community and expressed in praxis. If the appendix (ch. 21) has a single purpose, it is to make this clear to the reader. Jesus meets the disciples in the context of their everyday world, which provides the material of parable (21.3–11); and his invitation is to share a meal together (breakfast – the meal which his followers could have together before work began, although here it occurs after a night's labour). It is in table-fellowship – in the interrelatedness and interdependence of human community – that Jesus' presence is celebrated. And from this togetherness there emerges praxis: 'Follow me' (21.19). Readers must decide whether they see themselves as part of Peter's flock or whether they share in pastoral ministry itself as part of the call to discipleship (21.15–19). They are certainly invited to note the witness which the beloved disciple bears and to say, 'we know that his testimony is true' (21.24). The meaning of Jesus is indeed inexhaustible (21.25); but those who take the apostolic testimony to heart know him as living and transcendent reality: the resurrection and the life (11.25); 'My Lord and my God' (20.28).

3 A DIALOGUE WITH DISCIPLES

The 'farewell discourse' in the Fourth Gospel contains many elements of dialogue, including the celebrated example in chapter 14. This focuses not only on the symbols of the way, the truth and the life but also on mutual indwelling. Here, the Johannine art of involving the reader is particularly effective. Jesus is ostensibly in dialogue with his disciples; in effect, he is in dialogue with the reader.

'Let not your hearts be troubled ... ' The initial exhortation recalls the oracle of salvation in prophetic discourse, with its reassuring 'fear not'.[30] The ground of reassurance is found in faith in God and Christ (14.1b). The reason for the confidence lies in Christ's work in preparing a place for the believer in the Father's house (14.2–3). The reference is eschatological, the metaphor familiar: a house to accommodate many.[31]

The demand for further clarification – not least, in the reader's interest – comes from Thomas: 'Lord, we do not know where you are going; how can we know the way?' (14.5). The answer lies in understanding Jesus as the embodiment of 'the way', of reality ('the truth') and 'life' (14.6). He himself is the access to the Father. In him the Father is made manifest (14.7).

Philip now presses the reader's question: 'Lord, show us the Father...' (14.8). It is an implicit admission of imperception; but though it earns a rebuke (14.9), it furthers the dialogue. The revelation of the Father comes through the indwelling of Father and Son: hence the Father is discerned in Jesus' words and works (14.10–11). The mutual indwelling, however, includes the believing, obedient community (14.12–17), in whom the Spirit of truth dwells.[32] The disciples are therefore not to be left 'orphaned' (14.18). They will 'see' Jesus, although the world will not (14.19).

This is the cue for Judas (not Iscariot) to query the distinction between the believing community and the world (14.22). The answer reaches the heart of mutual indwelling and its essential expression in the praxis of love and obedience (14.23–4). Hence, 'the world' cannot receive the indwelling Spirit (cf. 14.26), for his coming presupposes a receptive and recollecting community (14.26) on whom Christ's benediction rests (14.27). But what is the connection between Jesus and the Spirit?

Jesus is about to be taken from his disciples: indeed, it is to their advantage that he goes away (16.7). The truth is incarnate in Jesus (14.16): it dwells in him, and he in it. After his departure, the Spirit of truth will dwell in the faithful. In this sense, they will not be left 'orphaned' (14.18). They will be enriched 'in spirit and in truth'. Hence, the believer will do even greater works after Jesus' physical removal from the earthly scene (cf. 14.12).

From the disciples' viewpoint, therefore, the Spirit comes in succession to the Jesus whom they knew. He proceeds from the Father (15.26), 'in my name' (14.26) and at Jesus' intercession (14.16). But the mutual indwelling is such that Jesus can also say, 'I will send him to you' (16.7). In the later resurrection story (20.19–23), which stands in close relation to this discussion, Jesus enacts the bestowal of the Holy Spirit by breathing on them (20.22).[33]

The Spirit is both differentiated from Jesus and closely related to him. The Spirit will be with the faithful, dwelling within them for ever (14.16–17). He will actively promote their understanding of the truth (16.13) and call to remembrance 'all that I have said to you' (14.26). Indeed, the interaction with the Son is extremely close. The Spirit glorifies the Son, 'for he will take what is mine and declare it to you' (16.14): a project which is possible because of the mutual indwelling of Father, Son and Spirit. The Spirit bears witness to the Son, as the disciples bear witness to Jesus from their experience of his ministry (15.26–7); hence the circle of indwelling embraces the disciples also. There is therefore a sharp differentiation between the world and the community of the Spirit. In 'yet a little while', Jesus says, the world will see him no more – 'but you will see me' (14.19). They will see him because they participate in the deeper level of reality to which the world is blind but to which the eyes of the disciples have been opened: the level of reality denoted in the Fourth Gospel by the term 'life'. It is characterized by what we may term an interactive indwelling: 'I am in my Father, and you in me, and I in you' (14.20). It is a community of love and obedience. Those who thus love the Son enjoy the Father's love and that of the Son (14.21). And it is this loving spiritual community which provides the context for the manifestation of Jesus himself after his physical presence is withdrawn from them (14.21b).[34]

Arguably, therefore, John has provided a clue to the interpretation of the appearances of the risen Christ.[35] If the manifestation of Jesus after his death (14.21) is linked to the resurrection, it is given to a community which felt itself orphaned but had deep love for Christ. That love can be seen in Mary's pathetic search for the body, as in Peter's joyous recognition of Jesus by the lakeside. Renan was not altogether wrong when he pointed to the 'divine power of love' as a factor in the resurrection faith, but he betrays the shallowness of his romantic interpretation when he goes on to claim that 'the passion of one possessed gave to the world a resuscitated God'.[36] The Fourth Gospel, though not ruling out the place of human imagination, points to the operation of the Spirit in the context of love. It is possible, therefore, to hold that the Spirit who 'dwells with you' (14.17) and can 'take what is mine and declare it to you' (16.14) is the channel by which the risen Jesus appeared to his disciples. And beyond these special manifestations, the transcendent Jesus who has gone to the Father also comes to the faithful as Lord through that Spirit which creates community in heaven and on earth and offers to them an abiding fellowship: 'Abide in me, and I in you. As the branch cannot bear fruit by itself, unless it abides in the vine, neither can you, unless you abide in me' (15.4).

1 i.e., they draw the hearer into a realm of discourse which transcends 'the flesh' and makes one open to the working of the Spirit and to 'the real' or ultimate dimension of being: cf. 2 Cor. 3.6–8; also 1 Pet. 3.18; 1 Cor. 15.45. Jesus' words therefore reflect the power and reality of God himself – veritable acts of God (cf. John 14.10); cf. Broer (1987).
2 Macgregor (1928), p. 81.
3 The place John gives to confessional and christological formulae tends to highlight the propositional element (cf. 3.15), but one should not overlook the fact that his standpoint is primarily relational.
4 cf. Smalley (1968–9), pp. 287–9; Black (1954), p. 85. The Greek preposition *epi* with the accusative expresses motion 'up to' or 'towards', with a hint of purpose (cf. the Aramaic '*al*), but in this sentence it is collocated with the participle 'descending' as well as 'ascending'. Hence the notion of 'up to' expresses the exaltation of the Son of Man, but not exclusively his elevation to heaven; cf. the Spirit 'descending' upon Jesus at baptism.
5 cf. Michaels (1966–67).
6 This is to take 'Son of God' in its basic sense.
7 cf. chapter 1 and the centrality of suffering in the post-exilic world-view and in apocalyptic.
8 cf. Smalley (1968–9), p. 289.
9 cf. Dodd (1954), p. 245 n.1.

10 The LXX of Gen. 28.12 is clear that the prepositional phrase refers to the ladder, not to Jacob; cf. Smalley (1968–9), p. 288. The concept of the angels ascending and descending 'upon him' is hard to clarify. The Markan concept (cf. 8.38 par.) is more readily grasped.

11 Here, *epi* with the accusative is taken to indicate direction: perhaps translating the Aramaic '*al*', 'to' or 'towards': cf. Smalley (1968–9); Black, (1954), p. 85. It is difficult to take seriously the suggestion that the Son of Man is at the top of the ladder (Robinson (1957), p. 168, n.1), since the phrase is collocated with 'descending' (*katabainontas*) rather than with 'ascending'.

12 Smalley (1968–9), p. 290.

13 The worship of the brazen serpent was known in Hezekiah's time; cf. 2 Kings 18.4. In Num. 21.4–9, the action seems to reflect sympathetic magic, but has a prophetic purpose: the cure comes from Yahweh. Cf. also Wisd. 16.5–7

14 cf. O'Collins (1987), pp. 188–200.

15 The non-judgemental aspect probably represents the humanity of the figure. In Heb. 2.14–18; 4.15, his intercessory function has the same effect. The story of Jesus and the woman taken in adultery (textual problems apart) is the acme of this understanding (7.53—8.11).

16 The Son of Man passes from the role of defendant to that of judge in the course of his ministry – above all, in the context of suffering and trial; cf. Moule (1967), pp. 82–99.

17 Bultmann (1971) ascribes John 6.51–8 to the work of the redactor; Brown (1966), p. 286, ascribed them to an alternative strand of tradition; Bornkamm (1968) takes them as an insertion. These positions, along with others, are reviewed by Barrett (1982), pp. 37–9.

18 cf. Nida (1960), p. 66.

19 Bultmann (1971), p. 219; cf. Ignatius, *Eph.* 20.2; for a critique, cf. Barrett (1982), pp. 43–4. As Barrett observes, it cannot be the Eucharist that imparts eternal life, for 'the eater still has to be raised up at the last day' (p. 43).

20 Barrett (1982), pp. 40–9.

21 ibid., pp. 47–8.

22 Macgregor ([11]1953) p. 59. In particular, diachronic exegesis tends to understand the reference to the body of Jesus as 'a post-resurrectional amplification', Brown (1966), p. 123; Bultmann (1971), p. 126. For holistic exegesis, attention focuses much more directly on the final form of the statement.

23 Barrett observes that the body which is raised up cannot be identified with the Church, in spite of the varied Pauline usages (e.g., Rom. 12.5; 1 Cor. 12.12–27; Col. 1.18, 24; Eph. 1.23). At most, a secondary reference can be posited: cf. Barrett (1978), p. 201. In this connection it is instructive to compare 2 Cor. 5.1–10 and Mark 14.58. The image of temple is related to life after death in 2 Cor. 5.1–10, and to the indwelling of the Holy Spirit in 1 Cor. 3.16; 6.19. In Philo, man is the temple of the Logos; cf. Barrett, ibid. What is essential is that Johannine logic is followed closely. The general connotation is hardly in dispute.

24 11.13 is an obvious comment to the reader; other passages invite the reader's response: for example, through the reader's identification with the disciples, or Jesus' question, 'Do you believe this?' (11.26).

25 Auerbach (1957) spoke of the text presenting the reader with the real world – indeed, the only real world: its claim is autocratic. Frei also (1974) understands biblical narrative in an autonomous and self-referential way: it not only presents a world but a person (Jesus Christ), declaring who he really

is. Existential interpretation and reader-response criticism emphasize the dialogue between reader and text, or encountering the text. Ricoeur speaks of the 'post-critical moment': the culmination of the hermeneutical process regarded as response to the 'witness' of the text: cf. Mudge's comment in Ricoeur (1981), pp. 1–40, and Ricoeur's reply, ibid., pp. 41–5.

26 In particular, the happy outcome might strike a false note: it is valid only in so far as it dramatizes the truth of the resurrection.

27 *othonia*, not *keriai*: cf. 19.40; 20.5–7. Although there are suggestive parallels with the burial of Jesus, the parallelism is not complete.

28 1 Kings 17 and 2 Kings 4 are also important. G. Rochais comments: '*A la base de notre récit il y a une prédication sur la messianité de Jesus et une catéchèse sur la résurrection generale* [Behind our narrative there is a sermon on the messiahship of Jesus and a catechetical lesson on the general resurrection]', Rochais (1981), p. 133; cf. his entire treatment of the subject, ibid., pp. 113–46.

29 cf. Cullmann (1953), p. 15.

30 cf. Isa. 41.10a, 13b; McDonald (1980), pp. 13–14; Westermann (1967), pp. 203–5.

31 The many *monai* ('abodes', 'homes') suggest room for all in the immediate presence of God (cf. 14.23). The Vulgate has *mansiones* ('mansions', AV), suggesting a hospice on the pilgrim's way; but it is doubtful if this reflects the intended sense.

32 'In relation to Christ the Spirit is "another Helper", in all respects Christ's own *alter ego*', Macgregor (1928), p. 309.

33 cf. *ruach* (Heb. 'breath' or 'spirit'): in later controversy, the *Filioque* clause in the Creed gave expression to the notion that the Spirit proceeds also from the Son.

34 The importance of the withdrawal or absence of Jesus is underlined, cf. 16.7. When Jesus' physical presence is removed, he will 'manifest' himself to his disciples in the loving fellowship and the Spirit will lead them into truth.

35 Meanings coalesce in John: the divine presence can be interpreted in terms of *parousia*, Spirit, 'mutual indwelling' and resurrection.

36 Renan (1897), p. 272.

7

Conclusion

Space permits only the briefest closing review of issues raised in the main chapters of this book. The arguments will not be re-presented here, but there may be point in drawing together some of the threads which have run through the previous discussion.

Observations are divided into two broad sections. In the first, a range of questions is set out to encourage reflection on the overall problem of handling the theme of resurrection in the New Testament. In the second, a few particular problems are addressed.

1 A RANGE OF QUESTIONS

The range of questions raised by the resurrection of Jesus is very wide. To comprehend the most important in a brief review, five are selected for comment: genre, history, eschatology, theology and praxis.

(i) *Genre*

A variety of genres is used to convey the meaning and truth of the resurrection: for example, confessional formula, sermon, dialogue, apocalyptic vision and narrative. Each genre engages the reader in a different way. The confessional formula invites belief in the sense of assent and commitment: to confess the resurrection of Jesus is tantamount to making the basic confession of Jesus as Lord (cf. Rom. 10.9; Acts 10.36). The sermon presents the Word of God: the resurrection of Jesus is presented as God's vindication of him as Saviour and Judge; hence, the call to decision, faith and baptism (cf. Acts 2.24, 31–39; 10.39–43). Dialogues explore meaning and truth, which are hammered out in tension with misconception or untruth: the radical statements which Paul makes in 1 Corinthians 15 – for example, in relation to the distinction between the physical and corporeal – are elicited through engagement with (and an element of concession to) his Greek opponents. Apocalyptic vision is an accepted form for expressing transcendence and invites the reader to relate to the ultimate scenario.

Narrative is the most extensively used. There is a story to be told or projected. The basic story is that of Jesus himself: an interpreted story, blending history and imagination. Its genius lies not in its recital of 'facts' – Jesus' enemies knew such 'facts' and rejected him. It lies in its invitation to 'see' Jesus through imaginative faith: 'see' him as Messiah, Lord, God with us... Resurrection stories both comprise and invite such imaginative engagement. Jesus is seen as 'God with us' in life and death

136

– and beyond death. The reader is invited to 'see' Jesus as the resurrection and the life, to 'rise' with him from death to new life, and to accept the paradox that the believer, even though he dies, yet shall he live…

It is important not to create generic confusion. Narrative is not history, though it may be historically significant. Both narrative and history are concerned with truth.

(*ii*) *History*

History is always mediated through sources, some of which may be narrative. It is arrived at through critical reflection and is therefore relative to the historian. The end product is a critical understanding of the past, but one subject to debate and correction, and so by no means free of controversy. On any but an eccentric or specifically ideological interpretation, Jesus is a historical figure.

History is concerned with causes, purpose and policy, motivation and goal. It takes account of the 'inside' as well as the 'outside' of events. Hence the historian is interested, for example, in the dynamics of Jesus' ministry. To be sure, he or she would set this in a relative context: 'Jesus believed that…' Jesus' self-understanding is a proper part of historical investigation. But historical debate also raises issues which go beyond the historian's remit: for example, the truth claims inherent in Jesus' ministry; the reality of the Kingdom. The 'inside' of the event passes into the realm of theology or philosophy.

The historical faith-communities which comprised the early Christian Church stood in both an external and an internal relation to Jesus. Externally, they stood in succession to the disciple-community round Jesus, the disciples representing a measure of continuity in the absence of Jesus. Internally, there was the strongest bond with Jesus; a bond different in kind from a simple continuation of Jesus' faith, for Jesus himself – crucified and risen – was focal to it. The historian once more relativizes and speaks of the *belief* of the early Church. The validation of the truth claims lies beyond the historian's remit. A similar analysis can be made of the experience of the individual believer.

History can be interpreted as a process in which new developments are born out of older stages. The emergence of the Christian Church from Judaism is a matter for historical study: indeed, the history of religions is concerned with this kind of issue. And within this realm of discourse, it is a historical judgement that belief in the risen Jesus as Lord and Messiah (Acts 2.36) marked the effective bifurcation of the traditions. This belief had, of course, major historical effects: for example, Christian mission as the in-gathering of Israel, world mission as the mark of the age of fulfilment. Many resurrection experiences were connected with a divine commission to participate in the new age; the prime example being that of Paul himself. And community life reflected a similar awareness.

The most that can be expected of historians is that in the pursuit of their method they show an *openness* to the validity of the faith professed.

The further interpretation of that faith is the work of theology. When theologians, however, interpret history theologically (as they have every right to do), their statements are described as 'meta-historical': that is, history interpreted metaphysically. Examples include 'God's mighty acts in history', 'an act of divine intervention', and 'the Christ event'. To speak of the resurrection of Jesus as a historical event is to use the category of meta-history.

(*iii*) *Eschatology*

The resurrection is to be classified as meta-history if only because it has an eschatological dimension. The language and concept of resurrection are derived, as we have seen, from Jewish eschatological discourse. The resurrection of Jesus is not simply a phenomenon of this world: it is a cosmic event. It is the 'first fruits' of the final age. It is the new creation, the reversal of the dispensation of Adam (1 Cor. 15.22–3). The crucified-and-risen Christ embodies and heads the renewed cosmos. For historical existence, therefore, he presents the ultimate demand and invitation; and, inevitably, he stands over against it as Judge.

There is, therefore, an eschatological perspective on history, which is expressed definitively in Jesus. Human existence is lived out in the 'penultimate' age – the age of 'not yet'; Jesus himself gave this-worldly expression to ultimate reality – for example, in his performance or living out of the Kingdom. By his resurrection-and-ascension, his divine sovereignty is established and the final destiny of the cosmos made manifest (cf. 1 Cor. 15.24–6).

(*iv*) *Theology*

Theologically, the concept of the resurrection of Jesus coheres with that of his ascension, exaltation or glorification, or his session 'at the right hand of God'. It is an affirmation of transcendence and lordship; of cosmic redemption and renewal. It has a triumphalist strain – victory over sin and death. But, above all, it is doxological: it is creation returning to the Creator in love and praise. The resurrection of Jesus is therefore the first-fruits of a great harvest. The believer is identified with him and will rise like him into the life of the new age.

To believe in the risen Jesus is therefore to open oneself to the Transcendent One. It is to open oneself to the power of the new age: the power of healing and forgiveness and renewal. It is to be part of something far wider than one's individual horizon or destiny. It is to be part of the reclaimed humanity which Christ embodied and represented, and therefore to be part of a new solidarity with him: the body of Christ, communal and transcendental. And this solidarity is doxological: living to the glory and praise of God. It is a community of thanksgiving (Eucharist) and service (liturgy), in heaven and on earth.

Yet there was an acute sense in the early Christian communities that Jesus had gone away from them. The Gospels include the heart-rending cries of Mary Magdalene over the absence even of the relics of her beloved Lord. Jesus declares that it is to his disciples' advantage that he goes away (John 16.7). He will be succeeded by the Spirit of truth (or truthful Spirit) who 'dwells with you, and will be in you' (14.17), and who 'will take what is mine and declare it to you' (16.14). The Spirit therefore is the means by which the transcendent becomes immanent for us and in us. He is the means by which the transcendent Father and Son are brought within our apprehension as accessible living presence. But the context required for the resolution of this paradox of transcendence and immanence, of absence and presence, is doxological: namely, the community of praise, the fellowship made open and sensitive to the working of God, the solidarity of devotion and service.

(v) *Praxis*

Through the mediation of the Spirit, the risen Jesus finds historical expression in his 'body'. Christian existence, grounded in community, faces two ways: to the transcendent and to action in the world. The two are brought into dynamic interaction within the fellowship of the Spirit. Thus there emerges the dialectic of theology and praxis.

In New Testament terms, the Spirit is not confined purely to personal experience or to introspective spirituality. In John 16.8–11, his operation is described in relation to the world. He will convict the world of its sin in rejecting Jesus; convince it that 'righteousness' comes through the recognition that Jesus, though no longer visible, is with the Father; and judge it, because the worldly power that condemned Jesus now stands condemned by God. Here are Christian perspectives on the world which originate with the cross-and-resurrection and which demonstrate the Spirit as the power which energizes Christian praxis. The resurrection faith is to be lived out in a world alienated from God, from the source of its true being ('righteousness') and thus under God's judgement. It is the dynamic of liberation and renewal, effectively symbolized in baptism, Eucharist and worship, and expressed in the world in terms of witness and invitation. It is the dynamic of God's love which renews the roots of faith and life and makes effective the reality of forgiveness. In the resurrection faith, the organic link between transcendence and immanence is lived out as 'worldly transcendence'. Christian spirituality is indivisibly expressed as love to God and neighbour: we love God in our service to neighbour, and we love our neighbour in our service to God.

The Eucharist may be singled out as the prime example of resurrection faith. Here is the fellowship of thanksgiving which expresses loving response to God and acceptance of one's neighbour. Here, divine self-giving engenders genuine humility in community interaction (John 13.2–11). The accounts of the Last Supper and the Lord's Supper are christologically focused. That is to say, they celebrate and share in the divine action in Christ. The 'body' and 'blood' are the new covenant, the new living relationship with God in Christ which reinforces the *koinonia* or common fellowship of believers and expresses itself in table-fellowship. Here is the complete model of 'worldly transcendence'. The 'recalling' of Jesus' practice informs the eucharistic celebration, and the eucharistic celebration gives expression to Jesus' practice. It is a continuation or re-presentation of the reality to which Jesus gave performance in his own ministry. It is therefore an act of witness, performed in solidarity with Christ for the world for whom he died. It is the action by which the Spirit takes what is Christ's and declares it to the community (cf. John 16.14–15). It is also the action by which the Spirit through the community declares 'the things that are to come' (16.13): the new humanity of which the risen Jesus is the living head.

2 PARTICULAR PROBLEMS

No review of resurrection matters would be complete without reference to two problems in particular: the empty tomb and the appearances of the risen Jesus. These are now considered briefly in relation to the foregoing discussion.

(i) The empty tomb

The narrative nature of the empty tomb traditions is the key to understanding their function. In the narratives, the fact that the tomb was empty is the basic problem. It is not celebrated: notes of joy tend to be secondary (cf. Matt. 28.8). It is disorientating: a nasty shock. The predominant responses are trembling and astonishment, fear, weeping, a sense of loss, disorientation... It does not carry a self-evident meaning for the disciples, who in the Lucan accounts write it off as an idle tale (Luke 24.11) or puzzling report (24.22–4) and who, in the Gospel of John, take no action on the basis of its discovery (cf. John 20.10). It frustrates the feminine urge to lavish devotion on the body. It makes an end, a break with the past.

Two illustrations must suffice. Mark 16.1–8 effects an astonishing closure. The women are so shattered by their experience at the tomb that they do not deliver the message they were expressly told to communicate to the disciples (16.7–8). W. H. Kelber has seen in this the *coup de grace* to the oral tradition stemming from Jesus' disciples.[1] There is not a continuous line, free from disjunction or interruption, linking the disciples' understanding of Jesus' ministry and the rise of the Church of Jesus Christ: hence Mark's tendency to be rather hard on the disciples. Disjunction there clearly is, but Mark's narrative is not so much about failure of oral tradition as the amazing climax to Jesus' ministry, accomplished through the disjunction of death. 'He has risen' takes precedence in Mark over 'he is not here' (16.6). The reality of his risen being will be realized in due course by the disciples in Galilee. Jesus belongs to the future, not the past. Those who, like the devoted women, cling to the past are disorientated and unserviceable.

The haunting tale of Mary Magdalene in John 20.1–18 bears out this interpretation. Her acute anxiety is occasioned by the removal of the body and the impossibility of locating it (20.2, 13, 15). She is not at all helped by the confirmation of this astonishing situation by Simon Peter and the beloved disciple. She is inconsolable, for she cannot attain her heart's desire, which is to take responsibility for the body of Jesus (20.15). She wants to hold on to the remains of the Jesus she knew. Even when she recognizes Jesus, she wants to take hold of him and keep him with her. But this is not possible, for Jesus henceforth belongs to the transcendent realm. He cannot be held on earth; he ascends to the Father (20.17).

The fact that the empty tomb tradition is articulated in narrative allows the narrator the freedom to combine human and divine elements and thus fuse together the 'outside' and the 'inside' meanings. The emptiness of the tomb is the basic presupposition which is not in itself explained, though it is verified. It is presented in narrative in the context of angelic messages – 'he is risen' – and of the appearances of Jesus himself. Thus the inner significance of the absence of Jesus is suggested. Here is the supreme act of God. Henceforth, Jesus will be found among the living, not the dead (Luke 24.5). The foundations of the old order have been shaken: hence Matthew's earthquake, the rending of the veil of the temple and the resurrection of the saints. But if one wants to find Jesus, one must look beyond the tomb – and beyond the past. He leaves no vestige of his physical presence to be venerated or embalmed, or to be the focus of a cult of the tomb. His life belongs to the future, to lived experience and the shaping of history.

If one decodes the story in this way, then the theological interpretation of the resurrection is given both direction and freedom. The corporeal aspect of the risen Jesus finds expression in the concept of 'the body of Christ' in which believers participate, rather than in the notion of a reanimated corpse. Nor is it adequate to cite Jewish beliefs about the nature of the resurrection body as evidence of physical resurrection. Some undoubtedly held such views; others did not. More to the point, perhaps, is that translated or elevated persons – Elijah, Enoch, Moses – leave no relics on earth. Jesus is raised to a new realm of being. That is all we need to know: the rest is commentary.[2]

(ii) The appearances

Narrative is also the vehicle for the transmission and understanding of the appearances of Jesus and governs the reader's understanding of them. The variety of the forms such narratives assume urges caution in proposing a standard form to which they relate. The shortest form tends to be a statement that 'he appeared' to certain people: indeed, this form occurs both in the summary statements in the shorter and longer endings of Mark and in the kerygmatic summary Paul uses in 1 Corinthians 15.5–8. Fuller forms indicate that resurrection narratives respond to or presuppose the basic problem of the loss or absence of Jesus to the disciple community. They are told in relation to the problem of devotion or discipleship in the aftermath of the trauma of his death.

The focus therefore is not simply the fact of Jesus' appearance to them (be it revelation or visualization) but how the risen Jesus relates to the disciple community, communally or individually, in its extremity. Matthew's narrative emphasizes the response of worship (28.8, 17) and the commission given by Jesus as sovereign Lord to make disciples of all nations (28.18–20). Luke's extended Emmaus Road narrative culminates in the recognition of Jesus in table-fellowship ('the breaking of bread', 24.30–1, 35; cf. Mark 16.14), and places emphasis on new perspectives in scriptural understanding, with a focus on the suffering and death of the Messiah. His subsequent narrative also links Jesus' presence with table-fellowship (24.41–3) – though there may well be an apologetic motif here (that is, he is a 'real' person who eats and drinks with them) – and emphasizes scriptural reinterpretation (24.44–9). Luke's narrative is therefore overtly concerned with the practice of the disciple community, whose role is that of witness (24.48), to accomplish which the power of the Spirit will be granted (24.49).

In John's Gospel, appearance narratives redirect the devotion of Mary Magdalene (20.11–18) and convey Jesus' benediction and commission to the disciple community (20.19–23). The Thomas episode deals with a specific dilemma and culminates in a supreme confession (20.24–9). In the appendix (ch. 21), emphasis falls once more on the shared meal, on mission and on pastoral concern.

The narratives take the reader through the joy and amazement that mark the human side of revelation of this order, and finally pose the question of the reader's faith and praxis. The context of the stories is the tension between faith and doubt (Matt. 28.17), faith and fear (John 20.19), or faith and grief (John 20.11); it is also the search for a more adequate understanding of the Scriptures – one that can hold together the paradox of messianic ministry and the ministry of suffering service and affirm their coming together as 'God with us'. In this way, the reader is offered a way of resolving the problem of faith (John 20.28) and discipleship (cf. 21.22–3). Fundamentally, the challenge is to affirm the witness that emerges from the encounters with Jesus (21.24).

The critical reader is tempted to go beyond the interpretation of narrative and import some kind of hermeneutical device from the modern world to explain, or at least throw further light on, the nature of the appearances of the risen Jesus. In the history of religious tradition, such narratives are related to the mythopoetic tendency within faith communities and are sometimes devalued in consequence.[3] A more disciplined form of this inquiry relates the resurrection appearances to similar phenomena in apocalyptic movements and thus assigns them to the category of prophetic or charismatic vision.[4] Psychological discussion may cover a wide area: from 'subjective vision' theories relating to certain individuals who then influenced the wider group, to socio-psychological interpretations and parapsychology.[5] Sociological approaches focus on the function of belief in the faith community.[6]

Without detracting from the value of any of these, it may be observed that concentration on any one of them inevitably leads to an element of reduction. The contribution of the literary perspective which has been attempted in this book is to keep before the reader the full scope of the subject as suggested by the New Testament authors. In this holistic scenario, the appearances are part of a much greater canvas which does not so much depict the risen Christ as interpret for us the lordship of Christ, crucified and risen. Included in the picture is the messianic community, heir to the tradition of Israel's faith and now established 'in Christ'. The appearances are but a moment in the birth of the new community: a declaration of its vocation, commission and communion. The disciples do not remain 'gazing into heaven' (Acts 1.10): they are commissioned to go out into the world in the strength of the Spirit. Yet that same Spirit leads them to recall and to grasp more fully the teaching of Christ – and not in word only, but in the shared life of Christian *koinonia*. Transcendence has been given a definitive worldly expression – in Christ. This paradoxical statement allows us to penetrate as far as we may into the mystery of the resurrection of Jesus.

1 Kelber (1983), p. 104.
2 The commentary ranges far and wide. There is Bultmann's oft-cited dictum to the effect that the bones of Jesus lie in the sands of Palestine. For Marxsen, (1970), p. 128, 'the miracle is the birth of faith'. On the other hand, there is the positive historicism of von Campenhausen (1968), pp. 42–89. A sensitive handling of the historical problem is found in O'Neill (1972). In an interview with the author, Professor O'Neill put it thus: 'My massive argument is that the preaching of the resurrection could not have arisen on any basis other than the empty tomb. There is positive evidence that the tomb was found empty... Negatively, nobody produced the body, although it would have been required for any refutation of the resurrection claims that a body be produced.'
3 cf. the discussion of Bultmann's position in chapter 2.
4 There are similarities; but note is to be taken of the way Paul distinguishes his fundamental experience of the risen Lord from other 'visions and revelations'. The risen Christ impinged directly not only on Paul's praxis but also that of the Church; it gave impetus to the mission to the Gentiles and so completed the act of God in Christ. The appearances of the risen Jesus are related to the establishment of the messianic community.
5 Perry (1959); Price (1967); cf. Selby (1976) pp. 9–19.
6 Thus, Robertson (1969), p. 14, takes religion 'as a major, and historically *the* major, provider of meaning in human societies'. In this sense, a sociological dimension is inherent in all narrative presentation. For a specific application to the resurrection, cf. Barton (1984).

Bibliography

Allison, D. C., Jr., *The End of the Ages Has Come*. Edinburgh, T & T Clark, 1987; Philadelphia, Fortress, 1985.

Alsup, J. E., *The Post-Resurrection Appearance Stories of Gospel-Tradition*. London, SPCK, 1975.

Anderson, H., *The Gospel of Mark* (New Century Bible). London, Oliphants, 1976.

Auerbach, E., *Mimesis*. New York, Doubleday, 1957.

Baillie, D. M., *God Was In Christ*. London, Faber & Faber, 1948.

Baillie, J., *And the Life Everlasting*. Oxford, Oxford University Press, 1934.

Barrett, C. K., *The Gospel according to St John*. London, SPCK, 1978.

— *Essays on John*. London, SPCK, 1982.

— 'The Background of Mark 10.45', Higgins (1959), pp. 1–18.

Bartholomew, G. L., (see Boomershine, T. E.).

Barton, S., 'Paul and the Resurrection – A Sociological Approach', *Religion* 14 (1984), pp. 67–76.

Bartsch, H. W., (ed.), *Kerygma and Myth* I, II (E. tr. R. H. Fuller). London, SPCK, 1954, 1962.

Beare, F. W., *The Gospel according to Matthew*. Oxford, Blackwell, 1981.

Betz, H. D., *Galatians*. Philadelphia, Fortress, 1979.

Black, M., *An Aramaic Approach to the Gospels and Acts*. Oxford, Clarendon Press, 1954.

Bock, D. L., *Proclamation from Prophecy and Pattern*. Sheffield, JSOT, 1987.

Boomershine, T. E., 'Mark 16.8 and the Apostolic Commission', *Journal of Biblical Literature* 100 (1981), pp. 225–39.

Boomershine, T. E. and Bartholomew, G. L., 'The Narrative Technique of Mark 16.8', *Journal of Biblical Literature* 100 (1981), pp. 213–23.

Boring, M. E., *Sayings of the Risen Jesus*. Cambridge, Cambridge University Press, 1982.

Bornkamm, G., *Geschichte und Glaube* 1 (Gesammelte Aufsätze iii). Munich, Chr. Kaiser Verlag, 1968.

Bousset, W., *Die Offenbarung Johannis*. Göttingen, Vandenhoeck und Ruprecht, 1896[5].

Brandon, S. G. F., *Jesus and the Zealots*. Manchester, Manchester University Press, 1967.

Broer, I., 'Auferstehung und ewiges Leben im Johannesevangelium', '*Auf Hoffnung hin sind wir erlöst*' *(Rom. 8.24)*, (eds. I. Broer and J. Werbick), Stuttgart, SBS 128 (1987), pp. 67–94.

Brooks, O. S., 'Matthew xxviii 16–20 and the Design of the First Gospel', *Journal for the Study of the New Testament* 10 (1981), pp. 2–18.

Brown, R. E., *The Gospel according to John* (Anchor Bible 29). New York, Doubleday, 1966.

Bruce, A. B., *The Synoptic Gospels*. London, Hodder & Stoughton, 1897.

Bruce, F. F., *1 and 2 Corinthians* (New Century Bible). London, Oliphants, 1971.

Bultmann, R., 'New Testament and Mythology' and 'A Reply to the Theses of J. Schniewind', *Kerygma and Myth* I, (ed. H. W. Bartsch, E. tr. R. H. Fuller), London, SPCK, 1954.

Bibliography

— *The Gospel of John*. (E. tr. G. R. Beasley-Murray), Oxford, Blackwell, 1971.

Burchard, C., 'The Importance of Joseph and Asenath for the Study of the New Testament: A General Survey and a Fresh Look at the Lord's Supper', *New Testament Studies* 33 (1987), pp. 102–34.

Caird, G. B., *Saint Luke*. Harmondsworth, Penguin Books, 1963.

Campbell, A. V., (ed.), *A Dictionary of Pastoral Care*. London, SPCK, 1987.

Campenhausen, H. von, 'The Events of Easter and the Empty Tomb', *Tradition and Life in the Church*, (E. tr. A. V. Littledale), London, Collins, 1968, pp. 42–89.

Cardenal, E., *Love in Practice. The Gospel in Solentiname*. (E. tr. D. D. Walsh), London, Search Press, 1977.

Carr, W., *Angels and Principalities*. Cambridge, Cambridge University Press, 1981.

Carrington, P., *According to Mark*. Cambridge, Cambridge University Press, 1960.

Casey, M., *Son of Man : The Interpretation and Influence of Daniel 7*. London, SPCK, 1979.

— 'Did Jesus Rise from the Dead?', (unpublished ms.), 1987.

Charlesworth, J. H., (ed.), *The Old Testament Pseudepigrapha*. London, Darton, Longman & Todd, 1983.

Chilton, B. and McDonald, J. I. H., *Jesus and the Ethics of the Kingdom*. London, SPCK, 1987.

Clayton, J. P., (see Sykes, S. W.).

Collange, J. F., *The Epistle of Saint Paul to the Philippians*. (E. tr. A. W. Heathcote), London, Epworth, 1979.

Collingwood, R. G., *The Idea of History*. London, Oxford University Press, 1946.

Conzelmann, H., *The Theology of St Luke*. London, Faber & Faber, 1969.

Cranfield, C. E. B., *The Gospel according to Saint Mark*. Cambridge, Cambridge University Press, 1959.

Cullmann, O., *Early Christian Worship*. (E. tr. A. S. Todd and J. B. Torrance), London, SCM, 1953.

— *Immortality of the Soul or Resurrection of the Dead? The Witness of the New Testament*. London, Epworth, 1958.

Cuming, G. T., *Studies in Church History II*. London, Nelson, 1965.

Delzant, A., 'Les Disciples D'Emmaus', *Recherches de Science Religieuse*, 73, 2 (1985), pp. 177–85.

Derrett, D. M., 'Where two or three are convened in my name…', *Expository Times* 91,3 (1979), pp. 83–6.

— *The Anastasis : The Resurrection of Jesus as an Historical Event*. Shipston-on-Stour, Drinkwater, 1982.

Dixon, W. MacNeile, *The Human Situation*. London, Arnold, 1937.

Dodd, C. H., *The Parables of the Kingdom*. London, Nisbet, 1936.

— *The Interpretation of the Fourth Gospel*. Cambridge, Cambridge University Press, 1954.

— 'The Appearances of the Risen Christ: an Essay in Form Criticism of the Gospels', *Studies in the Gospels*, Nineham (ed.), 1955, pp. 9–35.

Drury, J., *The Parables in the Gospels*. London, SPCK, 1985.

Dugmore, C. W., 'The Study of the Origins of the Eucharist: Retrospect and Revaluation', in *Studies in Church History II*, Cuming (ed.), 1965, pp. 1–18.

Dunn, J. D. G., *Jesus and the Spirit*. London, SCM, 1975.

— *Unity and Diversity in the New Testament*, London, SCM, 1977.

— *Christology in the Making*. London, SCM, 1980.

— *New Testament Theology in Dialogue*. (with Mackey, J. P.), London, SPCK, 1987.

Farrer, A. *The Glass of Vision*. London, Dacre Press, 1948.

— *A Study in Mark*. London, Dacre Press, 1951.

Fitzmyer, J. A., *The Gospel According to Luke I–IX* (The Anchor Bible). New York, Doubleday, 1981; *X–IX*, ibid., 1985.

Flender, H., *St Luke : Theologian of Redemptive History*. (E. tr. R. H. and I. Fuller), London, SPCK, 1967.

Forrester, D. B., McDonald, J. I. H., Tellini, G., *Encounter with God*. Edinburgh, T. & T. Clark, 1983.

Förster, W., *Palestinian Judaism in New Testament Times*. (E. tr. G. E. Harris), Edinburgh and London, Oliver and Boyd, 1964.

Fowler, R. M., *Loaves and Fishes : The Function of the Feeding Stories in the Gospel of Mark*. Decatur, GA, Scholars Press, 1981.

— 'Who is "the Reader" of Mark's Gospel?', *Society of Biblical Literature Seminar Papers*, 1983, pp. 33–53.

— 'Who is "the Reader" in Reader Response Criticism?', *Semeia* 31 (1985), pp. 5–23.

Frei, H. W., *The Eclipse of Biblical Narrative*. New Haven, Yale University Press, 1974.

Freire, P., *Pedagogy of the Oppressed*. London, Sheed and Ward, 1972.

Friedrich, G., 'Die formale structur von Mt. 28.18–20', *Zeitschrift für Theologie und Kirche* 80, 2 (1983), pp. 137–83.

Fuller, R. H., *The Formation of the Easter Narratives*. London, SPCK, 1972.

Funk, R. W., *Language Hermeneutic and the Word of God*, Missoula, Scholars Press, 1966[1].

Gärtner, B., *The Aeropagus Speech and Natural Revelation*. (E. tr. C. H. King), Uppsala, Almquist & Wiksells, 1955.

Gasque, W. W. and Martin, R. P., (eds.), *Apostolic History and the Gospel*, (Festschrift to F. F. Bruce), Exeter, Paternoster, 1970.

Gourges, M., 'A propos du symbolisme christologique et baptismal de Marc 16.5', *New Testament Studies* 27 (1981), pp. 572–8.

Grass, H., *Ostergeschehen und Osterberichte*. Göttingen, Vandenhoeck und Ruprecht, 1962[2].

Gundry, R. H., *Matthew, A Commentary on his Literary and Theological Art*, Grand Rapids, Eerdmans, 1982.

Gustafsson, B., 'The oldest graffiti in the history of the Church?', *New Testament Studies* 3 (1956), pp. 65–9.

Harries, R., *Christ is Risen*, London, Mowbray, 1988.

Hayman, A. P., 'Rabbinic Judaism and the Problem of Evil', *Scottish Journal of Theology* 29 (1976), pp. 461–76.

— 'Theodicy in Rabbinic Judaism', *Transactions of the Glasgow University Oriental Society* XXVI (1975–6), pp. 28–43.

Hengel, M., *Judaism and Hellenism* I, II. (E. tr. J. Bowden), London, SCM, 1974.

Héring, J., *The Second Epistle of Saint Paul to the Corinthians*. (E. tr. A. W. Heathcote and P. J. Allcock), London, Epworth, 1967.

Hester, J. D., 'The Use and Influence of Rhetoric in Galatians 2.1–14', *Theologische Zeitschrift* 42 (1986), pp. 386–408.

Higgins, A. J. R. (ed.), *New Testament Essays : Studies in Memory of Thomas Walter Manson*, Manchester, Manchester University Press, 1959.

Hooker, M. D., *Jesus and the Servant*. London, SPCK, 1959.

— *The Son of Man in Mark*. London, SPCK, 1967.

— *The Message of Mark*. London, Epworth, 1983.

Hooker, M. D. and Wilson, S. G., (eds.), *Paul and Paulinism, Essays in honour of C. K. Barrett*. London, SPCK, 1982.

Horsley, R. A., '"How can some of you say that there is no resurrection of the dead?" Spiritual elitism at Corinth', *Novum Testamentum* 20 (1978), pp. 203–231.

Hubbard, B. J., *The Matthean Redaction of a Primitive Apostolic Commissioning: an Exegesis of Matthew 28.16–20*. Society of Biblical Literature and Scholars Press, Dissertation Series No. 19, 1974.

Hurst, L. D., 'Re-enter the Pre-existent Christ in Philippians 2.5–11?', *New Testament Studies* 32, 3 (1986), pp. 449–57.

van Iersel, B., 'Terug van Emmaüs', *Tijdschrift voor Theologie* 18 (1978), pp. 294–323.

Isaacs, M. E., *The Concept of Spirit*. London, Heythrop Monographs No. 1, 1976.

Jeremias, J., *The Parables of Jesus*. (E. tr. S. H. Hooke), London, SCM, 1954.
— *The Eucharistic Words of Jesus*. (E. tr. N. Perrin), London, SCM, 1966.
— *Jesus' Promise to the Nations*. (E. tr. S. H. Hooke), London, SCM,[3]1981.

Jervell, J., *The Unknown Paul*. Minneapolis, Augsburg, 1984.

Jervell, J., and Meeks, W. (eds.), *God's Christ and His People*. Oslo, Universitetsforlagert, 1977.

Johnson, S. E., *A Commentary on the Gospel according to St Mark*. London, A. & C. Black, 1960.

Kaiser, O., *Isaiah 13–39: A Commentary*. (E. tr. R. A. Wilson), London, SCM, 1974.

Kee, H. C., *Community of the New Age: Studies in Mark's Gospel*. London, SCM, 1977.

Kelber, W. H., *The Oral and the Written Gospel: The Hermeneutics of Speaking and Writing in the Synoptic Tradition, Mark, Paul and Q*. Philadelphia, Fortress, 1983.

Kermode, F., *The Genesis of Secrecy. On the Interpretation of Narrative*. Cambridge, MA, Harvard University Press, 1979.

Kingsbury, J. D., 'Reflections on "the Reader" of Matthew's Gospel'. *New Testament Studies* 34, 3 (1988), pp. 442–60.

Knibb, M. A., *The Ethiopic Book of Enoch* (2 vols.). Oxford, Clarendon, 1978.

Koet, B.-J., 'Some Traces of a Semantic Field of Interpretation in Luke 24.13–35', *Bijdragen* 1 (1985), pp. 59–73.

Künneth, W., *The Theology of the Resurrection*. (E. tr. J. W. Leitch), London, SCM, 1965.

Lategan, B., 'Is Paul Defending his Apostleship in Galatians?', *New Testament Studies* 34, 3 (1988).

Legrand, L., 'Christ the Fellow Traveller. The Emmaus Story in Luke 24.13–35', *Indian Theological Studies*, Bangalore, 19, 1 (1982), pp. 33–44.

Lietzmann, H., *An die Korinther I.II* (rev. Kümmel). Tübingen, Mohr, 1949[(4)].

Lightfoot, J. B., *St Paul's Epistle to the Philippians*. London, Macmillan, 1913 (4th ed. revised).

Lindars, B., *Behind the Fourth Gospel*. London, SPCK, 1971.

Lindblom, J., *Prophecy in Ancient Israel*. Oxford, Blackwell, 1962.

McDonald, J. I. H., *Kerygma and Didache: The articulation and structure of the earliest Christian message*. Cambridge, Cambridge University Press, 1980.
– (see also under Chilton and Forrester).

Macgregor, G. H. C., *The Gospel of John*. London, Hodder and Stoughton, 1928, 1953.

Mackey, J. P., (see Dunn, J. D. G.).

Macmurray, J., *Persons in Relation*. London, Faber & Faber, 1961.

Macquarrie, J., *The Scope of Demythologizing*. London, SCM, 1960.

Malbon, E. S., 'Mythic Structure and Meaning in Mark: Elements of a Levi-Straussian Analysis', *Semeia* 16, 1980, pp. 97–129.

Manson, W., *The Gospel of Luke*. London, Hodder and Stoughton, 1948[6].

Marshall, I. H., *Luke : Historian and Theologian*. Exeter, Paternoster, 1970a.

— 'The Resurrection in the Acts of the Apostles', *Apostolic History and the Gospel* (eds. Gasque and Martin), 1970b, pp. 92–107.

Martin, J. O., 'Toward a Post-Critical Paradigm', *New Testament Studies* 33 (1987), pp. 370–85.

Martin, R. P., *Carmen Christi : Philippians 2.5–11 in Recent Interpretation and in the Setting of Early Christian Worship*. Cambridge, Cambridge University Press, 1967.

Marxsen, W., *The Resurrection of Jesus of Nazareth*. (E. tr. M. Kohl), London, SCM, 1970.

Meagher, J. C., *Clumsy Construction in Mark's Gospel*. New York and Toronto, Edwin Mellen Press, 1979.

Michaels, J. R., 'Nathaniel under the Fig Tree', *Expository Times* 78 (1966–67), pp. 182–3.

Michel, O., 'Der Abschluss des Matthaüsevangeliums', *Evangelische Theologie* 10 (1950), pp. 16–26.

Moltmann, J., *The Trinity and the Kingdom of God*. (E. tr. M. Kohl), London, SCM, 1981.

— *The Crucified God*. (E. tr. R. A. Wilson and J. Bowden), London, SCM, 1974.

Moule, C. F. D., 'From Defendant to Judge - and Deliverer', *SNTS Bulletin* III, 1953.

— *The Phenomenon of the New Testament*. London, SCM, 1967.

— (ed.), *The Significance of the Message of the Resurrection for Faith in Jesus Christ*. (E. tr. D. M. Barton and R. A. Wilson), London, SCM, 1968.

— 'Further Reflexions on Philippians 2.5–11', *Apostolic History and the Gospel* (eds. Gasque and Martin), 1970, pp. 264–76.

Mudge, L. S., (ed.), *Paul Ricoeur : Essays on Biblical Interpretation*. London, SPCK, 1981.

Munck, J., 'Paulus Tamquam Abortivus' in Higgins (ed.), 1959.

— *The Acts of the Apostles*. (Anchor Bible), New York, Doubleday, 1967.

Murphy-O'Connor, J., 'Christological Anthropology in Phil. 2.6–11', *Revue Biblique* 83 (1976), pp. 25–50.

Nestle-Aland, *Novum Testamentum Graece*. Stuttgart, Deutsche Bibelstiflung, 1979.

Nickelsburg, G. W. E., Jr., *Resurrection, Immortality and Eternal Life in Intertestamental Judaism*. Cambridge MA, Harvard University Press; Oxford, Oxford University Press, 1972.

Nida, E. A., *Message and Mission*. New York, Harper & Row, 1960.

Nineham, D., *The Gospel of St Mark*. Harmondsworth, Pelican, 1968.

— *The Use and Abuse of the Bible*. London, SPCK, 1976.

— (ed.), *Studies in the Gospels : Essays in memory of R. H. Lightfoot*. Oxford, Blackwell, 1955.

Norman, E. R., *Christianity and the World Order : The BBC Reith Lectures 1978*. Oxford, Oxford University Press, 1979.

O'Collins, G., *What are they saying about the resurrection?*. New York, Paulist Press, 1978.

— *Jesus Risen*. London, Darton, Longman & Todd, 1987.

O'Donoghue, N. D., 'An Approach to Interpretation' (unpublished seminar paper, 1983).

Bibliography

O'Neill, J. C., *Letter to the Romans*. Harmondsworth, Penguin Books, 1975.
— 'On the Resurrection as an Historical Question', *Christ, Faith and History* (Sykes and Clayton, eds., 1972), pp. 205–19.
Otto, R., *The Idea of the Holy*. (E. tr. J. W. Harvey), London, Oxford University Press, 1928.⁵
Pearson, B. A., *The 'Pneumatikos-Psychikos' Terminology in 1 Corinthians*. Missoula, Scholars Press, 1973.
Pedersen, J., *Israel, its Life and Culture I–II*. London/Copenhagen, Cumberlege/Korch, 1926; *III–IV*, ibid., 1959.
Perkins, P., *Resurrection*. London, Chapman, 1984.
Perrin, N., *Rediscovering the Teaching of Jesus*. London, SCM, 1967.
— *The Resurrection Narratives*. London, SCM, 1977.
Perry, M. C., *The Easter Enigma: an Essay on the Resurrection with special reference to the data of psychical research*. London, Faber & Faber, 1959.
Petersen, N. R., 'When is the End Not the End? Reflections on the Ending of Mark's Narrative', *Interpretation* 34.2 (1980), pp. 151–66.
Price, H., 'Is the Resurrection of Christ to be Explained by Theologians?', *Theology* 70 (1967), pp. 105–10.
Räisänen, H., 'Paul's Conversion and the Development of his View of his Law', *New Testament Studies* 33 (1987), pp. 404–19.
Ramsey, A. M., *The Resurrection of Christ*. London, Collins, 1961.
Renan, E., *Life of Jesus*. (E. tr. W. G. Hutchison), London, Walter Scott, 1897.
Rese, M., *Alttestamentliche Motive in der Christologie des Lukas*. Gutersloh, Mohn, 1969.
Ricoeur, P., *Essays on Biblical Interpretation*. (ed. L. S. Mudge), London, SPCK, 1981.
Rigaux, B., *Dieu l'a ressuscite*. Gembloux, Duculot, 1973.
Rist, M., *The Revelation of St John the Divine* (Interpreter's Bible 12). New York, Nashville, Abingdon, 1957.
Robertson, R., (ed.), *Sociology of Religion*. Harmondsworth, Penguin Books, 1969.
Robinson, B. P., 'The Place of the Emmaus Story in Luke-Acts', *New Testament Studies* 30, 4 (1984), pp. 481–87.
Robinson, J. A. T., *The Body*. London, SCM, 1952.
— *Jesus and His Coming*. London, SCM, 1957.
— *Redating the New Testament*. London, SCM, 1975.
Robinson, J. M., *The Problem of History in Mark*. London, SCM, 1962⁽²⁾.
— 'Jesus: From Easter to Valentinus (or to the Apostles' Creed)', *Journal of Biblical Literature* 101, 1 (1982), pp. 5–37.
Rochais, G., *Les Recits de Resurrection des Morts dans le Nouveau Testament*. Cambridge, Cambridge University Press, 1981.
Rowland, C., *The Open Heaven*. London, SPCK, 1982.
— 'The Vision of the Risen Christ in Rev. 1.13ff. The Debt of an Early Christology to an Aspect of Jewish Angelology', *Journal of Theological Studies* XXXI (1980), pp. 1–11.
Schenke, L., *Auferstehungsverkündigung und leeres Grab*. Stuttgart, Katholisches Bibelwerk, 1968.
Schillebeeckx, E., *Jesus, An Experiment in Christology*. (E. tr. H. Hoskins), New York, Seabury; London, Collins, 1979.
Schniewind, J., 'A Reply to Bultmann', *Kerygma and Myth* I. (ed. Bartsch), pp. 45–101.
Schweizer, E., *'soma', Theological Dictionary of the New Testament* (eds G. Kittel and G. Friedrich), vol. VII, London, SCM, 1971.

— *The Good News According to Mark*. (E. tr. D. H. Madvig), London, SPCK, 1971.

Segal, A. F., *Two Powers in Heaven*. Leiden, Brill, 1977.

Selby, P., *Look for the Living*. London, SCM, 1976.

Selwyn, E. G., *The First Epistle of St Peter*. London, Macmillan, 1964 (1st ed. 1946).

Skinner, J., *A critical and exegetical commentary on Genesis*. (ICC), Edinburgh, T & T Clark, 1910.

Smalley, S. S., *John – Evangelist and Interpreter*. Exeter, Paternoster, 1978.

— 'The Johannine Son of Man Sayings', *New Testament Studies* 15 (1968–69), pp. 278–301.

Smith, R. Gregor, *The New Man*. London, SCM, 1956.

— *Secular Christianity*. London, Collins, 1966.

— *The Doctrine of God*. London, Collins, 1970.

Sprott, W. J. H., *Human Groups*. Harmondsworth, Penguin Books, 1958.

Stanton, G., (ed.), *The Interpretation of Matthew*. Philadelphia, Fortress; London, SPCK, 1983.

Sukenik, E. L., 'The earliest record of Christianity', *American Journal of Archaeology* NS 51 (1947), pp. 351–65.

Suleiman, S. R., and Grossman, I., (eds.), *The Reader in the Text : Essays on Audience and Interpretation*. Princeton, Princeton University Press, 1980.

Sykes, S. W., and Clayton, J. P., (eds.), *Christ, Faith and History*. Cambridge, Cambridge University Press, 1972.

Talbert, C. H., 'An Anti-Gnostic Tendency in Lukan Christology', *New Testament Studies* 14 (1967), pp. 259–71.

Tannehill, R. C., 'The Gospel of Mark as Narrative Christology', *Semeia* 16 (1980), pp. 57–93.

Taylor, V., *The Gospel of Mark*. London, Macmillan; New York, St Martin's Press, 1966.

Telford, W. R., *The Barren Temple and the Withered Tree*. Sheffield, JSOT, 1980.

Theissen, G., *The Social Setting of Pauline Christianity*. (ed. J. H. Schütz), Edinburgh, T & T Clark, 1982.

Thompson, L. L., *Introducing Biblical Literature : A More Fantastic Country*. Englewood Cliffs, Prentice Hall, 1978.

Tillich, P., *The Protestant Era*. (E. tr. J. L. Adams), Chicago, University of Chicago Press, 1948.

Tompkins, J. P., (ed.), *Reader-Response Criticism : From Formalism to Post-Structuralism*. Baltimore, Johns Hopkins University, 1980.

Torrance, T. F., *Space, Time and Resurrection*, Edinburgh, Handsel, 1976.

Trilling, W., *Das Wahre Israel*. Munich. Küsel-Verlag, 1964.

Tyson, J. B., 'The Gentile Mission and the Authority of Scripture in Acts', *New Testament Studies* 33, 4 (1987), pp. 619–31.

Vermes, G., *Jesus the Jew : A Historian's Reading of the Gospels*. London, Collins, 1973.

— 'The Present State of the "Son of Man" Debate', *Journal of Jewish Studies* (1978), pp. 123–34.

Via, D. O., *The Ethics of Mark's Gospel in the Middle of Time*. Philadelphia, Fortress, 1985.

Wanamaker, C. A., 'Philippians 2.6–11: Son of God or Adamic Christology?' *New Testament Studies* 33, 2 (1987), pp. 179–93.

Wedderburn, A. J. M., 'The Problem of the Denial of the Resurrection in 1 Corinthians XV', *Novum Testamentum* 23 (1981), pp. 229–33.

Bibliography

Westermann, C., *Basic Forms of Prophetic Speech*. (E. tr. H. C. White), London, Lutterworth, 1967.

Wilckens, U., *Die Missionsreden der Apostelgeschichte*. Neukirchen, GMBH, 1963.

— *Resurrection*. (E. tr. A. M. Stewart), Edinburgh, St Andrew Press, 1977.

Wilder, A., *Early Christian Rhetoric*. London, SCM, 1964 (rev. 1971).

— 'The Parable of the Sower: Naivete and Method in Interpretation', *Semeia* 2 (1974), pp. 134–51.

Williams, J. G., *Gospel Against Parable*. Sheffield, Almond, 1985.

Williams, R., *Resurrection*, London, Darton, Longman & Todd, 1982.

Wilson, R. McL., 'Gnosis at Corinth', *Paul and Paulinism* (eds. Hooker and Wilson), London, SPCK, 1982, pp. 102–14.

Wilson, S. G., (see Hooker, M. D.).

Wink, W., *Naming the Powers: The Language of Power in the New Testament*. Philadelphia, Fortress, 1984.

Ziesler, J., *Pauline Christianity*. Oxford and New York, Oxford University Press, 1983.

— 'Matthew and the Presence of Jesus', *Epworth Review* 11, 1 and 2 (1984), pp. 55–63, 90–95.

Index of Biblical References

Index of Subjects

Index of Modern Authors

Index of Modern Authors

161